CENTRAL ASIA

A Global Studies Handbook

GLOBAL STUDIES: ASIA

CENTRAL ASIA

A Global Studies Handbook

Reuel R. Hanks

A B C ⬤ C L I O

Santa Barbara, California • Denver, Colorado • Oxford, England

Library of Congress Cataloging-in-Publication Data

Hanks, Reuel R.
    Central Asia : a global studies handbook / Reuel R. Hanks.
        p. cm. — (Global studies. Asia)
    Includes bibliographical references and index.
    ISBN 1-85109-656-6 (hardback : alk. paper)
    ISBN 1-85109-661-2 (eBook)
    1. Asia, Central. I. Title. II. Series.

    DS327.5.H36 2005
    958—dc22
                                                        2005014716

08   07   06   05   10   9   8   7   6   5   4   3   2   1

This book is also available on the World Wide Web as an eBook.
Visit http://www.abc-clio.com for details.

ABC-CLIO, Inc.
130 Cremona Drive, P.O. Box 1911
Santa Barbara, California 93116–1911

The Acquisitions Editor for this title was Alicia Merritt,
the Project Editor was Carla Roberts, the Media Editor was
Ellen Rasmussen, the Media Manager was Caroline Price,
the Editorial Assistant was Cisca Schreefel, the Production
Manager was Don Schmidt, and the Manufacturing Coordinator
was George Smyser.

This book is printed on acid-free paper.
Manufactured in the United States of America

Contents

Series Editor's Foreword

It is imperative that as many Americans as possible develop a basic understanding of Asia. In an increasingly interconnected world, the fact that Asia contains almost 60 percent of all the planet's population is argument enough for increased knowledge of the continent on our parts. In addition, there are at least four other reasons why it is critical that Americans become more familiar with Asia:

First, Americans of all ages, creeds, and colors are extensively involved economically with Asian countries. U.S.-Pacific two-way trade surpassed U.S. trade with Europe in the 1970s. American companies constitute the leading foreign investors in Japan. With the world's second-largest economy, Japan is also the second-largest foreign investor in the United States.

The recent Asian economic crisis notwithstanding, since World War II, East Asia has experienced the fastest rate of economic growth of all the world's regions. Recently, newly industrialized Southeast Asian countries such as Indonesia, Malaysia, and Thailand have joined the so-called Four Tigers—Hong Kong, the Republic of Korea, Singapore, and Taiwan—as leading areas for economic growth. In the past decade China has begun to realize its potential to be a world-influencing economic actor. Many Americans now depend upon Asians for their economic livelihoods, and all of us consume products made in or by Asian companies.

Second, it is impossible to be an informed American citizen without knowledge of Asia, a continent that directly impacts our national security. America's war on terrorism is, as this foreword is composed, being conducted in an Asian country—Afghanistan. (What many Americans think of as the "Mideast" is, in actuality, Southwest Asia.) Both India and

Pakistan now have nuclear weapons. The eventual reunification of the Korean Peninsula is fraught with the possibility of great promise or equally great peril. The question of U.S.-China relations is considered one of the world's major global geopolitical issues. Americans everywhere are affected by Asian political and military developments.

Third, Asia and Asians have also become an important part of American culture. Asian restaurants dot the American urban landscape. Buddhism is rapidly growing in the United States, and Asian movies are becoming increasingly popular. Asian Americans, though still a small percentage of the overall U.S. population, are one of the fastest-growing ethnic groups in the United States. Many Asian Americans exert considerable economic and political influence in this country. Asian sports, pop music, and cinema stars are becoming household names in America. Even Chinese-language characters are becoming visible in the United States on everything from baseball caps to T-shirts to license plates. Followers of the ongoing debate on American educational reform will constantly encounter references to Asian student achievement.

Fourth, Asian civilizations are some of the world's oldest, and their arts and literature rank as some of humankind's most impressive achievements. Anyone who is considered an educated person needs a basic understanding of Asia. The continent has a long, complex, and rich history. Asia is the birthplace of all the world's major religions, including Christianity and Judaism.

Our objectives in developing the Global Studies: Asia series are to assist a wide variety of citizens in gaining a basic understanding of Asian countries and to enable readers to be better positioned for more in-depth work. We envision the series being appropriate for libraries, educators, high school, introductory college and university students, businesspeople, would-be tourists, and anyone who is curious about an Asian country or countries. Although there is some variation in the handbooks—the diversity of the countries requires slight variations in treatment—each volume includes narrative chapters on history and geography, economics, institutions, and society and contemporary issues. Readers should obtain a sound general understanding of the particular Asian country about which they read.

Each handbook also contains an extensive reference section. Because our guess is that many of the readers of this series will actually be traveling to Asia or interacting with Asians in the United States, introductions to language, food, and etiquette are included. The reference section of each handbook also contains extensive information—including Web sites when relevant—about business and economic, cultural, educational, exchange, government, and tourist organizations. The reference sections also include capsule descriptions of famous people, places, and events and a comprehensive annotated bibliography for further study.

—*Lucien Ellington*
Series Editor

Preface and Acknowledgments

The three countries of Central Asia addressed in this work remain largely unknown to Americans, and it is my hope that *Central Asia: A Global Studies Handbook,* will serve to introduce the region to students, businesspeople, travelers, and others. Although Central Asia is located almost exactly on the opposite side of the globe from North America, it is vital that we develop a knowledge and understanding of this mysterious and remote place for several reasons.

Central Asia sits at the hub of a great cultural crossroads—this has been the case for thousands of years—and it is a geographic fact that holds as much significance today as when the army of Alexander the Great carried Greek culture to the heart of Asia. Today three great emerging countries converge at the margins of Central Asia: Russia, China, and India. In addition, the Middle East lies adjacent to Central Asia, representing the world's most vital and politically unstable repository of petroleum, and not far to the west resides Europe, one of the massive engines of the global economy. Central Asia stands poised to play a leading role in the interplay between all these forces in the twenty-first century.

Beyond the importance of location, Central Asia has a growing significance for several other reasons. In recent years large deposits of petroleum and natural gas have been discovered in Kazakhstan, and in the future that country may arise as a significant player in the global oil market. In terms of geostrategic importance, Central Asia has already proven its stature: Alliances with both Uzbekistan and Kyrgyzstan allowed the United States to launch military strikes deep within Afghanistan in 2001 and 2002 and successfully oust the Taliban regime from that country. Ironically, even Central Asia's many problems make it important. Economic underdevelopment, political authoritarianism and a lack of democratic institutions, expanding populations, and environmental problems all challenge the future development of the region—yet, it is a region where instability is likely to have repercussions well outside its immediate borders.

Ideally, this volume would cover all five countries of what is generally termed former Soviet Central Asia: Kazakhstan, Uzbekistan, Kyrgyzstan, Tajikistan, and Turkmenistan. The latter two countries are not included here simply because all five states could not be addressed in a single work, and the absence of Turkmenistan and Tajikistan does not imply by any means that those countries are unimportant either in Central Asia, or globally. Hopefully, a future volume of this series will address these countries specifically, although a considerable amount of the information presented here, especially concerning culture and history, applies to Turkmenistan and Tajikistan as well.

Readers may notice a certain amount of redundancy in the discussion of history across the three narrative sections. I have written the book this way so that those who are interested in obtaining information about a single country may read only about that country and still encounter a comprehensive treatment of the country's history, without resorting to other parts of the book. On the other hand, those who wish to read the entire book may choose to skim some of the introductory historical discussion in the latter two narrative sections, because much of this information is presented in "Uzbekistan's Geography and History." There is much similarity in the sections on etiquette as well, and some readers may wish to approach these passages selectively.

In addition, I have deliberately avoided the use of the terms "Uzbeki," "Kazakhstani," and "Kyrgyzstani" as indicators of national identity (a problematic concept itself in the region). These terms are gradually appearing more frequently in the literature on Central Asia, but they are still not widely used by Central Asians themselves and may be confusing to those encountering Central Asia for the first time. I hope it will be obvious from context when I use the terms "Uzbek," "Kazakh," and "Kyrgyz" to mean a specific ethnic identification and when these labels are intended to signify a broader social and national context, as in "Uzbek Institutions," a heading that includes the institutional structure in the country of Uzbekistan. In rendering place-names, I have not attempted to rigorously follow either the Russian variants or those of the native languages but rather have used names that seem to be most widely encountered in Western writing. In some cases, particularly in Kazakhstan, both Russian and Kazakh place names are presented.

I have been studying and visiting Central Asia for almost twenty years, and every additional encounter with the region brings me something new and interesting. As a scholar who has devoted his career to the region, I am hopeful that this work will stimulate others to learn about, and perhaps even visit one or all of the three countries examined, to travel if for no other reason than "for lust of knowing what should not be known," to quote James Elroy Flecker's famous passage. Indeed, the culture, history, and people of Central Asia are all very much worth knowing, and perhaps this modest effort at introduction will fuel the desire to know more among others.

Although I am listed as the author, this work is the product of a collective effort, and without the encouragement and support of many people behind the scenes, this volume would not have reached print. The editorial staff at ABC-CLIO is a wonderful collection of professionals, and I am fortunate to have worked with them. I am particularly indebted to Alicia Merritt at ABC-CLIO and to Professor Lucien Ellington, the editor of the Global Studies series for Asia, for their steady encouragement and patience, as I worked to write this book. In addition, Carla Roberts and Ellen Rasmussen provided invaluable assistance and advice in preparing the manuscript for publication. Finally, I am especially grateful to my wife, Oydin, for her love and help; and to my parents, who taught me stay the course, even though it led me to places so far away.

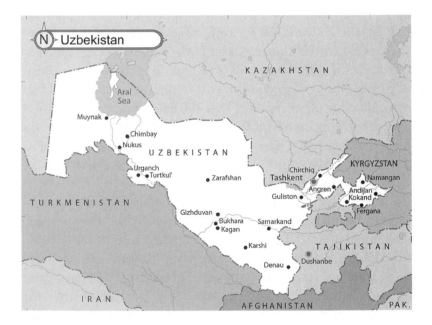

All maps provided by Digital Wisdom.

UZBEKISTAN

PART ONE
NARRATIVE SECTION

The Geography and History
of Uzbekistan

Uzbekistan lies at the very core of Central Asia, a rather inde-
terminate region that includes all of Uzbekistan's immediate
neighbors: Kazakhstan, Kyrgyzstan, Tajikistan, Afghanistan,
and Turkmenistan. Uzbekistan is the only Central Asian state
that shares a common border with all of these countries. Not
only does Uzbekistan represent the physical heart of the
region, but metaphorically, as well, it stands as its cultural,
historical, and political axis. A great many of Central Asia's
ancient urban centers of learning and commerce, arising
along the track of the Silk Road, lie within the confines of the
modern Uzbek state. Some of these same cities now represent
vital magnets for foreign investment and tourism, thereby
extending the economic role they have played in this corner
of Asia for the past two thousand years.

Yet ironically, although its culture and monuments are
ancient, Uzbekistan is one of the world's newest countries.
Before 1991, no independent state designated as "Uzbekistan" had ever existed, and no precisely delineated territory
associated with the ethnicity of "Uzbek" was established
before 1924, when the Uzbek Soviet Socialist Republic was
created from the remnants of several independent city-
states and part of Russian Turkistan. Therefore, a specific
geographic homeland associated with the Uzbeks has
existed for less than eighty years—a space determined not
by the Uzbeks themselves, but by the efforts of Soviet cartographers, ethnographers, and political administrators.
This lack of self-determination continues to play a role in
issues of Uzbek national identity, state cohesion, and relationships with neighboring countries. Modern Uzbekistan is

a polyglot of more than one hundred ethnic groups, highlighting the country's multiethnic character as well as the region's long history of invasion, trade, and cultural diffusion and integration. At the dawn of the twenty-first century, the central challenge for Uzbekistan is not only to encounter the future, but simultaneously to discover, articulate, and comprehend the past.

The abruptness of independence compounded a host of serious challenges confronting the new state, including profound environmental damage, rapid demographic expansion, economic mismanagement and underdevelopment, and political instability. Some of these problems appeared during the Soviet era, whereas others emerged as the country charted its way through the first decade of post-Communist development. At the same time, Uzbekistan benefits from significant deposits of valuable natural resources; impressive production of agricultural commodities, especially cotton; a large amount of military equipment inherited from the Soviet Union; and a reasonably well-developed transportation infrastructure and industrial capacity. The country's potential for tourism is only beginning to be exploited, and, along with an advantageous geopolitical location, gives some basis for optimism for Uzbekistan's economic future. What appears certain is that for the first time, the future will be directed exclusively by the citizens of Uzbekistan, who now face the challenges of independence and nation building.

PHYSICAL AND HUMAN GEOGRAPHY

Central Asia lies at the confluence of all major regional components of the Eurasian landmass. To the east lie the vast deserts of western China; to the south and southwest, South Asia and the Middle East; to the west, Europe; and, directly northward, the steppes of Russia. Although landlocked, Uzbekistan's position as the nucleus of the region historically endowed certain geographic and economic advantages, at

River and cotton fields seen from space. Cotton fields and irrigation canals along the Amu Darya River. Growing cotton in this arid region requires large amounts of irrigation water. (NASA/Corbis)

least until the 1500s when maritime commerce overtook land-based trade between Europe and Asia. Its location at the crossroads of Asia, Europe, and the Middle East has played a vital role in attracting both trader and invader and has thus dramatically influenced the culture, economic development, and urbanization of modern Uzbekistan.

Uzbekistan extends across almost 1,000 miles from west to east and covers nearly 173,000 square miles, about the same area as Sweden or Morocco. In the west, most of the country is blanketed by a sandy desert, the Kyzyl Kum (Red Sand),

and much of the remainder of Uzbekistan is arid steppe. Indeed, human habitation in this corner of Central Asia would be almost impossible were it not for the life-giving waters provided by the country's two main rivers, the Amu Darya and the Syr Darya. The larger of the two, the Amu Darya, originates in the Pamirs and serves as the boundary between Uzbekistan and Afghanistan, and the Syr Darya arises in the Tien Shan range and flows westward through Kyrgyzstan and eastern Uzbekistan before entering Kazakhstan. Almost all of Uzbekistan's major cities lie on or adjacent to these rivers, or one of their tributaries, underscoring the relationship between human settlement and water in this parched corner of Asia.

For millennia the riverine system of Uzbekistan has supported an extensive network of irrigation, allowing for the production of a wide spectrum of agricultural commodities. From the middle of the nineteenth century on, and especially during the Soviet era, cotton production was increasingly emphasized, as previously unexploited land was brought under cultivation. Particularly after World War II, as the acreage devoted to cotton production increased, demand for additional water also rose, leading to the extraction of enormous amounts of water from the Amu Darya, Syr Darya, and other rivers. These rivers are virtually the only source of inflow for the Aral Sea, however, and the overuse of their waters has led to what is arguably the world's worst example of environmental mismanagement, the collapse of the Aral Sea. This disaster severely affects the entire region and illustrates how ramifications of Soviet policy continue to plague Uzbekistan and its neighbors.

Approximately 80 percent of Uzbekistan is desert or semi-desert, and the physical geography of central and western Uzbekistan may be characterized as a series of island-like oases, scattered across a vast and hostile ocean of sand, dust, and stone. The oases lie along the streams that snake out of the mountains lying along the eastern and southeastern mar-

Samarkand shepherd posed near a hillside, ca. 1910.
(Library of Congress)

gin of Uzbekistan and flow in a westerly or northwesterly direction toward the Turan Plain, occupied by the remnant of the Aral Sea. Here, in a zone of true desert and dry steppe, average elevations drop to around 200 to 300 feet above sea level, making this the lowest region in the country. To the west, the Ustyurt Plateau separates the Turan Lowland from the Caspian Basin. The plateau represents only a slight increase in elevation, however, and is predominantly a waste-land of rock outcroppings, saline marshy lowlands, and sandy ridges.

Beginning just west of Bukhara and extending northwest-ward to the Aral Sea, the Kyzyl Kum desert occupies most of western Uzbekistan (Sinnott 1992). Not quite as large as its cousin to the southwest, the Kara Kum, the Kyzyl Kum nevertheless covers approximately 110,000 square miles. The name derives from the red tinge of the sand in many locations, and the desert is nearly devoid of vegetation except for the saxaul bush. The saxaul is a xerophytic, salt-tolerant species that is virtually the only naturally occurring source of wood and charcoal in this section of Central Asia. Saxaul is also important in anchoring dunes, thereby reducing wind erosion and dune migration.

The agricultural heartland of the country lies at the eastern terminus, in the Fergana Valley. Here rich alluvial soils, laid down by thousands of years of deposition, provide the substrate for a rich variety of grains, vegetables, melons, fruits, and the ubiquitous cotton. The valley, running along an east-west axis, is almost 200 miles long and approximately 100 miles across at its widest point. It is enclosed by the Pamir Alay Range to the south, the Fergana Mountains to the east, and a subchain of the Tien Shan to the north. The Naryn River and Kara Darya enter the valley from the east and join to form the Syr Darya, which then exits the valley and flows unimpeded in a northwesterly direction toward the Aral Basin. A complex system of canals, aqueducts, and irrigation works provides water to the valley's fields and terraces, and much of the water flowing out of the surrounding peaks is used entirely within this vast oasis.

Climate and Ecology

In technical terms, virtually all of Uzbekistan is a desert, because only a few locations receive more than ten inches of precipitation annually. Even in the verdant and fecund Fergana Valley, most locations average around ten inches, and much of this precipitation falls in the form of snow during the winter months.

The extreme aridity of the region may be explained by a combination of factors. First, the high mountains to the south and southeast create a rain shadow effect, blocking any moisture-laden subtropical air masses from entering the region from the south, and westerly winds, which might otherwise bring some additional rainfall to the region, deposit most of their moisture while crossing the Caucasus Mountains. Second, Uzbekistan's position at the heart of the Eurasian landmass magnifies the continental characteristics of the climate, resulting in a wide annual range of temperatures. Outside the alpine regions, summers may be dangerously hot, with high temperatures commonly exceeding 100 degrees Fahrenheit in July and August. Winters are unexpectedly cold and dry, with prevailing winds from the northeast, as a result of the pressure generated by the Asiatic High. In recent years, the collapse of the Aral Sea has led to an exacerbation of temperature ranges in western Uzbekistan near the former shoreline, accompanied by a decline in relative humidity (see following section).

Uzbekistan has the unfortunate distinction of hosting what is most probably the worst case of environmental mismanagement in human experience, the collapse of the Aral Sea. Before 1960, the Aral was the fourth largest lake on the planet. Over the next thirty years, the entire ecosystem of the Aral underwent a catastrophic decline, as prodigious amounts of water were siphoned off from the Aral's only sources of inflow, the Amu Darya and the Syr Darya, to grow the region's *beloe zoloto* (white gold)—cotton. By the early 1990s, the Aral had lost two-thirds of its volume, and in many locations the shoreline had retreated by more than 20 miles. The sea had become so saline that a once-thriving commercial fishing industry had completely disintegrated, as virtually all valuable species of fish had vanished. Accompanying these problems are a multitude of associated difficulties, including widespread salinization of soils because of overirrigation, massive salt and dust storms that are carried hundreds of miles to the east by prevailing winds, and the degradation of local water supplies, especially wells.

The residents of Karakalpakstan, the large, autonomous

A fishing trawler on the dry bed of the Aral Sea near Muynak. The writing on the stern reads "Muynak Fishing Port." The Soviet environmental legacy continues to haunt Central Asia. (Photo courtesy of Reuel Hanks)

region that occupies almost all of far western Uzbekistan, have paid a heavy price for this debacle, and their quality of life has been tragically eroded. The economy in many locations has essentially collapsed, with high rates of unemployment, particularly in those communities that relied on the fishing industry. Additionally, in the late 1980s, this region had some of the highest infant mortality rates in the USSR, and infection rates for anemia, hepatitis A, and related blood disorders were also alarmingly high. As wells dried up because of the collapse of the local water table, many people turned to the nearby irrigation channels for water, unaware that this source was contaminated with fertilizers, heavy metals, and pesticides that continue to be applied to agricultural fields in copious amounts. In recent years, this situation has been ameliorated to some degree via education efforts and the provision of alternative water sources, yet it appears there is little hope that either the Aral itself or those living around it will return to the conditions that both enjoyed before 1960.

Political Geography

During the Soviet era, what was the Uzbek Soviet Socialist Republic was divided into provinces (Russian: *oblasti;* Uzbek: *viloyatlar*), which were further subdivided into smaller units. Karakalpakstan, the large territory occupying most of western Uzbekistan, was considered an ASSR, or Autonomous Soviet Socialist Republic. Independent Uzbekistan has maintained this structure, with some slight modifications to the number and shape of individual provinces. Karakalpakstan maintains a de jure autonomous status, although in reality the government is subservient to the national administration in Tashkent. Each province is controlled by a *hakim,* or local governor, who is responsible for local policy and ultimately answers to the country's president—a position that, since independence, has been held by Islom Karimov, the former first party secretary of the Uzbek Communist Party.

The eastern portion of the country is projected toward the very heart of Eurasia, and the richness and potential of the Fergana Valley explains this distinctive shape and the convoluted borders in this part of Central Asia. When the Soviet administration divided the region into "republics" in the 1920s and 1930s, the Fergana Valley was also split, providing Uzbekistan with the lion's share of the agricultural land and cities, but also giving a portion to Tajikistan and Kyrgyzstan, both of which were formed as Soviet Socialist Republics (SSRs) after the creation of the Uzbek SSR (Tajikistan was a subunit of the Uzbek SSR until 1929).

The division of Central Asia into constituent republics during the early Soviet era was a watershed event, for it was this process that provides the contemporary political geography of the region. With few exceptions, the borders inherited from the Communist period have remained essentially intact since independence in 1991, and the imperfections and ambiguities of the Moscow-directed approach of *divide et impera* (divide and conquer) remain as well. A clear example of such ambiguity is the presence of large minorities of Uzbeks in northern Tajikistan and western Kyrgyzstan, as well as Uzbekistan's control of Samarkand and Bukhara, both historically Tajik cities. Particularly in the latter case, ethnic distinctions were blurred by centuries of cohabitation and the fact that many, if not most, residents were bilingual and were themselves viewed by outsiders as a distinct group, the Sarts. The boundaries imposed during Soviet administration therefore do not precisely correspond to the actual ethnic geography of Central Asia, leaving open the possibility of irredentism and related political conflict. Indeed, border issues in the region have been the source of some friction in recent years between Uzbekistan and Kazakhstan, and two Uzbek enclaves remain entirely inside Kyrgyz territory, Sokh and Shakhimardan. The latter were created during the Soviet era and are officially part of Fergana viloyat.

Population Characteristics

Ethnic and Religious Geography

Uzbekistan is a multiethnic state, with close to 100 distinct ethnic groups residing in the country. The largest group are the ethnic Uzbeks, who make up slightly more than 70 percent of the population. The Uzbeks are fundamentally of Turkic stock, but many ethnic strains may be detected among them, the result of a history of intrusion of progressive waves of invaders and settlers from all points of the compass, but especially from the Eurasian steppe lands. Traditional Uzbek society is subdivided into clan and tribal affiliations, which although weakened during the Soviet period nevertheless continue to influence political and economic relationships.

The second largest ethic group remains the Russians, although their proportion in the total population has steadily shrunk since the 1980s and now stands at about 6 percent. This relatively small figure conceals the economic importance of the Russians, who comprise a disproportionate share of the country's professional and business people. The Uzbek regime has made a special effort to court the remaining Russian community, as the continued emigration of Russian teachers, doctors, engineers, and others only exacerbates the country's economic woes. Overwhelmingly, the Russians are urban dwellers and remain concentrated in the larger cities, and Russian continues to function as a lingua franca because few Russians can communicate in Uzbek.

Other minority groups are also predominantly urbanized, such as Koreans, Tajiks, Armenians, and the few remaining Jews. Bukhara, a city famous for its once-thriving Jewish community, has seen most of that group emigrate in recent years. Both Bukhara and Samarkand are "Tajik" cities, in the sense that a majority of their inhabitants speak that tongue as a first language, although virtually all residents are also conversant in Uzbek, and usually Russian as well. The use of Tajik and the percentage of Tajiks in the country are politically sensitive issues in Uzbekistan today, and some scholars hold that the officially sanctioned figure of 5 percent is intentionally underreported.

Uzbekistan has long been a part of the Islamic realm, and most Uzbeks today classify themselves as Muslim. Nearly all Islamic believers belong to the Sunni branch, and various Sufi *tariqa* (orders) have held considerable influence in Central Asia for centuries. This is especially true for the Naqshbandi, founded by the late Bakhautdin Naqshband, whose body lies in a large mausoleum complex a few miles outside of Bukhara. Islam in modern Uzbekistan must be understood in historical context, however, particularly in light of the impact that Soviet antireligious policy had on the status and development of Islam, Russian Orthodoxy, and other religions. The repression of religious practice and belief during the seventy years of Soviet administration resulted in the loss of religious knowledge among Uzbeks, especially regarding traditions, dogma, and ritual.

Since independence, many Uzbeks of all ages have become reacquainted with the basic aspects of the faith, and the early 1990s witnessed a remarkable expansion of the religious landscape, as many mosques and medressehs (Islamic seminaries), previously controlled by the Soviet government, were returned to believers. In addition, hundreds of new religious structures were built to accommodate the resurgence of interest in Islam. In the late 1990s, the Uzbek regime began to crack down on "unofficial" Islamic organizations, and this along with the detonation of several bombs in Tashkent in 1999 (allegedly by Islamic radicals) and incursions by the Islamic Movement of Uzbekistan (IMU) in 1999 and 2000 led to widespread repression of any nonsanctioned Muslim group. The passage of severely restrictive antireligious legislation in 1998 curtailed the emergence of Islamic religiosity, although some clandestine organizations continue efforts at proselytism.

Uzbek, a Turkic language with many borrowings from Persian and Russian, gained official status just before independence and has increasingly displaced Russian as the language of education and commerce, although Russian continues to be widely spoken in larger urban areas. Written using the Cyrillic alphabet since the 1940s, Uzbek is increasingly written using the Latin script, which is expected to replace Cyrillic entirely in the near future. Several dialects of Uzbek are used across the country, and the literary language, not developed until the Soviet era, is based on the Tashkent dialect. As noted previously, both Russian and Tajik are commonly spoken in some cities, and during the Soviet period, most literature was published in Russian, sometimes along with an Uzbek-language edition. Ironically, Uzbekistan's most famous man of letters, the fifteenth-century Timurid poet Mir Alisher Navoi, did not write in Uzbek but composed most of his poetry in Chaghatay, a Turkic precursor of modern Uzbek.

Navoi, a national hero in contemporary Uzbekistan, considered the Uzbeks of his era to be uncivilized and antithetical to the "forces of good" (Allworth 1990, 37).

Distribution and Growth

The total population of Uzbekistan today stands at about 26 million, about the same as Peru. From antiquity, people have been unevenly distributed across this portion of Central Asia because proximity to the region's water resources was essential to the support of any significant population cluster. This is still true today, as the highest population densities are found in the Fergana Valley and in the oasis urban centers dotted along the major rivers and their tributaries. Andijan viloyat has the highest population density at nearly 486 people per square kilometer, and its neighboring regions of Namangan and Fergana are also high; at 226 and 352 people per square kilometer respectively, these represent the highest population densities in all of Central Asia, exclusive of the major metropolitan areas. In sharp contrast is the population density for Karakalpakstan, at only 8.6 people per square kilometer, again reflecting the inhospitable nature of the country's western deserts and their paucity of available water.

Since the 1950s, Uzbekistan's population has grown rapidly. Between 1950 and 1979, annual rates of increase averaged above 3 percent, declining somewhat in the 1980s and 1990s but still remaining relatively high, particularly compared with rates of increase elsewhere in the former Soviet realm. The emigration of much of the Slavic population over the last twenty years has only partially offset the high birthrates among Uzbeks, and population growth remains particularly high in rural districts, where average family size commonly exceeds six persons. These trends have resulted in a youthful population structure—in 1996, nearly 43 percent of the population was 16 years of age or younger, a distribution that is certain to maintain high population growth rates through at least the next generation. Goskomstat, the Uzbek government planning agency, predicted in the early 1990s that the country's population would approach 36 million by 2015, an increase of almost 50 percent in just 25 years.

Migration and Urbanization

The most significant migration for Uzbekistan, and indeed for the region as a whole, has been the steady out-migration of Slavs, mostly Russians, from the region over the last several decades. This movement began well before Uzbekistan and other Central Asian republics achieved independence but accelerated once the Soviet Union collapsed, with most Slavs moving to Russia, Ukraine, or other countries. Although rates of emigration have slowed, the trend continues today. The motivating factors behind this shift are economic, social, and cultural. Many Slavs now feel alienated, as Uzbek (which the great majority of Slavs do not speak) replaces Russian as the dominant tongue and Islamic traditions have once again taken root in Uzbek society. Additionally, some Russians believe that greater economic opportunities await them in Russia. Uzbeks, on the other hand, have historically shown a very low propensity to migrate, both outside Uzbekistan and even internally from region to region.

The dominant primate city is Tashkent, which with its surrounding region accounts for about 4 million people, or a sixth of the country's total population. Much if not most of Uzbekistan's industrial capacity is there as well, and the city boasts the only metro system in Central Asia. Overall, however, only 40 percent of the population is urbanized, and surprisingly, the percentage of urbanized population has actually declined in recent years. This is due to two factors: the out-migration of the Slavic population, which was almost exclusively urban, and the high fertility and birthrates in rural districts. Oddly, among the country's regions (outside Tashkent), Karakalpakstan possesses the highest percentage of urbanized population at 48 percent because of the limited agricultural opportunities there. The trend toward deurbanization in Uzbekistan does not bode well for future economic development because employment in the agricultural sector is saturated, and job growth will have to occur in industry, construction, and other activities traditionally connected to urban areas.

HISTORY
Early History

The oasis centers of Uzbekistan have been occupied for millennia and have supported a number of civilizations and empires. Samarkand was the capital of the Sogdian Empire and already an old city when Alexander the Great arrived at the gates in 329 B.C. According to some sources, Alexander was smitten not only by the city's beauty, but also by one of its daughters, Roxanna, whom he took as a bride before continuing on his quest. Even today "Iskander" is a common name among Uzbek males, and some residents of the Fergana Valley claim descent from soldiers in Alexander's army, a claim circumstantially supported by the frequent appearance of gray or blue eyes and lighter hues in both hair and complexion among certain groups there.

In the centuries following Alexander's appearance, the region the Greeks referred to as Transoxiana (the land beyond the Oxus River, i.e., the Amu Darya) became a central part of the global trading network known as the Silk Road, allowing for the transfer of goods, technology, and ideas between East and West. Indeed, Sogdian merchants based in Samarkand and other settlements played a key role in expanding trade across the region and in developing a transcontinental network for the distribution of silk commodities. The fabric eventually reached the Roman Empire following this path, where it was prized for its strength, durability, and comfort. Western coins and artistic forms traveled in the opposite direction, and several faiths diffused along the

Silk Road and its branches, including Buddhism, Manichaeism, and Nestorian Christianity. The Silk Road was pivotal as a conduit for commerce and culture for centuries and was crucial to expanding and enriching the region's urban centers.

The wealth and grandeur of Central Asia's urban landscape frequently became the target of invaders in the centuries following Alexander's incursion. Huns, Turkic groups, Chinese, and others attempted to control the strategic heart of Asia over the next eight centuries, but the invaders who would leave the most lasting imprint on Central Asia's culture were Muslim armies under the direction of Qutaiba ibn Muslim, who subjugated Bukhara and Sogdiana in the first decade of the 700s. In 751, a decisive victory near the Talas River by Muslim forces over the army of Tang China ensured that Central Asia would remain within the Islamic cultural realm. Within a century, many if not most of the residents of Bukhara, Samarkand, Tashkent, and neighboring urban centers were practicing Muslims, although complete conversion of the surrounding nomadic peoples would require many more centuries.

In the succeeding centuries, Central Asian intellectuals contributed an impressive body of work to Islamic theology, literature, science, and art. Bukhara, the capital of the Persian Samanid dynasty, developed into one of the foremost centers of Islamic study and thought, and scholars residing in the oasis centers of the region made significant advancements in mathematics and science. Scholars such as the mathematician al-Khorezmi, whose name became corrupted in English to "algorism," and later the philosopher-physician Ibn Sina (Avicenna in the West) made profound contributions to the advancement of science and human knowledge. Young men traveled to Central Asia from all corners of the Muslim world to study at the region's medressehs, and trade flourished as Central Asia became culturally and commercially integrated with the larger Islamic realm.

The Kalon Minaret in Bukhara. The minaret is almost 150 feet tall and has stood for nearly 900 years. (Photo courtesy of Reuel Hanks)

By the eleventh century, several Turkic dynasties were competing for control of Transoxiana. The Karakhanids, a warlike people from the east, struggled for control of Transoxiana for a century with a second Turkic power, the Ghaznavid Empire, until both were subjugated by yet another Turkic group, the Seljuks. The Seljuks created a sultanate that stretched from the Mediterranean Sea to what is today eastern Afghanistan, but disunity and dissension among the Seljuks led to their demise in the twelfth century at the hands of the Khwarizm shahs, a Turkic clan who had adopted many aspects of Persian culture. At the same time, Transoxiana was occupied by the Kara-Khitai, a Mongol people from the steppe lands of Inner Asia. The arrival of the Kara-Khitai set the stage for the most significant Mongol incursion in Central Asian history a century later—the invasion of the hordes of Genghis Khan.

The Mongol conquest of Transoxiana under Genghis Khan may be said to begin in the year 1218, when the Great Khan's forces absorbed the fractured Kara-Khitai Empire. This acquisition of territory meant the Mongols shared a common border with the Khwarizm Empire, a state with which the Mongols sought commercial and political ties to secure their western flank. The pillaging of a Mongol caravan by a Khwarizmian official led to outright war, however; within three years, all the great cities of the region had been taken and sacked by Mongol armies, and Central Asia had been joined to the vast domain of the Mongols. The devastation of the urban geography was staggering: most of the population of Bukhara and Samarkand was either killed or enslaved, and entire cities were wiped off the map. In the aftermath of this brutal conquest, the Chagatai Khanate emerged, a state that was administered by Mongols but populated mostly by Turkic peoples. Riddled with conflicts and intrigue, the Chagatai Mongol rulers held Transoxiana for almost a century and a half. Their empire would be replaced by a local Turkic chieftain—Amir Timur, or as he is often called in the West, Tamerlane. Once the Mongols' vassal but eventually their master, he would establish an imperial realm reaching from the Euphrates River to the Fergana Valley.

Amir Timur's impact on the history and culture of Central Asia, particularly Uzbekistan, is immeasurable. Born at Kesh (modern Shakhrisabz), not far from Samarkand, Timur chose the latter as his capital, and he and his successors built the city into one of the most beautiful and important urban centers in Asia. Under the Timurids, as Timur and his dynasty came to be called, magnificent structures were erected in Samarkand that were gilded with glazed tiles, as Timur brought artisans skilled at making and utilizing such decoration from the Middle East to Central Asia. The city became not only a center of architectural wonder, but also a hub of commerce and learning. Ulug Bek, Amir Timur's grandson, constructed a spectacular medresseh in the heart of Samarkand and also designed and built an observatory on the city's outskirts, where he observed the heavens and made significant contributions to the astronomical knowledge of his time.

Following his death in 1405, Amir Timur was succeeded by one of his sons, Shah Rukh. This Timurid prince was a cultured and competent leader who patronized the arts and held the heart of his father's empire together despite the fractious nature of the many Timurid princes and potentates who laid claim to Amir Timur's legacy. His reign of more than forty years witnessed an erosion of Timurid power in Persia and Azerbaijan, but also a flourishing of arts and literature. Upon his death in 1447, his son Ulug Bek inherited the Timurid throne in Central Asia but was executed by his own son after only two years. During the brief reign of Ulug Bek, a new military power suddenly appeared in Transoxiana, the Uzbeks. The arrival of the Uzbeks presaged the end of Timurid control of Transoxiana and surrounding regions, although a Timurid prince displaced by them, Babur, would leave an indelible mark on Indian civilization. By 1500, an Uzbek prince,

Muhammad Shaybani Khan, had taken Bukhara and Samarkand and firmly established an Uzbek dynasty in the heart of Asia.

The Shaybanid dynasty, as this Uzbek empire came to be called, lasted less than a century but firmly entrenched the Uzbeks in Transoxiana. At the same time, the trade that had passed through Central Asia via the caravan routes of the Silk Road began to diminish, a result of both the chaotic and fractured political geography of Central Asia and the increasing competition of ocean-borne commerce. As Shaybanid control waned over the next century and a half, it was replaced by several city-states, centered on Khiva, Bukhara, and, somewhat later, Kokand in the Fergana Valley. Despotic and often poorly administered, these relatively isolated entities waged war on one another but were individually too weak to gain control of the entire region. By the middle of the nineteenth century, Transoxiana and its once magnificent cities had slipped into obscurity.

The Imperial Russian Period

From the 1600s, the Russian Empire displayed an interest in Central Asia and the riches the region was believed to hold. Much of this interest was not sanctioned by the Russian crown but was the work of Cossack adventurers who raided settlements in the Khorezm oasis. As early as 1603, a party of Cossack soldiers attacked Urgench, the capital city of the Khivan Khanate, and over the next century several other parties of raiders attempted to repeat this event. By the reign of Peter the Great, Russian interest in Central Asia had been stimulated by the region's possible role as a link to India, as well as by persistent rumors of considerable deposits of gold located there. A large expedition to Khiva in 1717 met with violent failure, however, and for the next century and a half the Russian Empire was content to solidify its position on the Kazakh steppe, building an extensive system of forts and towns, and gradually bringing the nomadic peoples of that region under Russian control. This process would eventually steer the Russians into direct confrontation with the city-states of Transoxiana.

Thus, the nineteenth century would bring yet another conquering power to Transoxiana, but this time from the north. Imperial Russia's interest in Central Asia was greatly magnified by several geopolitical events. First among these was the increasing attention paid by the British to Central Asia, particularly toward Afghanistan but also toward the khanates of Khiva, Bukhara, and Kokand. By the 1800s, the Russian crown had come to regard Central Asia as lying within its rightful sphere of influence and viewed Great Britain's campaigns and intrigues there as a clear attempt to expand the British Empire into this sensitive and vulnerable region. The result would be a century-long contest for influence, immortalized by Rudyard Kipling in his novel *Kim* as the "Great Game."

A second event that intensified Russian interest in the Muslim realm along its southern margin occurred literally on the opposite side of the Earth yet was to have a profound and lasting effect on Central Asia. The U.S. Civil War disrupted supplies of raw cotton to the cotton textile industries of Europe, leading manufacturers to search for alternative supplies. Russian producers in particular recognized the potential of Central Asia to produce irrigated cotton and actively sought the Russian government's assistance in obtaining cotton from the region. The combination of political and economic interests ensured that Russian involvement in the affairs of the khanates continued to deepen, and as the weakness and backwardness of these states became evident, their conquest and annexation became a primary focus of Russian foreign policy.

The pivotal year in the Russian conquest of Central Asia was 1865. By then, Russian military strategists had determined to wrest the city of Tashkent away from the Khanate of

Kokand and utilize the city as a base of operations for eventually subjugating the entire region. Tashkent was taken by General M. G. Cherniaev in June of 1865, and within two years, the city along with surrounding territories had been organized into the governor generalship of Turkistan. The military officer chosen to serve as the first governor general of this new corner of the Russian Empire was General K. P. von Kaufman, an ambitious and capable proponent of Russian expansionism. By the mid-1870s, Bukhara and Khiva had been reduced in size and made vassal states of Russia, and the Khanate of Kokand had been directly absorbed into the empire.

Russia's Central Asian subjects remained restive however, even under the potent threat of superior tsarist military might. This restiveness was expressed through frequent local revolts, often directed by Islamic religious leaders. The most violent and widespread of these uprisings occurred in 1898 and originated in the city of Andijan, in the heart of the Fergana Valley. There a Sufi sheikh, Madali, declared a jihad, or holy war, against the Russian occupiers and, with a small army of followers, attacked the local garrison at Andijan. Simultaneously, forces loyal to the sheikh attacked other neighboring cities, including Margilan and Osh, and the revolt appears to have had widespread support throughout the Fergana Valley. The Muslim rebels lacked sophisticated weaponry, including artillery, and although they may have outnumbered the Russian defenders of the cities, the rebels did not fare well in direct combat with them. Quickly suppressed, the Andijan Revolt nevertheless surprised Central Asia's Russian administrators with both its ferocity and its broad base of support and led to fundamental changes in Russian governance.

Russian control of Central Asia also led to less violent but more profound changes in the attitudes and perspective of the indigenous elite. Some Central Asian intellectuals recognized that the backwardness of their region was a key factor in the Russians' ability to conquer and control them. In response, a number of scholars, poets, and others initiated the Jadidist reform movement. Jadidism means "New Method," and this movement began as an effort to reform the educational system in Central Asia, where in 1900 only a tiny percentage of the local population was literate. Eventually the efforts of the Jadids evolved into a political movement, which sought the overthrow of the despotic rulers in Bukhara and Khiva and which also served to expand an emerging nationalism among the native Central Asians. Russia's defeat in the Russo-Japanese War and the failed revolution of 1905 strengthened nationalist sentiment among Central Asia's educated classes. Many Jadids would eventually join the Bolshevik uprising in 1917 and the years immediately after, only to be purged and liquidated in the 1920s and 1930s.

The pervasive discontent that characterized the European regions of the Russian Empire during World War I was also a feature of the social landscape of Central Asia. In 1916, on the eve of the Bolshevik Revolution, Russian Turkistan was wracked by a violent uprising that continued for several months, resulting in thousands of deaths and extensive property damage. The trigger for the revolt, but certainly not the sole cause, was a military draft decree, calling up units of Central Asians to help in Russia's struggle with the Central Powers. Soldiers from Central Asia were not to be assigned to combat units but were to serve as support troops. Nevertheless, the draft ignited fierce resistance, most of which appears to have been organized and led by Muslim mullahs. As had been the case in the Andijan uprising, the revolt originated in the Fergana Valley but quickly spread to a much greater area than had been the case in 1898.

Although the revolt of 1916 was suppressed by the end of the year, intrigue and instability were still very much a part of the Central Asian political scene. The February Revolution in 1917 and the abdication of the tsar only exacerbated these characteristics, leading to great uncertainty and chaos in the Russian administration based in Tashkent. Famine in the summer of 1917, along with increasing tensions between native Central Asians and Russian settlers, helped to bring revolutionary sentiments to a head. On September 12, the Bolshevik Party in Tashkent staged a coup and briefly seized power—thus the Bolshevik Revolution actually began in Central Asia, because this event preceded the Bolshevik uprising in St. Petersburg by several weeks. As a result, many Central Asians anticipated an end to Russian colonialism and cultural domination, without realizing that the new regime would ultimately prove far harsher than the former.

The Soviet Period

The brutality and chaos that marked the 1917 Russian Revolution were no less pronounced in Central Asia than elsewhere in the former Russian Empire. The struggle between the "Reds" and the "Whites" was made more complex by the emergence of nationalism among the native intelligentsia. An independent government, composed of both local and Russian representatives, was set up at Kokand but crushed by Bolshevik forces directed from Tashkent, where the Bolsheviks had seized power early in the revolution. Two groups of Jadids in the semi-independent states of Khiva and Bukhara, the Young Khivans and Young Bukharans (after the reformist Young Turks of Turkey, led by Mustafa Kemal Ataturk), seized power and established "People's Republics," but these were shortly absorbed by local Bolshevik forces. Some Jadids willingly joined the Bolshevik cause, whereas others did so out of political necessity. Mikhail Frunze, the Russian general leading the Red Army in Central Asia, had beaten the White forces and consolidated control of most of the region by 1922, but this was not the end of resistance to Bolshevik rule.

Active resistance to Communist rule continued in Central Asia, particularly in the Fergana Valley and remote districts, for another decade. Those fighting the Soviet authorities were labeled *Basmachi* (bandits) by the regime, and indeed some in their ranks probably were no more than common criminals. Many others, however, were Islamic officials, disaffected Jadids, former military men, and others who were opposed to the Soviet government. The Basmachi were splintered and frequently fought in small, clandestine units, but in 1922 leaders of the various factions met in Samarkand and attempted to adopt a unified strategy of resistance, articulating their goal of establishing an independent state governed by Central Asians. Several key figures from this meeting were later caught and beheaded by the Soviet authorities, and the movement remained underground. The rebels lacked the organization and support to overthrow Soviet power, but the Soviets in their turn lacked the ability to eradicate completely the Basmachi, who often operated from bases across the border in Afghanistan. Rebel activities sporadically continued in some remote corners of Central Asia into the 1930s, before the Basmachi were entirely subdued.

By the mid-1920s, the Soviet regime was secure enough to consider the problem of administering Central Asia. The Russian imperial designation of Turkistan was jettisoned, and the vast territory was divided into political units based on the nationalities (in reality, various ethnic groups) identified by Russian and Soviet ethnographers and anthropologists—that is, Uzbeks, Tajiks, Kazakhs, Kyrgyz, and so on (Carlisle 1994). According to the Soviet constitution promulgated in 1922, at least some of these peoples qualified to be awarded the territory of a Soviet Socialist Republic (SSR), the constituent unit of the Union of Soviet Socialist Republics, or USSR. The first of these was created in Central Asia in 1924, with the formation of the Uzbek SSR. Attached to the Uzbek SSR was the Tajik ASSR, which would eventually be separated and elevated to SSR status in 1929.

Such political organization was unprecedented in Central Asia; never before had a distinct territory been identified with the Uzbeks and other ethnic groups. Indeed, considerable confusion reigned over ethnic self-identification, and many people, including urban residents known as Sarts, did not easily fit into any specific ethnic category. Others merely chose the ethnicity of the territory in which they lived, regardless of their actual ethnic affiliation. This was particularly true in cities such as Samarkand and Bukhara, which were placed in the Uzbek SSR but held populations that were mostly Tajik. Nevertheless, the delimitation of Central Asia into ethnopolitical units and the resultant identities these created were more resilient than expected and would lay the basis for the emergence of independent states sixty-seven years later.

Soviet attitudes toward Islam in Uzbekistan underwent a series of modifications during the approximately seventy years of Communist control, although in general the approach toward the faith was hostile. During the 1920s, religious lands were confiscated and the *khudzhum* campaign, an effort to "liberate" Muslim women by forcibly removing their veils, was implemented, although on the other hand, most mosques were allowed to remain open in Uzbekistan and elsewhere (Masswell 1975). After the rise of Josef Stalin in 1928, a harsh policy of eradicating the physical manifestations of Islam was pursued, resulting in the closure of hundreds of mosques and medressehs, and the liquidation of most of the Muslim leadership.

The Stalinist repression was relaxed during World War II, when four regional Muslim Spiritual Boards were created in the USSR, with the board for Central Asia located in Tashkent. After the war, this accommodation with Islam continued until 1959, when Stalin's successor, Nikita Khrushchev, abruptly returned to the confrontational stance of the 1930s. After another period of relative religious tolerance in the 1970s, Islam was again vilified and suppressed for most of the remainder of Soviet rule. The Uzbek SSR played an important part in maintaining Islamic belief under the Soviets, as the only two official medressehs operating in the USSR after World War II were located there, the largest in Bukhara and a second in Tashkent.

Destruction of Uzbekistan's traditional culture was not the only negative aspect of Soviet control. Soviet economic policy had a profound, and in some cases devastating, effect on the Uzbek SSR. Collectivization of agricultural lands dramatically changed the structure of production, which was now determined by the government planning agencies, not by individual farmers. The Five Year Plans, introduced during the Stalin era, imposed increasing production quotas five years into the future regardless of crop failure or drought. Cotton became the dominant crop in sown acreage and was a vital export for the Soviet regime, earning badly needed hard currency on the international market. The Uzbek SSR was the Soviet Union's leading republic in cotton production. Cotton production was so lucrative that the crop was often referred to as "white gold" in the Uzbek media. As new acreage was brought into production, however, the demand for water steadily increased. The main sources of irrigation water were the Amu Darya and Syr Darya rivers, and as increasingly larger amounts of water were extracted from them, they failed to replenish the Aral Sea. The resulting collapse of the Aral and its surrounding ecosystem, as noted earlier, represents the most serious environmental problem Uzbekistan inherited from the Soviet administration, a problem that continues to defy solution.

A second result of the economic policies of the Soviet period was an emphasis on agricultural production and extraction of natural resources at the expense of industrial development. This was the case across the Central Asian republics but was particularly pronounced in Uzbekistan, where a tiny percentage of the cotton produced was processed within the republic; rather, the great bulk of the crop was shipped to mills and factories in Russia, Ukraine, and other parts of the European USSR.

In many ways, this relationship mirrored the classic mercantile systems established by European colonial powers in the seventeenth and eighteenth centuries, and it led to the same consequences: a skewed economic structure highly dependent on the production of raw materials, with little local industrial capacity. In Central Asia, only northern Kazakhstan received abundant capital investment in heavy and light industry. While the USSR was in existence, Central Asians were its poorest residents, a partial consequence of the economic directives issued from Moscow. The relocation of entire factories to Tashkent and a few other cities in the Uzbek SSR during World War II helped to spur industrial development, but Uzbekistan and its neighbors remained well behind most of the remainder of the Soviet Union in industrial development.

In a few social and educational spheres, Soviet administration resulted in significant advances in the quality of life for many residents of the Uzbek SSR. Gains were achieved in terms of raising literacy rates and general levels of education, particularly among women, and infant mortality was reduced dramatically by improvements in health care, promoted and implemented by the Soviet regime. When Tashkent was struck by a catastrophic earthquake in 1966, thousands of volunteers from around the USSR migrated to the capital to assist in its reconstruction, and many settled there. Tashkent evolved into one of the most modern cities in Asia, with broad boulevards and an impressive subway system. Yet the improvements in these aspects of life did not offset the repressed resentment many Uzbeks felt toward not only the Soviet system but in some cases toward Slavs themselves.

The sudden rise of Mikhail Gorbachev to the position of general secretary of the Communist Party of the Soviet Union in early 1985 heralded changes that few could have predicted. Gorbachev's policy of glasnost (openness) eventually cleared the way for public debate and criticism of the status quo, enabling even the most fundamental aspects of Soviet policy and administration to be challenged. This process emerged more slowly in the Central Asian republics than in other corners of the USSR, but by the late 1980s, several independent political organizations in the Uzbek SSR had appeared, including Birlik (unity). Birlik strove to promote the status of the Uzbek language, which had remained secondary to Russian throughout the Soviet era.

The new liberalization of glasnost also brought forth more sinister impulses among some in the Uzbek SSR. During the summer of 1989, ethnic rioting erupted in the Fergana Valley between Uzbeks and Meskhetian Turks, leading to at least 100 fatalities and to the end of the myth of "socialist brotherhood" in Uzbekistan. Following the lead of other republics, the Uzbek SSR issued a declaration of sovereignty in June 1990, an indisputable sign that the old order was crumbling. Yet few inside the USSR or abroad could have imagined how imminent Soviet collapse was—within a year and a half, the Uzbek SSR, along with the fourteen other constituent republics, would abruptly gain independence, a status that brought both hope and anxiety for the people of the new country of Uzbekistan.

Independent Uzbekistan

It is probably true that the Central Asian republics were the least prepared for independence once the USSR was officially disbanded in December of 1991. A few attempts had been made in Uzbekistan to form a political opposition at the end of the Soviet era, including the Islamic Renaissance Party (IRP), Birlik, and a splinter group from Birlik, Erk (Will) (Gleason 1997, 122). The Uzbek Communist Party (later the People's Democratic Party) had either suppressed these groups by force, as was the case with the IRP, or harassed and prevented them from organizing and disseminating their message via the media, as was the case with Birlik, which was not allowed to register as a political party. Only Erk was allowed to function briefly as an official political party. In the country's first presidential election, held in December 1991, the former first party secretary of the Uzbek Communist Party, Islom Karimov, ran against Muhammad Solih, the leader of Erk. Karimov won the election with a large majority, although the support Solih received was somewhat surprising given his lack of access to broadcast media and other restrictions placed on his campaign by the Karimov regime.

Following his first election as president, Karimov moved rapidly to dismantle his emerging opposition. Leaders of Birlik, Erk, and other potential rivals were silenced, sometimes through physical assault, and most were driven into exile. Islamic authorities who disagreed with the regime's approach toward the faith were arrested or simply "disappeared." The Uzbek government retained control of all media (just as had been the case under Communism), and although a parliament, the Oliy Majlis, was established in 1994, most of the governmental power resides directly with the office of the president. The Uzbek constitution, promulgated in 1992, limited the president to two terms, but Karimov sidestepped this provision in 2000 when he ran for a third term and was elected.

From its first days as a sovereign state, Uzbekistan has faced daunting economic challenges. The imbalances created by the Soviet emphasis on the cotton "monoculture" meant that the economy was heavily skewed toward production of cotton and other raw materials, with the manufacturing and service sectors badly underdeveloped (Craumer 1995). To make matters worse, the demographic growth Uzbekistan has experienced for the last several decades continues, resulting in an expansion of the workforce and rising levels of unemployment.

From the early 1990s, the Karimov regime adopted a policy of "gradualism," allegedly designed to maintain stability while the country made the transition from a command economy to a capitalistic system, subject to market forces. As a result, privatization of land was delayed, and although a national currency, the *som,* was introduced in 1994, it was not made convertible on international currency markets until October 2003. The authoritarian, repressive nature of the Uzbek administration, along with bureaucratic obstacles and widespread corruption, kept many foreign investors at bay, although a few large-scale projects, such as the Daewoo automobile plant built in Aksaka, were successfully completed. Throughout the 1990s, the country remained woefully short of investment capital, a problem only made worse by its distance from major markets, lack of direct access to global shipping routes, and the immediate proximity of two unstable neighbors, Tajikistan and Afghanistan. By the late 1990s, the political stability of Uzbekistan itself was called into question by acts of domestic terrorism and short-lived but highly publicized incursions by Islamic militants.

From 1991 to 1994, interest in Islam increased exponentially. Thousands of new mosques were built, courses in classical Arabic became widely available, and the Uzbek media, which only a few scant years before had reviled the faith, began to present a more balanced, and often favorable, image of the country's Islamic heritage. Islamic organizations that might challenge President Karimov's power and position, however, were promptly crushed, just as the secular opposition had been. These included the Islamic Renaissance Party and a smaller group based in the city of Namangan, *Adolat* (justice) (Bohr 1998). Two of the leading figures in Adolat would emerge in the late 1990s as key players in the Islamic Movement of Uzbekistan (IMU), Tohir Yuldash and Juma Namangani. In general, any Muslims in Uzbekistan who attempted to organize and proselytize outside of the government-sponsored Islamic structure were apt to be accused of "fundamentalism" by the Uzbek authorities.

Tashkent was rocked by a series of explosions in February 1999, which killed at least sixteen people and injured many more. The incident was quickly declared to be an assassination attempt on President Karimov by Islamic radicals, although those responsible have never been identified with certainty. Over the next three summers, parts of eastern Uzbekistan were briefly invaded by fighters of the newly proclaimed Islamic Movement of Uzbekistan (IMU), which openly sought the removal of the Karimov regime by armed force. Aided by the Taliban and quite possibly by Osama bin Laden, many if not most of the followers of the IMU were killed or dispersed by U.S. bombing and raids in the battle for Mazar-i-Sharif in northern Afghanistan during the late fall of 2001. A second radical Islamic group, Hizb-ut-Tahrir (Party of Liberation), appears to have significant support within Uzbekistan. Unlike the IMU, Hizb-ut-Tahrir, through its literature and Web site, calls for political change via non-violent means. More violence rocked the country in the spring of 2004, when a series of bombings and gun battles occurred in Bukhara, Tashkent, and other locations. A previously unknown group, Jamoat (society), claimed responsibility for these actions, which claimed almost fifty lives, including those of the terrorists.

In the wake of the terrorist attacks on the United States on September 11, 2001, the Central Asian countries acquired a new significance as "frontline" states in the struggle against international terrorism. Uzbekistan immediately declared itself an ally of the United States in the "war on terror" and allowed U.S. forces to use an airbase near Termez as a staging point for the campaign against the Taliban regime. This dramatically improved the Karimov regime's standing with the United States and had the added effect of decimating the IMU, which had been an irritant for several years and now found itself bearing the full brunt of U.S. military might. The Karimov administration had virtually overnight gained more sympathy for its policies directed against the "fundamentalists," who allegedly represented the most serious threat to the country's stability.

CONCLUSION

The elimination of the IMU as a viable fighting force and the imprisonment of thousands of suspected Islamic sympathizers have perhaps increased the longevity of the Karimov government. Fundamental challenges to Uzbekistan's stability remain, however: a moribund economy, severe ecological damage, a growing and increasingly frustrated population, widespread corruption, and a rigid authoritarian government with virtually all power invested in the person of President Islom Karimov. Uzbekistan appears to be as distant from democracy today as it was during the era of the Soviet Union. The failure to develop democratic institutions, including an independent judiciary, a free and open media, and a multi-party political system, means that political transition, which must inevitably come, will likely be chaotic and possibly bloody. After more than a decade of independence, Uzbekistan seems to have made little concrete progress in meeting its potential and addressing its most pressing problems. Ultimately, the people of Uzbekistan will choose a path to stagnation or to recovery—both will require great sacrifice and tenacity, with uncertain outcomes.

References

Allworth, Edward. 1990. *The Modern Uzbeks: From the Fourteenth Century to the Present*. Stanford, CA: Hoover Institution Press.

Bohr, Annette. 1998. *Uzbekistan: Politics and Foreign Policy*. London: The Royal Institute of International Affairs.

Carlisle, Donald. 1994. "Soviet Uzbekistan: State and Nation in Historical Perspective." In *Central Asia in Historical Perspective*, edited by Beatrice F. Manz. Boulder, CO: Westview Press.

Craumer, Peter. 1995. *Rural and Agricultural Development in Uzbekistan*. London: The Royal Institute of International Affairs.

Gleason, Gregory. 1997. *The Central Asian States: Discovering Independence*. Boulder, CO: Westview Press.

Massell, Gregory. 1975. "Family Law and Social Mobilization in Soviet Central Asia: Some Comparisons with Communist China." *Canadian Slavonic Papers* XVII, Nos. 2 and 3, pp. 374–403.

Sinnott, Peter. 1992. "The Physical Geography of Soviet Central Asia and the Aral Sea Problem." In *Geographic Perspectives on Soviet Central Asia*, edited by Robert A. Lewis. New York and London: Routledge.

The Economy of Uzbekistan

The phoenix is an important symbol of modern Uzbekistan, appearing on the coinage and official documents. The representation is appropriate, because the country, like the mythological creature, attempts a resurrection from the ashes of Soviet Communism. Yet the rebirth of a society is a more complex and time-consuming procedure than legend would have us believe. Like all components of Uzbek life, the economy of Uzbekistan remains in a condition of flux and transition, and rebirth in the form of fundamental restructuring has been neither a quick nor a painless process. Entering the arena of the global marketplace has been made more difficult by developmental imbalances inherited from the Soviet era, geographic isolation and distance from markets, the generally low level of personal income and investment, and the reluctance of the Karimov regime to undertake difficult but necessary reforms.

Uzbekistan's economy remains heavily focused on the primary sector, with agriculture and extraction of natural resources representing leading activities. Agriculture's share of total GDP (gross domestic product) has held constant since independence at about 34 percent, and it remains the largest employer in Uzbekistan, accounting for about 33 percent of the total workforce in 2000 (United Nations 2001). The dependency on agriculture may also be seen in the country's export structure, where cotton exports alone accounted for approximately half of total exports by value in the late 1990s. Since independence, a sizable and burgeoning service sector has emerged and helped to fuel a rather modest annual rate of economic growth of slightly more than 2 percent during the 1990s, according to Uzbek government statistics, although estimates by the World Bank, International Monetary Fund, and other sources indicate growth at lower levels. The twin evils of high unemployment and high inflation continue to plague the Uzbek economy and deter foreign investors. A long-overdue move in October 2003 to make the national currency, the som, convertible in international financial markets is expected to have a favorable impact, but this event alone will not solve the country's economic dilemma, which must be addressed by fundamental economic restructuring.

AGRICULTURE

Agriculture is the most important economic sector in the Uzbek economy. Approximately a third of the country's GDP comes from agriculture, and this portion of the economy likewise provides about a third of the jobs in Uzbekistan, although the percentage of employment in agriculture has declined significantly from the mid-1990s. Given that most of Uzbekistan is desert, it is remarkable that the country is a significant agricultural producer at all, and even more remarkable that, in a typical year, Uzbekistan ranks among the top countries globally for the production of raw cotton and cotton fiber, as well as being self-sufficient in wheat production. Virtually all agricultural production is accomplished via irrigation, and the system of canals and viaducts that provide water to the fields and orchards is both ancient and extensive, having been built up over the course of many centuries.

Cropping Pattern

Because of the dependency on the irrigation network, the geographic pattern of crop production is closely linked to the rivers of Uzbekistan, which are the main sources of water—a limited amount of water for irrigation is obtained from wells. The areas of production therefore tend to lie adjacent to the streams, in a mosaic similar to that of beads on a string. The agricultural heartland of the country is the Fergana Valley, a

Cotton harvesting in Uzbekistan. Women and students do much of the harvesting by hand. (David Turnley/Corbis)

densely populated region of relatively abundant water and fertile soils. In the western two-thirds of Uzbekistan, cultivation is closely associated with the pattern of streams and canals that branch off from the Amu Darya, the main source of water for this parched section of the country. Although irrigation is essential to agricultural production, overirrigation of much of the land has resulted in widespread problems with salinization. This occurs when subsurface mineral salts are brought to the surface via capillary action, despoiling the topsoil.

Cotton remains a key crop, particularly as a source of foreign earnings, and accounts for 1.5 million hectares of the sown acreage, or 37 percent of the total cultivated area. Cotton fiber continues to represent the main source of foreign income for Uzbekistan, accounting for more than 50 percent of exports in the late 1990s. Much of the cotton crop is planted, cultivated, and harvested by hand, and in a typical year, soldiers and students are called into the fields for several weeks in the early fall to help gather the crop. Cotton is grown across Uzbekistan, and various regions compete to have the largest harvest.

Besides cotton, Uzbekistan produces other cash crops of significance. Sericulture, or the cultivation of silk worms, is an ancient activity in the Fergana Valley, where silk has been produced for centuries. In the wake of independence, the silk industry in Uzbekistan experienced a decline, as a shortage of modern equipment and the low quality of silk hindered production and reduced potential exports. As in other areas of the economy, investment is badly needed to upgrade production and processing facilities and to improve efficiency. If a willing foreign partner can be found, success can follow, as the case of tobacco illustrates. In the early 1990s the Uzbek government teamed with British American Tobacco (BAT) in an effort to revitalize the country's tobacco production. BAT invested millions of dollars into the local tobacco industry, and by the mid-1990s, Uzbekistan was producing approximately 12 billion cigarettes a year, for both domestic consumption and export (Craumer 1995, 26).

Primary food crops include wheat, rice, maize (corn), and potatoes, with the country achieving self-sufficiency in wheat in the mid-1990s. Although wheat production skyrocketed in the 1990s, rice production dropped significantly. Rice and maize are grown in the irrigated lowlands along the country's major rivers, along with a variety of other food crops, including grapes, apricots, and other fruits; several types of nuts; and the best known of Uzbekistan's food crops (at least among citizens of the former Soviet republics), the famous melons of Uzbekistan. Two major types of melons are produced. Westerners would quickly recognize watermelons, and massive piles of these and other melons are found on the street corners in every Uzbek city in late summer. The second type of melon, virtually unknown in the West, is a yellow, elongated variety of sweet melon, usually slightly smaller than a watermelon, called locally *dinya,* or simply "melon." Both the watermelon and dinya are enjoyed as a dessert from

July until October, and many people keep melons through the winter.

Land Ownership and Reform

When Russian imperial administration of Central Asia was implemented in the last half of the nineteenth century, Russian officials inherited a complex, long-standing system of land tenure in which not only rights to land ownership but also access to irrigation water were well established. Although in theory the local khan or emir controlled all land, in reality much of the arable area was the property of thousands of individual farmers. In addition, a considerable amount of land was held by local religious authorities, in a system of ownership known as *waqf.* Individual plots were small, ranging from less than an acre to perhaps several dozen. A sizable number of farms were worked by tenant farmers or sharecroppers, and the tsar's authorities eventually decreed that ownership of land would be transferred to those who actually worked the property, a reform that gave thousands of landless peasants a share of the region's agricultural wealth for the first time.

In the two decades after the Bolshevik Revolution, virtually all agricultural land in the Soviet Union was collectivized, meaning that it became the property of the state, and farmers worked the land on collective farms, or *kolkhozi*. This centralization of agricultural control was widely, and sometimes violently, opposed by those who held a share of the agricultural land, yet despite this resistance, by the late 1930s nearly all land in production was under the direct control of the state. Farmers were allowed to work a small amount of land as a "private plot," but the Soviet government held the remaining acreage, and government planners determined the type of crop to be raised, as well as setting production quotas for the collective. In Uzbekistan, the collectivized system of agriculture led to many serious imbalances, including the development of the cotton monoculture in which cotton was produced at the expense of other crops. In addition, widespread environmental problems, inefficient use of water and other resources, and damage to the land from overirrigation, lack of crop rotation, and other poor farming practices resulted from poor agricultural policy.

Since the 1990s, the Uzbek government has slowly implemented a restructuring of land ownership, gradually moving to withdraw the state as the main agricultural landowner. This limited privatization of land has resulted in about 10 percent of the arable land being distributed to *dekhqan* farmers (small-plot landowners), and ownership of most livestock has been transferred into private hands. In addition, the government has withdrawn "state orders" (in reality, quotas that had to be delivered to the government) on many agricultural goods, although not on the most economically important crops, cotton and grain. Most of the production of both cotton and wheat takes place on the government-supported cooperative farms called *shirkat*. The ultimate goals of agricultural land reform are to increase employment opportunities in the countryside and to raise the standard of living there, because a majority of those living below the official poverty line reside in rural regions (Agafonoff 1997).

Returning collectivized agricultural land is difficult for a number of reasons. First, legal records of ownership prior to the Soviet takeover were sparse, and many of those records that were in existence were destroyed or lost during the decades of Communist control. Claims of ownership based on the period before collectivization are therefore often impossible to verify and enforce. Second, dividing the land up equitably among the collective farmers is difficult because there are significant variations in the quality of land and the accessibility of water. In addition, how will the collective's allotment of irrigation water be divided up fairly among all the new landowners? Then there is the matter of the collective's jointly held equipment, seed, fertilizer, farm buildings, and other assets—how can these be distributed in a fair manner?

Ultimately, these questions must be answered if productivity and living standards are to rise in the Uzbek countryside, and although progress has been slow to this point, privatization of farmland remains a goal of the Uzbek administration.

INDUSTRY

Upon achieving independence, Uzbekistan inherited a rather modest industrial base. Unlike its giant neighbor, Kazakhstan, Uzbekistan had received relatively little industrial investment during the Soviet period, except during World War II, when a considerable number of enterprises were relocated to Central Asia to prevent them from falling into German hands. The amount of industrial investment was low despite the fact that Uzbekistan possesses large deposits of natural gas and gold, sources of wealth from which the country continues to benefit. Under Soviet administration, Uzbekistan was exploited as an enormous repository of raw material, especially raw cotton, almost all of which was shipped to Russia, Ukraine, and other parts of the USSR for refinement. The end result was a retardation of industrial development in Uzbekistan. Most of the industrial development that did reach Uzbekistan was highly concentrated in Tashkent and a few remaining cities, leading to additional distortions and imbalances in economic development.

The Uzbek government has found it difficult to overcome this legacy, and new industrial growth has been sporadic and limited since independence. Industrial output also experienced a serious decline in the years immediately following independence, but has rebounded somewhat in recent years. One of the major reasons for the relative lack of new industrial enterprises has been a dismal rate of foreign direct investment (FDI), a crucial source of investment capital for a country like Uzbekistan, where few local people have the money or the trust to invest in the national stock market, a new innovation in itself. A study by the European Bank for

Reconstruction and Development discovered that, in 2000, Uzbekistan had the lowest rate of FDI per capita of any of the former Soviet states; in the late 1990s, the country experienced a net capital *outflow,* an alarming omen for the Uzbek economy (United Nations 2001, 10).

To compound the problem, many of the projects that have attracted foreign investors have met with limited success. A prime example is the large automobile plant built by the South Korean firm Daewoo at Asaka, not far from the city of Andijan in the Fergana Valley. When the plant was constructed in the mid-1990s, it was heralded as a major advance for both the local and national economies, and Uzbek authorities expected a wave of foreign investment to follow. Not only did the projected surge of investment fail to materialize, but the Daewoo plant has not lived up to expectations in terms of production or job creation. Although it produces many of the automobiles seen on Uzbekistan's roads, it operates below capacity and has not generated as many jobs as the Uzbek government had hoped. According to a study by the World Bank published in 2003, Uzdaewoo, the joint venture company established by Daewoo and the Uzbek government, was operating at only 20 percent of its capacity (World Bank 2003). A thriving export market for Daewoo cars, another expected benefit, has not developed. In reality, much of the FDI sent to Uzbekistan has flowed into extractive industries such as mining, oil and gas, and other activities that do not generate long-term employment opportunities for local workers. The low level of FDI is particularly disheartening when viewed against the fact that Uzbekistan represents the largest market in Central Asia and the most centralized location.

Given the disappointing rate of foreign investment, it is vital that small-scale local businesses emerge in Uzbekistan. Recently Uzbek authorities have increasingly emphasized the development of so-called SMEs, or small to medium businesses (World Bank 2003). A number of obstacles have hampered the development of small-scale entrepreneurship, including a general lack of business knowledge, such as the basic techniques of accounting, management, and marketing; a shortage of available and affordable credit from commercial banks; and poor enforcement of laws governing ownership and contractual obligations. The Uzbek regime has moved to encourage SMEs in recent years by supporting business incubators in various regions, reducing restrictions and paperwork for registering new businesses, and working to increase lines of credit. According to official calculations, SMEs made up almost 30 percent of total GDP in 1999, although it is likely this estimate is too optimistic. There is certainly room for expansion of this sector in the Uzbek economy, an opportunity that must be seized if Uzbekistan's economy is to enjoy sustained growth.

SERVICE SECTOR

The service sector of the Uzbek economy is made up of activities that do not fall in the agricultural or industrial branches of production. This makes for a broad category, which includes transport and communication, construction, trade, information and computer services, health, education, banking and insurance, and a number of additional components. Although the share of both agriculture and industry in Uzbekistan's GDP declined during the 1990s, the service sector expanded to more than 40 percent, making it the largest part of the economy by this measure. By the end of the first decade of Uzbek independence, services had also slightly surpassed agriculture in terms of total employment, accounting for 41 percent, a fraction more than the agricultural sector.

Several factors have fueled the expansion of the service sector. Before 1991, many services simply did not exist in the Uzbek economy, because the country was only tenuously connected to the global economy, and in the relatively isolated Soviet system, such services were not provided. Few consumer goods were imported under the command economy of the USSR, but following independence, outlets offering imported goods from Europe, Turkey, East Asia, and other locations quickly appeared. Foreign automobile dealerships, stores offering processed food from abroad, and cybercafés are just some of the new businesses that emerged in the 1990s in Uzbekistan. Commercial banking, a stock market, insurance, and other financial services also contributed to the expansion of the service sector, although growth of these businesses has been somewhat stunted because of the country's economic difficulties, especially high inflation rates, low wages, and low rates of personal savings.

The service sector represents one of the few positive areas in the Uzbek economy over the last decade. Continued and accelerated expansion of this part of the economy could greatly assist in job creation, increased rates of saving and investment, and a reduction in poverty, although because of the concentration of poverty in rural regions, service sector expansion alone will not dramatically raise living standards among Uzbekistan's poor in the short term. Moreover, there is considerable room for growth in several types of services, particularly in tourism, the potential of which has yet to be reached. If the government's recent emphasis on SME development bears fruit, then the economy may eventually be weaned of its dependency on cotton and gas exports, and shortcomings in the agricultural and industrial sectors may be offset by enlargement of services.

POVERTY

Poverty is a relative measure and is almost always considered in the context of income distribution. That is, someone (or in the United States, a family of four) achieving an income level below a recognized benchmark (the "poverty line") is identified as living in poverty, according to the standards of that society or country. What constitutes "poverty" is different from country to country. A family of four living just below the

Wooden scaffolding supports a group of laborers as they tile a dome in Ichan-Kala, the walled inner city of Khiva, in Uzbekistan. (Diego Lezama Orezzoli/Corbis)

poverty line in the United States in 2002 (annual income of $18,390) would be considered upper class in Uzbekistan, where in 2000 the average monthly wage was approximately $40 if measured at the official exchange rate for the som and dollar, considerably less if measured at the black market rate. A definition of poverty based on income level may mask other deficiencies in living standards, such as access to basic services, education, health care, and other factors that enhance one's quality of life. For example, an individual with a relatively low income living in Tashkent, the capital city, would generally enjoy a higher quality of life than someone with a somewhat larger income living in rural Karakalpakstan, or perhaps even in Nukus, the largest city in that region. Gauging poverty strictly through monetary income is problematical in many societies, and this is particularly the case in Uzbekistan.

A central contributor to poverty and low quality of life in Uzbekistan is unemployment and underemployment (Dosumov 1996). The latter occurs when an individual is listed as being employed by an enterprise but in reality spends little time there and performs a minimum amount of work. Most international agencies agree that official data from the Uzbek government during the 1990s on the level of unemployment in the Uzbek economy consistently and dramatically underrepresented the percentages of those out of work. In the late 1990s, for example, official rates of unemployment were less than 1 percent of the workforce, whereas international donor agencies estimated the real rate to be as high as 25 percent in some areas of the country. Two factors threaten to compound and worsen the employment situation: the low level of foreign investment and the large number of young people who will enter the labor force through 2015.

The Uzbek economy has also been victimized by high rates of inflation since the economic transition began, although the level of inflation has diminished significantly since the early

Woman searching for potable water. Searching for water in Muynak has become a daily chore for the people who inhabit this town, which once bordered on the Aral Sea. The Aral is rapidly disappearing and taking with it the local economy and health of the local population. (David Turnley/Corbis)

1990s. During the first five years of independence, the inflation rate averaged a staggering 527 percent per year. Under such hyperinflation, wages could not keep pace with price increases, confidence in the local currency was low, and there was little incentive to save, because the value of one's savings eroded almost overnight. This meant that capital for local investment remained at low levels because banks had limited reserves to loan, and interest rates were high, yet another negative result of runaway inflation. The local currency, the som, was not yet convertible on international markets, and a thriving illegal market in currency trading quickly appeared. The second half of the 1990s saw a reduction in the average annual inflation rate to about 42 percent—still high, but greatly improved from the early years of economic transition.

Accompanying the challenges of unemployment and inflation is a general problem with low—and in many cases,
delayed—salaries. In many instances, the pay scale for professionals is so low that highly skilled specialists must take on
secondary work, often involving long hours, to earn additional
income. It is not unusual, for example, to encounter a taxi
driver or repairman who is also a university professor, a doc-
tor, or an engineer. Not only are salaries low, but often the
money is not paid on schedule, to workers and administrators
alike; sometimes delays can be of several months' duration.
When the salary is finally delivered, no interest is paid, meaning that in Uzbekistan's inflationary economy, the real purchasing power of the money has significantly declined. There
are few social services available to those whose salary payment has been postponed; most people survive simply by borrowing money from friends or family members.

Those living in poverty in Uzbekistan are overwhelmingly
concentrated in rural districts, where unemployment and
underemployment rates are high, wages are relatively low,
and educational opportunities minimal. Within the country,
there are stark contrasts in the percentage of the population
in poverty, according to region. A study by the World Bank
in 2002 found that less than 10 percent of the population of
Tashkent was below the poverty line, whereas in
Kashkadarya oblast (province), in the southern part of the
country, more than 60 percent of the population was poor
(World Bank 2003). In addition, more than 40 percent in the
Kashkadarya region lived in extreme poverty, meaning that
they subsisted on no more than the equivalent of one dollar
per day. Six other oblasts exceeded the national average of
27.5 percent, concentrated mostly in the Fergana Valley and
in the far western reaches of the country. Ominously, these
same regions are experiencing the highest rates of population growth in Uzbekistan, indicating that poverty rates
there are likely to increase in coming years.

TRANSPORTATION AND COMMUNICATION

Uzbekistan has the dubious distinction of being one of only two "double-landlocked" countries in the world, the other being the tiny state of Liechtenstein, located in the heart of Europe. Double-landlocked means that not only is the country landlocked, but all the states bordering it are landlocked as well.

Thus, Uzbekistan finds itself a long way from the major shipping lanes of the global economy, presenting yet another economic disadvantage the new state must overcome. On the other hand, there are potential advantages to the country's location if sufficient transportation linkages can be developed. Emerging economies in Russia, China, and South Asia represent potential markets for exports from Uzbekistan and its neighbors in Central Asia. The challenge for Uzbekistan is creating the infrastructure to integrate its economy with these emerging centers of commerce, as well as building linkages to the greater global economy.

In the case of transportation, once again the country must overcome the legacy of the recent past. Transportation connections during the Soviet days were overwhelmingly focused on integration with other Soviet republics, not toward the global marketplace, and over the last decade Uzbekistan has worked to improve its connections with the rest of the world. Considerable success has been achieved in the case of air transportation. Uzbekistan has a national airline, Uzbekistan Airways, which flies to many world cities, including New York, London, and Tokyo. Other major carriers also serve Tashkent, including Lufthansa, Turkish Airways, and Aeroflot. In the late 1990s, the Tashkent airport underwent major renovation, and it is now the most modern and busiest in Central Asia. There are air connections to every large and medium-sized city in the country as well, although flying is expensive for most Uzbeks.

Less success has been met with the effort to improve ground transportation infrastructure. Outside of Tashkent oblast, roads are in generally poor condition and require constant repair; railroads are out of date and use rolling stock (cars and locomotives) that are decades old. A highway runs from Tashkent to Termez, on Uzbekistan's southern border with Afghanistan, and with the ouster of the Taliban regime in that country, hopes are growing that a continuous and reliable highway might be constructed linking Tashkent with Karachi, Pakistan, thereby providing Uzbekistan with an outlet on the Indian Ocean. Uzbekistan has sought other outlets as well. Along with Azerbaijan, Georgia, and Turkmenistan, Uzbekistan has agreed in principle to the establishment of a "trans-Caspian transport corridor" that would link Tashkent to the Black Sea port of Poti, in the Republic of Georgia. The construction of additional road and rail linkages to surrounding countries, and ultimately to the broader world market, is absolutely essential to Uzbekistan's economic future. Investment for such projects is limited, however, and the country must find ways to attract the necessary capital to support large-scale transport infrastructure construction.

TOURISM—A POTENTIAL ENGINE OF GROWTH?

Uzbekistan has only begun to tap its potential as a tourist destination, but to increase the number of visitors, a number of challenges must be overcome. The country, and the greater Central Asian realm as a whole, suffers from several disadvantages in the attempt to attract tourists from outside the region. The first disadvantage is Uzbekistan's great distance from many of the major countries that are the source of much of international tourism, especially the United States, Japan, and Australia. Flights from these locations to Central Asia require 10 to 20 hours, depending on route and transfers.

*Registan Square, in the center of Samarkand. (Photo courtesy of
Reuel Hanks)*

Even tourists from western Europe cannot reach Tashkent in
less than 5 to 6 hours via air.

The second disadvantage is the outside world's general lack
of knowledge of the region, coupled with a lackluster effort on
the part of the Uzbek administration to advertise the country's attractions and entice tourists to visit (Trushin 1998).
These problems, together with rather high visa fees and a
complex, bureaucratic, and intimidating entry procedure,
work to curtail the number of visitors to Uzbekistan. Finally,
the infrastructure and services required for enlarging the
tourist industry in Uzbekistan have been slow to emerge,
although recent years have seen a number of new first-class
hotels built in Tashkent, Samarkand, and other major cities.
Many other parts of the country lack even third-class accommodations, however, and relatively few tour companies are
yet operating outside the major destinations of Tashkent,
Samarkand, Bukhara, and Khiva.

If these problems can be overcome, Uzbekistan has a wealth of fascinating, beautiful, and historical places to offer visitors. Not only do the ancient Silk Road cities cited in the previous paragraph feature magnificent historical architecture and authentic Central Asian culture, but the mountains of eastern Uzbekistan, which contain several national parks, provide spectacular scenery with opportunities for trekking, hiking, and mountain climbing in the summer and skiing in the winter. The key to bringing significantly more tourist dollars (or other currencies) to Uzbekistan lies in marketing the country to international travelers and providing amenities and services at bargain prices that induce them to travel the long distances required to reach the region.

ECONOMIC PERFORMANCE AND BARRIERS TO GROWTH

The Karimov government's emphasis on "gradualism" in making the transition from a command economy to a free market system has avoided some of the shocks other post-Communist states have suffered over the past decade. On the other hand, this cushioning has come at a price; hidden subsidies have kept energy and food prices artificially low, allowing citizens of Uzbekistan to maintain minimum living standards, but postponing the inevitable adjustments that may result in more severe shocks to the economy in the long term. The gradualist policy has not been successful in holding back unemployment and poverty, particularly in the countryside where most Uzbeks live, nor have the problems of corruption, patronage, and a bloated, inefficient bureaucracy been adequately addressed. Although the astronomical rates of inflation of the early 1990s have been reduced, incentives for saving and investment remain minimal, even for those who are relatively well off.

The slow rate of reform has meant that Uzbekistan has fallen behind in a number of key categories that bear directly on the country's economic future. The disappointingly low level of FDI over the last decade, the slow rate of privatization of agricultural land, a declining level of exports, and a continued dependency on the export of unprocessed cotton all represent long-term structural problems. With the country's demographic situation—nearly half of the population is under age twenty—it is unlikely that Uzbekistan can afford another decade of gradualism. The country possesses a number of characteristics that should be attractive to foreign investors, including a high literacy rate, low labor costs, and a location adjacent to several large, emerging markets in Russia, China, and South Asia. These advantages must be promoted, because it is difficult to imagine how the country will achieve economic stability, and eventually prosperity, without bringing more foreign investment on board.

CONCLUSION

Time is running out for fundamental economic restructuring in Uzbekistan. Population expansion, declining living standards, widespread unemployment or underemployment, and rapidly increasing prices will eventually bring on an economic, and most likely a social, crisis unless dramatic changes are undertaken swiftly and comprehensively. Some signs indicate the Karimov regime recognizes that a critical juncture is on the horizon and may be willing to accelerate reforms. For example, after years of promises and delays, the som was made convertible in October 2003, a move widely welcomed by international donor agencies and economists alike. There are also signs that the government has recently adopted a more serious approach to privatization of agriculture and the establishment of small businesses. Time alone will tell whether these changes represent harbingers of more expansive reforms or whether they simply represent another effort to keep the Uzbek economy temporarily afloat and maintain the current administration in power.

References

Agafonoff, Alexander, et al. 1997. *The Labor Market, Income, and Expenditures of the Population of the Republic of Uzbekistan.* Seattle: Jackson School of International Studies, University of Washington.

Craumer, Peter. 1995. *Rural and Agricultural Development in Uzbekistan.* London: The Royal Institute of International Affairs.

Dosumov, Rustam. 1996. "Uzbekistan: A National Path to the Market." In *Central Asia in Transition: Dilemmas of Political and Economic Development,* edited by Boris Rumer. Armonk, NY: M.E. Sharpe.

Thompstone, Stuart. 1994. "Uzbekistan's Economic Prospects." In *Political and Economic Trends in Central Asia,* edited by Shirin Akiner. London: British Academic Press.

Trushin, Eshref. 1998. "Uzbekistan: Foreign Economic Activity." In *Central Asia: The Challenges of Independence,* edited by Boris Rumer and Stanislav Zhukov. Armonk, NY: M.E. Sharpe.

United Nations. 2001. *Uzbekistan: Common Country Assessment.* Tashkent, Uzbekistan.

———. 2003. *Uzbekistan: Common Country Assessment.* Tashkent, Uzbekistan.

World Bank. 2003. *Republic of Uzbekistan: Country Economic Memorandum.* Report Number 25625-UZ, April 30, 2003.

Uzbek Institutions

Uzbekistan's experience as a component of the Russian, and later the Soviet Empire, is quite different from those post-colonial countries that emerged in Africa and Asia in the decades just after World War II. Because of the totalitarian character of the Soviet regime and the Leninist doctrine of *sblizhenie,* or "melding" of the USSR's nationalities, little overt progress toward developing a specific Uzbek national identity was achieved by independence. Political and social institutions that sought to evolve and function outside the official structure of the Communist Party (Communist Party of the Soviet Union, or CPSU) were repressed. Only in the last years of Soviet control, during the era of the so-called glasnost (openness) policy, did the political environment in the Uzbek SSR allow for the formation of alternative movements, which based their platforms on issues related to Uzbek national identity—in particular, environmental devastation and the status of both the Uzbek language and Islam in the republic.

In effect, independence arrived before a clear concept of Uzbek national identity emerged, and thus the intervening years since 1991 have witnessed a continued evolution of the process of nation building. Although allowing the two key components of Uzbek identity, Islam and the Uzbek language, a role in solidifying the basis for the Uzbek state, the Karimov government has also guarded against what it views as immoderate Uzbek nationalism. Thus, use of Uzbek as the national language has been tempered by official recognition of Russian as a language of "interethnic" communication, allowing Russians and other minority groups, most of whom have little or no command of Uzbek, to continue to employ Russian as their first language. Yet despite this accommodation, Slavs have continued to emigrate in large numbers, further weakening an already fragile economy.

In the first years of independence the Uzbek administration welcomed the Islamic renaissance that swept the country. Thousands of new mosques were built, many with the help of foreign donors, and many mosques closed by the Soviets were reopened. By the late 1990s, however, the Uzbek authorities had recognized that Islam could serve as a political platform that might challenge the monopoly of power they enjoyed, as events in neighboring Tajikistan and Afghanistan confirmed. In response, many mosques were closed, and one of the world's most repressive laws governing religion was implemented in 1997, initiating an anti-Islamic campaign. Rather than bringing stability, the repression led to bombings in Tashkent and small-scale invasions by Islamic militants, which only served to distract from broader, more general discontent over the country's economic and ecological situation. "Stability," even in the context of an authoritarian political system, still seems a distant goal for the young nation. In light of Uzbekistan's evolution toward the status of a nation state, the objective of this chapter is to present a summary of the recent and contemporary political landscape in Uzbekistan, along with a discussion of the major social institutions.

GOVERNMENT AND POLITICS

The complexities of Uzbekistan's government and political dynamics must be examined in the context of the late Soviet period. The last three decades of Soviet control had a great effect on what followed and set the political tone for independent Uzbekistan. All the major political players in contemporary Uzbekistan came of age during this period, and many aspects of Soviet politics still resonate today, as the country remains essentially a single-party state. The characteristics of Uzbek politics in the past and today are tightly linked to the character and personality of the individual at the top of the political hierarchy in Uzbekistan. During the Soviet era, this was the first party secretary of the Uzbek Communist Party; in independent Uzbekistan it is the country's president. The approach here will therefore follow a chronological framework, divided into sections focused on the Soviet and independent periods. The section addressing Soviet politics is further divided into periods according to the first party secretary in power at the time.

The Rashidov Regime (1959–1983)

During the Soviet period in the Uzbek Soviet Socialist Republic, as Uzbekistan was then called, all political power was concentrated in the Communist Party and its structures. This meant that the head of the Uzbek branch of the party, the first secretary, was the most influential figure in the republic. Sharaf Rashidov was elected to this position by the party hierarchy in 1959 and would remain in power for twenty-four years, an unusually long period of time for someone holding this position. During the decades he controlled the Uzbek SSR, Rashidov succeeded in building a personal power base that reached all levels of administration in the republic, and his tenure was marked by cronyism and corruption on a wide scale. Rashidov also rose to prominence within the all-union branch of the Communist Party, when, during the Leonid Brezhnev regime, he was elected to the Politburo, the body that formulated policy for the entire Soviet Union (Gleason 1997).

The stability resulting from Rashidov's long turn at the helm of the Uzbek Communist Party allowed for the development of considerable autonomy from Moscow, particularly regarding local policy decisions. By placing his handpicked lieutenants into government positions at all levels and in virtually every ministry from state security to agriculture, Rashidov was able to run the Uzbek SSR as his personal domain, with little interference from authorities in Moscow.

Although a Communist, Rashidov in fact followed the mold of authoritarian leadership that had characterized Central Asian politics for centuries. The tradition of such strongmen carries a certain grudging respect among many Uzbeks, due to both the historical lack of democratic institutions and the stability and continuity represented by absolute authority.

Rashidov's decades-long stretch as the Uzbek SSR's leader came to an abrupt end in 1983 when he died under mysterious circumstances. Officially perishing due to natural causes, persistent rumors held that in fact he had committed suicide. The extensive system of patronage and entrenched privilege built up over his tenure survived his demise, however, although a new administration in Moscow would quickly attempt to dismantle the Rashidov power structure via an "anticorruption" campaign.

The Usmankhozhayev Administration (1983–1988)

Two major campaigns marked the political dynamics of the Uzbek SSR during the mid-1980s. In 1983, the so-called "cotton affair" was revealed, a major scandal that brought to light the depth of corruption among Uzbekistan's elite power brokers. Investigators sent by Moscow discovered that authorities in the Uzbek Communist Party had defrauded the country on a massive scale by falsifying figures for cotton production and delivery. Rashidov's successor, Inamzhon Usmankhozhayev, would eventually be discredited and removed for his role in this and other questionable activities, along with a number of high-ranking party officials both within the Uzbek SSR and at the national level.

The second policy change to occur during this period was a shift to a more antagonistic stance toward Islam in the republic. During the years of the Brezhnev administration, a softening of the repressive policies of the early 1960s had taken place, but with the death of Brezhnev in 1983 the new leadership returned to a confrontational, antagonistic approach toward religious believers, especially Muslims. In the Uzbek SSR, this shift was manifest in a rise in propaganda against the "outdated customs" of the region (i.e., Islam), as well as a harsher tone adopted by party officials, academics, and journalists.

The renewed campaign against Uzbek culture and the growing cotton scandal created considerable tensions among the republic's elite, many of whom were implicated in the scandal, or accused of secretly engaging in Islamic or other "backward" activities. Although Mikhail Gorbachev had emerged as the Soviet leader in 1985 and articulated his famous policy of glasnost the same year, little indication of a more open, tolerant approach toward Islam in Uzbekistan was evident until late 1988. That same year, Usmankhozhayev was abruptly removed, along with a number of other high-ranking party officials, and charged with corruption.

The Nishanov/Karimov Period (1988–1991)

The purge of the Uzbek Communist Party undertaken by Gorbachev in 1988 enabled him to place Rafik Nishanov in the position of first party secretary in Uzbekistan, and with the dismissal of the old order, some anticipated fundamental changes in social policy in the republic as well. For the first months of Nishanov's tenure, however, the status quo was maintained in regard to the tone of anti-Islamic rhetoric, although a few concessions to Uzbekistan's religious heritage also were made, such as allowing the restoration of some historical mosques. Opposition movements (not actual political parties), especially Birlik, a group led by Uzbek writers and intellectuals, became stronger as well. Nishanov's control of the Uzbek Communist Party was brought to an abrupt halt in the summer of 1989, when ethnic violence between Uzbek and Meskhetian Turks in the Fergana Valley resulted in hundreds of deaths. Less than a month later, Nishanov resigned his post.

Nishanov's successor was Islom Karimov, who had established a power base in Samarkand and risen steadily through the Uzbek Communist Party's ranks. Karimov inherited a republic in crisis, and initially he largely avoided the harsh condemnations of Islam and the burgeoning opposition groups in Uzbekistan that had been typical of Nishanov. Karimov acquired a reputation for ensuring "stability," and for promoting Uzbekistan's heritage, particularly with the passage of legislation making Uzbek the republic's "official language" just a few months after he took office. In 1990, his position was renamed president, replacing the old title of first secretary of the Uzbek Communist Party. This status enabled him to ride out the political maelstrom of the USSR's collapse, and due to the party's continued monopoly on political power and the uncertainty brought about by the sudden decline of the Soviet state, Karimov was the only political figure in position to become independent Uzbekistan's first president.

Independence (1991–)

The attempted coup against Mikhail Gorbachev in August 1991 was initially met with silence in the Uzbek SSR as the authorities there waited for a winner to emerge from the chaos. By the end of the month, the party organs had declared independence, renaming the Uzbek SSR the Republic of Uzbekistan. This was effectively a change in name only, for there was little modification of domestic policy, and most opposition groups remained marginalized from the political process. In December 1991, Islom Karimov won the country's first election for president, but his only opposition was Muhammad Solih, the leader of Erk. Solih was not provided full access to the media and was able to mount only a limited campaign, yet he still garnered almost 15 percent of the vote.

Former head of the Communist Party in Uzbekistan, Islom Karimov became president in 1991. (North Atlantic Treaty Organization)

This would be the last time a bone fide alternative to Karimov would be presented to the Uzbek electorate.

Through the 1990s, the Karimov regime became increasingly authoritarian. The leadership of Birlik, the largest and most influential opposition group, was attacked, and most fled the country. Other dissidents, including Solih, Karimov's opponent in the first presidential election, also eventually left the country out of fear for their personal safety. Other potential rivals, especially a number of influential Islamic leaders, simply disappeared. The Oliy Majlis, or parliament, is packed with Karimov supporters, and control of the country's regions is maintained through a system of *hakims,* or governors, all of whom are directly beholden to Karimov (Melvin 2000). Although the Uzbek constitution promulgated in 1992 had limited a president to two terms, Karimov has circumvented this restriction through the use of popular plebiscites (a plebiscite is a general vote on an issue or proposal) to extend his term of office and in 2005 had ruled Uzbekistan for nearly fifteen years. International human rights advocates continue to criticize the country for its poor record.

In addition to the executive branch and the Oliy Majlis, a separate judicial branch of government exists. Three high courts hear cases, depending on the nature of the case in question: a constitutional court, a supreme court, and the higher economic court, the last hearing cases involving business disputes or violations. Again, international human rights organizations have frequently criticized the Uzbekistan court system because the judicial branch is not independent of other government branches. In fact, the judicial system is controlled by the president because he appoints the judges who sit on the courts, although as a matter of procedure the Oliy Majlis also must approve the appointments. There is no system of checks and balances between the branches of government in Uzbekistan, with the powerful and dominant presidency exercising control over both the legislature and the judiciary. Karakalpakstan has it own higher courts that are, in theory, independent of those seated in Tashkent, but in reality they are subordinate to the national courts.

Economic reform has proceeded slowly under Karimov. His government has followed a policy termed gradualism, designed to implement changes slowly and avoid the shocks experienced by other post-Communist states during the transition from Communism to capitalism. Part of Karimov's overall plan to preserve so-called stability, the slow pace of reform has been criticized by international lending agencies and has allowed the widespread networks of patronage and corruption to remain in place throughout much of the Uzbek economy. Levels of foreign direct investment (FDI), a vital source of development capital, have stayed relatively low, while inflation and unemployment rates have continued to climb through most of the period of independence. It is anyone's guess how long this situation will hold, given Uzbekistan's high rate of population growth and continued political instability.

Although pursuing apparent stability and economic restructuring, the Uzbek regime has also been faced with the task of building national identity in a territory that did not exist before 1924. This has led to a strange, arbitrary restoration of the country's historic monuments, achievements, and culture, wherein selected elements are highlighted and others are downplayed or ignored. Karimov has spoken frequently of the importance of spirituality to the country, for example, but the role of Islam in Uzbek culture has received limited and muted discussion at best. Whereas the making of national myth always involves recasting history, in Uzbekistan some figures have emerged as national heroes who were neither Uzbek nor well disposed toward those who were, such as Babur, a Timurid prince driven from Central Asia by Uzbek forces and the founder of India's Mogul dynasty.

Ironically, the tactics employed by the Karimov government to promote and ensure stability appear to have had the opposite effect. Since the late 1990s, the country has been rocked by acts of terrorism, including bombings and brief incursions by Islamic rebels based in Tajikistan and Afghanistan. The elimination of the Taliban and the alliance with the United States in the "war on terrorism" may have temporarily solidified the regime's standing internationally, but it seems unlikely that this new status will help solve the country's systemic problems in the long term. At the time of this writing, almost fourteen years after the demise of the Soviet Union, independent Uzbekistan remained a repressive state with no democratic institutions, facing serious and growing economic difficulties. Although some changes have come about in the economic system and connections with the outside world have been greatly enhanced, politically the "transition period" has in fact been largely a continuation of the Soviet-style, single-party state. As with any dictatorship, the political future of Uzbekistan will likely be marked by intrigue, uncertainty, and unforeseen challenges.

RELIGION AND SOCIETY

The dominant faith of Central Asia is Islam, and Islam has provided the worldview of the majority of the region's inhabitants for more than a thousand years. The basic framework of Islam originated on the Arabian Peninsula and emerged from the revelations given to Muhammed, the most important prophet of Islam. These messages, believed by Muslims to be the direct word of God, or Allah in Arabic, were eventually compiled into the Koran, Islam's holy scripture. There are many divisions among the global Muslim community in terms of belief, dogma, and ritual, but the Five Pillars of the faith are common to all branches of Islam. The pillars are universal requirements of all believing Muslims and begin with the profession of faith, wherein a person declares, preferably before other Muslims, that "there is but one God, Allah, and Muhammed is his prophet." Stated with sincerity, this decla-

Uzbek Muslims pray in the Shakh Zainutdin mosque in central Tashkent, November 9, 2001. (Reuters/Corbis)

ration alone is sufficient to bring one into the faith and is repeated on a daily basis by devout Muslims.

The second pillar is daily prayer. Muslims pray frequently and at established intervals. Prayers are said at dawn, noon, midafternoon, sunset, and in the evening and may be done alone or in congregation. Prayer may be performed at any location, as long as the worshipper faces the direction of the holy city of Mecca, located in Saudi Arabia. Muslims are expected to be generous, and the third pillar, the giving of alms, reflects this charitable obligation. In some Islamic countries, a "charity tax" is collected by the state authorities; in others, donations are voluntary, and individuals usually give to the local mosque.

The final two pillars of the faith are the month of fasting, or *Ramadan,* and the holy pilgrimage to Mecca, called in the Muslim world the *hajj.* Ramadan occurs during the ninth month of the Muslim lunar calendar, and for this period

Muslims may not eat, drink any fluids, have sexual relations, or smoke while the sun is out. Between sunset and dawn, these activities are permissible. Only small children, pregnant women, and the sick are allowed to ignore these restrictions, but adults who avoid the official time of Ramadan must make it up on their own later. Every Muslim who is healthy enough and can afford the costs of the journey to Mecca is expected to make the hajj at least once during his or her lifetime. The hajj transpires during the twelfth month of the Muslim calendar and typically lasts ten to twelve days. While there, the devout visit many of the holy sites of Islam and perform rituals that symbolize the events and actions of Mohammed's final visit to Mecca before his death in the city of Medina a few months later in the summer of A.D. 632.

Islam was brought to Central Asia in the century after the Prophet Mohammed's death, and over time it displaced the religions already entrenched there: Zoroastrianism, Buddhism, Manichaeism, Nestorian Christianity, various shamanistic faiths, and others (Golden 1990). By the ninth century, the faith was dominant in virtually all the urban oasis centers, although in the countryside, and particularly among shamanistic nomadic peoples, Islam was adopted much more slowly with certain traditional elements incorporated into the faith, resulting in a hybrid known colloquially as "folk Islam." From this time to the present, Sunni Muslims have outnumbered various groups of Shiites in Central Asia, and the Sunnis are the dominant sect in Uzbekistan.

By the Middle Ages, various orders of Sufism, sometimes referred to as Islamic mysticism, had taken root in Central Asia and in fact the region produced its own Sufi movements. The most influential of these was the Naqshbandi order, whose late founder, Baha al-Din Naqshband, is buried only a few miles from the city of Bukhara in a magnificent shrine complex. Historically, Sufism served as a counterweight to conservative, orthodox observance in Islam, because Sufis stress a direct, devotional relationship with Allah rather than more formalized, doctrinaire, and structured patterns of worship emphasized by the *ulema,* the community of Islamic scholars and teachers (Schubel 1999). Numerous Sufi adepts were influential in Uzbekistan's history. For example, Alisher Navoi, considered Central Asia's greatest poet and man of letters, was a devotee of the Naqshabandi order. In recent years, there has been considerable interest in reviving the Sufi traditions of Uzbekistan, part of a larger effort to recover the country's Islamic traditions and forge a national identity at least partially based on this heritage.

During the Soviet period, religious belief was stigmatized and defamed by the regime as a result of the state ideology. In part, this policy was pursued to ensure that the "predictions" of Marxism concerning religion in a Communist society were borne out: according to Marx, religiosity as a manifestation of the "opium of the masses" would whither away and vanish with the creation of such a society. The campaign against Islam in Central Asia relented only occasionally, as it did during World War II when Josef Stalin's administration desperately required the support of the citizenry. It was in the wake of Germany's attack on the USSR that the government created an organizational structure for Soviet Islam with the implementation of four "spiritual boards," headed by a Muslim official (mufti) and responsible for promoting the officially sanctioned version of the faith. Although this strategy was a de facto recognition of Islam's persistence in Soviet society, it did not mean that the campaign to eradicate Muslim religiosity was abandoned. Vigorous efforts to eliminate "religious vestiges" and "outdated traditions" in Uzbekistan and other Muslim regions continued until the late 1980s.

Religiosity was never eradicated, however, and after the demise of Soviet authority, an Islamic renaissance swept Central Asia. This movement was particularly strong in Uzbekistan, where many of the most important institutions of Soviet Islam reposed, and where the population enjoyed a long and profound connection to the faith. In the first half of the 1990s, thousands of mosques were constructed in Uzbekistan along with many new medressehs (schools for training Islamic scholars). Most Uzbeks and Tajiks, the two largest Muslim groups in Uzbekistan, retain a strong cultural linkage to Islam, and these two groups account for at least 80 percent of the population.

The decades of Soviet repression did have some effect in terms of limiting knowledge of Islam among the general population, however. The Soviet regime restricted access to the Koran and to Islamic teachers for many people, with the result that today many Muslims in Uzbekistan have only a tenuous understanding of the rituals, doctrines, and precepts of the faith. For example, Ramadan is not widely observed in Uzbekistan, and relatively few Muslims in Uzbekistan have the wherewithal to make the hajj. The Islamic proscription against the consumption of alcohol and pork are frequently ignored, as Uzbeks and other Muslim groups have absorbed Slavic drinking and eating habits since the Russian conquest of the region.

Yet in the wake of Soviet collapse and with the abandonment of Marxism-Leninism as the guiding ideology, many in Uzbekistan have sought to reclaim their Islamic heritage and reconnect with a Muslim self-identity. This movement can be seen in the limited data available on Islamic religiosity collected in Uzbekistan since 1991. Some small-scale surveys indicate that a majority of young Uzbeks regard themselves as "Muslims," although this self-label is frequently applied more in an ethno-historical context than as a purely religious identification. Moreover, the knowledge of Islam's requirements and prohibitions among young people is typically limited and often inaccurate, a residue of seventy years of Soviet repression. Yet despite the incomplete information about Islam and persistent persecution of those whom the government deems extremist, the desire for more knowledge about the Islamic foundations of Uzbek culture has clearly grown since the disintegration of the USSR.

Since Uzbekistan's independence, official policy toward Islam has evolved from that of considerable tolerance and noninterference to repression reminiscent of the Soviet era. The Karimov regime has been intent on pursuing a dualistic, sometimes contradictory policy toward Islam. Those aspects of the faith that are useful for building national identity and do not challenge the regime's monopolistic grip on power are tolerated and even promoted, such as the country's Islamic heritage. On the other hand, any manifestations of Islam that are organized outside of the official government-controlled structure and that may show potential for politicization have been immediately crushed. Most often this has been done under the pretext of limiting the influence of Islamic so-called fundamentalists or extremists, who were frequently labeled *Wahhabis* in the Uzbek media, after the fundamentalist sect of Sunni Islam dominant in Saudi Arabia.

In the late 1990s, the Uzbek government intensified the campaign against unofficial Islam. Arrests of alleged Wahhabis increased, and in 1998, the Uzbek government implemented the Law on Freedom of Conscience and Religious Organizations, a highly restrictive piece of legislation that effectively allows the regime to ban any religious group on the basis of security, bans the private teaching of religion, and even prohibits the wearing of religious clothing in public, except by those officially recognized as clerics (Hanks 2004). Some have characterized the Uzbek religious law as among the most repressive in the world.

The effect of the campaign against Islam was to radicalize the opposition. In early 1999, several bombs exploded in Tashkent in what was claimed by the Uzbek leadership to be an attempt on President Karimov's life. The government quickly declared the explosions to be the work of Islamic extremists and arrested several dozen alleged perpetrators, all said to be members of the Islamic Movement of Uzbekistan (IMU), a shadowy group based in the remote mountain valleys of Tajikistan and Afghanistan. Although the IMU denied responsibility for the Tashkent bombings, in the summer of 1999 and the next year, small groups of IMU fighters infiltrated several border regions of Uzbekistan and Kyrgyzstan and had to be ousted by military force. Allied with the Taliban government in Afghanistan, much of the IMU was destroyed by the U.S. military campaign in northern Afghanistan in the fall of 2001.

In the wake of the demise of the IMU, the Uzbek regime has identified yet another radical "threat" to its stability, Hizb-ut-Tahrir (HT). HT is an international organization that has branches in many Islamic countries and has as its main goal the reestablishment of the Muslim caliphate, the position of Islamic spiritual and secular authority left vacant after the fall of the Ottoman Empire. Although its rhetoric is anti-Western and anti-Semitic, HT claims to pursue its agenda through nonviolent means, and indeed, there is no evidence that it has engaged in terrorist acts in Central Asia. Nevertheless, the Uzbek government has outlawed the group, and anyone found in possession of HT literature is subject to a long prison sentence; in fact, several thousand people have met such a fate. Thus, the role of Islam in Uzbek society remains controversial and ill defined.

EDUCATION

The educational system of independent Uzbekistan still shares many characteristics with its Soviet predecessor, although there have been a number of attempts to modernize both structure and curricula in recent years. Despite a one-dimensional ideological foundation, the Soviet educational system produced impressive results in Central Asia, particularly in regard to increasing general literacy rates and enfranchising females. The majority of these gains were achieved by the 1950s, however, and few substantial changes occurred after that time. The transition to post-Soviet education, like similar shifts attempted in the political and economic spheres, has been hampered by shortages of funding, low levels of training, and the inertia of a bloated and entrenched state bureaucracy.

The Educational System

Uzbekistan's educational system is controlled by two government bodies, the Ministry of People's Education, which governs all grades and programs below the postsecondary level, and the Ministry of Higher Education, which regulates institutions and activities at the postsecondary level. Since independence, the Uzbek government has implemented two major laws designed to reform the country's educational system. The first of these was initiated in 1992, only six months after the disbanding of the Soviet Union, and introduced several new ideas, including protection of children's rights and a right to correspondence education. The second law governing education reform, passed in 1997, extended the compulsory period of education to twelve years, requiring students who have completed the ninth grade to complete the final years of their compulsory education at either academic lyceums or professional colleges. Curricula at the former are designed to prepare students for university, while the professional colleges provide vocational training.

The relationship between student and teacher in Uzbek classrooms at all levels, including university, is much more formal than in the United States. When the instructor enters the classroom each day, all students stand until the teacher indicates that they are allowed to sit. When a student responds to a question, whether voluntarily or when called upon by the teacher, the student stands when giving the response and remains standing until told to sit. Showing disrespect to the teacher is not only considered unacceptable behavior by the school administration but is also looked down on by other students. The title *domla* (teacher) carries great esteem among Uzbeks and is used in reference to religious leaders as well as secular educators.

Primary education begins at age six and lasts through grade four; secondary education begins in grade 5 and extends through grade nine. As of the late 1990s, approximately 5.5 million students were enrolled in grades 1 through 11 in Uzbekistan, with half that number in primary education. Because of the multiethnic nature of Uzbekistan's society, instruction at the primary level is offered in a number of languages, including Uzbek, Russian, Kazakh, Karakalpak, Tajik, Turkmen, and Kyrgyz; at the universities, courses are typically taught in Uzbek or Russian. After independence, curricula were modified to include a greater emphasis on Uzbek culture, literature, and history, and coursework on economics, marketing, ecology, and technology was expanded. However, disciplines in the social sciences, such as sociology, anthropology, political science, and others that were heavily influenced by Soviet ideology, continue to suffer from a lack of teachers trained in these areas, as well as a shortage of suitable teaching materials.

Higher education is provided by an array of universities, institutes, and specialty or professional schools, the latter offering diplomas or certificate programs in business, languages, or other subjects. Most of the universities and institutes are state-funded, whereas many of the specialty schools are frequently partially privately funded. Admission to university is competitive, and entry has become more difficult since independence—in the first three years of independence, the number of students admitted to institutions of higher education fell by almost 20 percent (337,000 to 272,000), although graduation rates through the same period increased substantially, from 53 percent to 63 percent (Tibi 1995). Once admitted, students may initially pursue a bachelor's degree (*bakalavr*), usually requiring four years of study, followed by a master's degree (*magistr*), and ultimately a doc-

University students in Tashkent. (Photo courtesy of Reuel Hanks)

torate. The percentage of the adult population in Uzbekistan who have at least some postsecondary education (not necessarily leading to a degree) is approximately 14 percent, although given the drop in admissions just after independence, this percentage may be expected to decline.

A number of serious challenges plague the educational system in Uzbekistan. First, there is an increasing problem with basic infrastructure, particularly in rural areas, where both the quality and quantity of schools falls short. Many rural schools now carry double shifts of students, and many schools do not have basic plumbing or heating. Teaching equipment remains unsophisticated, often consisting of only a crude chalkboard, and textbooks are frequently unavailable or out of date. There is a growing shortage of teachers at all levels, a situation made worse by the continued emigration of ethnic Russians, many of whom are highly skilled instructors. Teachers' salaries are well below the average salary in the government sector, and nearly a quarter of those currently teaching do not have a postsecondary education. Many educators, including university professors, take second jobs to supplement their meager income. Pedagogical methods and strategies remain mostly rooted in the Soviet era, and despite the increasing number of students entering the system, government expenditures on education actually dropped through most of the 1990s. If the country is to be competitive in the global economy, these problems must be addressed immediately by the regime.

Literacy

As mentioned earlier, one of the most impressive achievements of the Soviet educational system in Central Asia was the elevation of literacy rates across all levels of society. At the dawn of the twentieth century, literacy rates were abysmally low in the region, with perhaps less than 5 percent of the total population able to read, and among women the rate was probably close to zero. By the time the Soviet Union collapsed, literacy in the region was nearly universal because the Soviet administration had introduced compulsory education at an early date. It is unclear how the proposed shift from the Cyrillic alphabet to the Latin will affect literacy rates, although a drop in literacy over the short term would not be unexpected, as some people will lag behind in learning to read the new script.

In addition, there is concern that deceases in government budgets for education and declining rates of enrollment at the primary level might ultimately result in a drop in literacy. During the 1990s, Uzbekistan experienced an approximately 10 percent reduction in the percentage of children enrolled in primary education, and preschool programs have been curtailed as well. One of the many challenges to the country is maintaining the impressive achievements of the twentieth century in literacy, in the midst of wholesale societal change.

Religious Education

Before the late 1980s, religious education in Uzbekistan was limited in scope. For much of the Soviet period, the only functioning medresseh in the USSR was the Mir-i-Arab medresseh located in Bukhara, which accommodated a few dozen students. The Islamic renaissance that swept Central Asia in the final years of the Soviet experiment, and the initial years of independence, resulted in a flowering of Islamic schooling, particularly in Uzbekistan. Many of the unsanctioned Islamic institutions have now been closed, but the Uzbek government itself inaugurated an Islamic university in Tashkent in 1999, which is open to both male and female students.

The Law on Freedom of Conscience and Religious Organizations (see previous section, "Religion and Society") enabled the Uzbek regime to crack down on independent Islamic education, a practice that the government links, rightly or wrongly, to Islamic radicalism. Underground Islamic schools apparently function in the country, but because of their clandestine nature, the number of schools and the number of students attending them is difficult to calculate with any accuracy. It seems likely that such activity may be fairly widespread in rural districts, if only because many young Uzbeks are curious about their religious heritage and are unable to gain such knowledge via the state-sponsored education system.

CONCLUSION

The transition from totalitarianism to a free market and civil society has been slow and arduous for Uzbekistan. The country faces mounting problems in the political and social spheres, as political repression, corruption, economic stagnation, and fundamental cultural changes continue to transpire on a broad scale. The pervasive control of the Soviet regime has been replaced by the authoritarianism of the Karimov government, which seems unwilling to institute painful but necessary democratic and economic reforms, preferring instead to maintain the status quo through repression and political patronage. Although this system may provide seeming stability in the short term, it also retards the development of institutions essential to the long-term emergence of a democratic, prosperous Uzbekistan and leaves the future of the country uncertain.

References

Allworth, Edward. 1990. *The Modern Uzbeks: From the Fourteenth Century to the Present.* Stanford, CA: Hoover Institution Press.

Gleason, Gregory. 1997. *The Central Asian States: Discovering Independence.* Boulder, CO: Westview Press.

Golden, Peter. 1990. "The Karakhanids and Early Islam." In *The Cambridge History of Early Inner Asia,* edited by Denis Sinor. Cambridge: Cambridge University Press.

Hanks, Reuel. 2004. "Religion and Law in Uzbekistan: Renaissance and Repression in an Authoritarian Context." In *Regulating Religion: Case Studies from Around the Globe,* edited by James T. Richardson. New York: Kluwer Academic.

Melvin, Neil. 2000. *Uzbekistan. Transition to Authoritarianism on the Silk Road.* Amsterdam: Harwood Academic.

Schubel, Vernon. 1999. "Post-Soviet Hagiography and the Reconstruction of the Naqshbandi Tradition in Contemporary Uzbekistan." In *Naqshbandis in Western and Central Asia,* edited by Elisabeth Ozdalga. Istanbul: Swedish Research Institute in Istanbul.

Tibi, Claude. 1995. "Education." In *Social Policy and Economic Transformation in Uzbekistan,* edited by Keith Griffin. Geneva: International Labour Office, United Nations Development Programme.

Uzbekskiia Sovetskiia Sotsialisticheskiia Respublika [Uzbek Soviet Socialist Republic]. 1981. Edited by K. A. Zufarov (main editor). Tashkent: Central Publishing House of the Uzbek Soviet Encyclopedia.

Uzbek Society and Contemporary Issues

Uzbekistan is a society in wholesale transition at multiple levels: economic, political, and cultural. After seventy years of Soviet rule during which much of Uzbek traditional culture was proscribed or harshly criticized, Uzbeks are now rediscovering and celebrating their heritage. At the same time, a second process of discovery is taking place—the discovery and widespread adoption of many aspects of Western culture and social practices. Under the Soviet administration, both traditional Uzbek social norms and those of Western society were viewed as "backward" and "decadent" and inferior to "scientific socialism," a system grounded in the principles of Marxism-Leninism.

Just twenty years ago, only those who wished to be branded as radical, antisocial, or, in Soviet parlance, "hooligans" would openly adopt and display social and cultural elements from the West, especially those associated with the United States. Today, among the youth of all major ethnic groups in Uzbekistan, wearing Western clothing, listening to Western music, watching Western television programs (especially music videos) and studying Western languages are not only acceptable, but considered desirable, especially in urban areas. Contact with foreigners, once a practice that might bring a visit from the secret police, is now commonplace and carries no social stigma. Indeed, the contrary is true—many perceive interaction with foreigners to enhance one's social standing (as well as one's economic prospects).

Yet this is not to say that Uzbek society is free of tension and contradiction. The popularity of Western cultural forms and the recovery of Uzbek traditions, along with the social and cultural residues from the Communist era, do not necessarily work in concert and result in a dynamic, eclectic cultural milieu where the traditional and the modern sometimes clash. Added to this mix are marked differences between Slavic groups and Muslims, wide divisions between rural inhabitants and city dwellers, and the usual generational gaps, all resulting in social tensions and a complex, dynamic culture. The aim of this chapter is to introduce and explain some of the complexities and challenges inherent in Uzbek society, with the goal of furthering understanding of both causes and effects, and, in the final section to frame this fascinating, complicated country in a larger global context.

ETHNICITY AND SOCIAL SYSTEM
Ethnic Groups

Uzbekistan is truly a multiethnic state, with nearly 100 distinct groups scattered across the country. The largest ethnic group is the Uzbeks, who constitute approximately 75 percent of the population. Although some Uzbeks were deeply influenced by Russian culture and adopted Russian as their first language, most Uzbeks speak Uzbek fluently and use Russian only for communicating with other ethnic groups. Uzbek is a Turkic language and is now written increasingly in the Latin script, although from the 1940s the Cyrillic alphabet was used. A complete shift to the use of Latin script for Uzbek is anticipated within the next several years. Closely linked to the other Turkic tongues of Central Asia, Uzbek nevertheless contains many words borrowed from Russian and Persian.

The origins of the people identified today as Uzbeks are obscure. Considerable historical evidence locates the group's ancestral homeland in the steppe region north of the Aral Sea. During the fifteenth century, a confederation of nomadic tribes was formed there by a warlord known as Uzbek Khan, and some commentators hold that these Turkic tribes represent the first body to be collectively identified as Uzbeks by the surrounding peoples (Allworth 1990). A century later, Uzbek forces conquered most of the urban centers of Central Asia, where they mixed with the local population of Persian speakers and those speaking a local Turkic dialect, Chagatay. Modern Uzbek is evolved from the latter. Over time, many urban dwellers became identified as Sarts, characterized by their use of both Persian (Tajik) and Chagatay (Turki) for business and everyday communication, although ethnically and culturally they often did not differ markedly from their monolingual counterparts in the countryside. Some clan and tribal loyalties may still be found among Uzbeks, although these are not as prevalent as they are among the Kazakhs and Kyrgyz. An Uzbek today likely carries the genetic imprint of a great variety of ethnic and racial types who have traversed and settled Central Asia over the centuries, and one may see the influence of Middle Eastern, Asiatic, and European stock in the faces of a single family.

Uzbeks frequently may be identified via their traditional dress, especially men, who often don an embroidered skull-cap, or *doppa*. The style and embroidery on the hat not only signify that the wearer is an ethnic Uzbek, but may also indicate which part of the country he is from, because certain regions produce caps that are distinct. Brides sometimes wear a brightly colored doppa as part of their wedding accoutrement, although typically the doppa is reserved for men. In addition, traditional Uzbek men may wear a *chapan*, a colorful heavy cotton or silk robe held closed by a sash, along with long boots. Uzbek women in the countryside usually appear in public only when wearing a scarf and may wear an ankle-length smock or a dress of multicolored silken material known as *atlas*. The more conservative dress of female Uzbeks distinguishes them from their Russian, Korean, and Armenian counterparts, who frequently sport the latest fashions from Europe and the United States.

During the period when Josef Stalin controlled the USSR, a

Young women on a street in Khiva. The woman on the left is wearing a traditional scarf concealing her hair, a sign of modesty in Muslim society. (Photo courtesy of Reuel Hanks)

number of ethnic groups were relocated by force to Central Asia, with many of these peoples taking up residence in Uzbekistan. Among these were sizable numbers of Crimean Tatars and Meskhetian Turks, who were shipped to the region because their loyalty to the Soviet state was considered suspect. Since the late 1980s, most of the members of both of these groups have left the country. This is, particularly the case with the latter, after violent ethnic riots between Meskhetians and Uzbeks in 1989 left several hundred people dead. In Tashkent, Samarkand, and other large cities, one may find substantial communities of Koreans and Armenians. Both groups are highly urbanized and typically use Russian as a language of interethnic communication, although in most cases they maintain their original languages as well. The Koreans were yet another group brought to Central Asia during the Stalin era who settled predominantly in urban areas and who have maintained much of their culture, including their unique cuisine. For many centuries the city of Bukhara held a large and unique Jewish community, but since independence many Bukharan Jews have emigrated to Israel or the United States.

As recently as the 1970s, Russians made up nearly 10 percent of the population of Uzbekistan, but over the last several decades, the percentage of Russians in the population has steadily dwindled as increasing numbers migrated to Russia and other destinations (Gleason 1997). This process accelerated after Uzbekistan's independence, and by the year 2000, Russians made up only about 5 percent of the country's population due to both out-migration and much lower birth rates than Uzbeks and other groups. Many Russians and other Slavs left as Uzbek came to replace Russian as the language of government and commerce, and as a resurgence of Islamic tradition occurred in the early 1990s that many Russians saw as a potential threat.

The Russians were historically heavily concentrated in the

major cities of Uzbekistan, and several neighborhoods and districts of Tashkent remain predominantly Russian today. In addition, Russian continues to function as a language of common communication among all the ethnic groups in the country because few members of the minority ethnic groups mastered Uzbek, and some government documents, newspapers, and television programs continue to use Russian. The emigration of the Russian community has been of some concern to the Uzbek administration, as many positions in business, technical, and academic fields were filled by ethnic Russians, and their departure undermines an already unstable economy.

Tajiks, speaking a language close to the Farsi spoken in Iran, make up a significant portion of the urban population in several key cities and in fact may represent a majority of the residents of both Samarkand and Bukhara. Their actual numbers are in dispute: official government figures put the proportion of Tajiks at about 5 percent of the total population, but other sources claim the number is closer to 15 percent. One is certain to hear Tajik spoken in the bazaars of Samarkand and Bukhara as frequently as Uzbek—in fact, probably more often. The number of Tajiks in Uzbekistan is a sensitive issue because both Samarkand and Bukhara were historically "Tajik" cities, and the Uzbek government fears that acknowledging the large number of Tajik-speakers in these places might lead to territorial claims by Tajikistan, whose border with Uzbekistan comes within 25 miles of Samarkand.

Social System

The majority of the population lives in rural areas, and many people continue to live on collective farms, or *kolkhozi,* although some limited privatization of farmland has taken place in recent years. In other regions, the local population is organized as a *kishlak,* or village, which may vary in size from a few families to several thousand people. In both urban and rural settings the family is the basic social unit, and family ties, both within and beyond the immediate family, are a vital part of Uzbek life. Loyalty to and respect for elders is expected of all family members, and extends to society as a whole— younger men will usually address an older man, even a stranger, as *aka,* meaning "elder brother," a sign of respect and courtesy. It is common even in urban areas for married sons to take up residence in close proximity to their parents' home, perhaps even moving into the same apartment or house.

Above the family is the social structure known as the *mahalla,* or "neighborhood association." The mahalla usually consists of dozens of families living in proximity who may not be related by blood or marriage but share the same geographic space and thereby are considered part of the association. Generally one or several older, experienced men are selected to organize and administer the activities of the mahalla, arranging ceremonies, which may range from a *sunna toy* (circumcision) ceremony to a funeral for a member of the mahalla. In some cases the mahalla elders may help a family financially, especially if there has been a recent death in the family, or they may admonish a younger member of the neighborhood who has transgressed socially and thereby may have brought shame not only on himself, but also upon the entire mahalla. There is frequently a parallel structure for women, and social conformity is enforced through the mechanism of social pressure and, in extreme cases, social ostracism.

Social linkages are reinforced through the observance of life rituals and ceremonies. One of the most important of these is marriage, an event that carries great significance to the entire family and often the whole mahalla. Marriages are typically arranged by the parents, even in urban areas (except in the case of the major minority groups), and traditional Uzbek weddings are lavish and complicated affairs. In rural areas, the practice of paying a bride price, or *kalym,* is still observed, although this is less common in the cities (Olcott 1991). Kalym may be paid either in cash or in the form of goods and commodities, and the price is negotiated between the fathers of the groom and bride, with elders of the mahalla sometimes serving as intermediaries. The morning of the wedding, the prospective father-in-law arrives at the residence of the bride and announces his presence by blowing loudly on a long brass horn, or *karnai.* This event is to call the bride forth ceremonially, although the actual wedding will not take place for several more hours. Once begun, the wedding festivities will often continue into the early hours of the morning, although the bride and groom retire earlier. Weddings with 400 to 500 guests in attendance are standard in Uzbekistan, and along with other celebrations and rituals reinforce the fabric of Uzbek society.

WOMEN'S STATUS IN SOCIETY

The impact of the Soviet colonial period on women in Central Asian society was profound and lasting and resulted in a Muslim society that is more egalitarian than many others in Asia. Under Soviet control, Slavic and native Central Asian women were granted access to educational opportunities previously unavailable to them, and Soviet law and policy restricted or outlawed some Islamic customs, such as polygamy and the wearing of the *paranja* (veil). It is difficult and inaccurate to speak of women in a comprehensive sense in Uzbekistan, however, because there are significant differences among various groups of women in society. There are, for example, major differences between Slavic and Muslim women, rural and urban women, and more recently, between the Soviet and post-Soviet generations of women, the latter increasingly exposed to, and influenced by, trends and standards external to traditional Uzbek society.

In urban areas in Uzbekistan, it is common for women of

Several generations of Uzbek women from Kokand. Women raise children and provide much of the country's labor supply. (Photo courtesy of Reuel Hanks)

all ethnic groups to work outside their home, and it is equally common to find women in administrative positions in universities, factories, hospitals, and businesses. In the countryside, particularly on the collective farms, women are often employed as agricultural workers and frequently do some of the most difficult physical work, such as picking cotton. Unlike some of the more restrictive Muslim societies, Uzbek women may go shopping or on other errands without being accompanied by a relative and may have contact with men outside the family, even foreigners. Physical contact with men is limited, however, although many women in Uzbekistan today will shake hands when meeting a stranger, especially if the occasion is professional. Although it is somewhat rare to encounter a woman driving in Uzbekistan, this is not due to any social taboo—driving is simply seen as a male activity, and women living in urban areas do not need this skill to traverse the city because public transport is available and relatively inexpensive.

The quality of life for rural women in Uzbekistan is considerably lower than that of their sisters in the major cities (Akiner 1997). Lack of basic infrastructure, especially shortages in the provision of clean drinking water and proper sanitation, fewer employment and educational opportunities, and greater social pressure to marry and have large families at a young age all contribute to a more difficult existence for women in the countryside. As already noted, rural women make up a large percentage of the workforce on the collective farms, and they perform much of the hard physical labor of cultivating and harvesting cotton and other crops, usually by hand. In some regions, particularly Karakalpakstan, it is common for girls to marry in their early teens and to have several children by the age of twenty. Interethnic marriage is relatively rare, even among the Muslim groups, and marriages are typically arranged by the parents. Pressure on the new bride to please and accommodate her in-laws and husband can be extremely stressful. Some girls attempt suicide rather than face the social stigma of leaving a bad marriage or being rejected by her husband's family.

Slavic, Armenian, and Korean women are concentrated in the major urban centers, and their lives differ in several important ways from those of their Uzbek and other Muslim counterparts. Marriages are not necessarily arranged, although interethnic marriages are still rare, especially for the Armenian, Korean, Jewish, and other non-Slavic, non-Muslim minorities. Women from these groups typically are more apt to dress according to Western standards, and whereas wearing short skirts, tight-fitting jeans, or shorts in public would be extremely provocative behavior for a female Uzbek, these garments frequently appear on young women from the major minority groups. Living mostly in the cities, women from the country's larger minorities generally enjoy greater access to educational and employment opportunities.

RECREATION AND POPULAR CULTURE

For much of the twentieth century, popular culture in Uzbekistan was limited to what the Soviet censors approved, and contact with outside cultural influences was limited. Some aspects of foreign culture were deemed acceptable, and others were condemned as decadent and undesirable. American jazz music, for example, was popular among Soviet music lovers, and at least one Soviet leader, Yuri Andropov, was alleged to own an impressive collection of the work of Western jazz musicians. On the other hand, it was not until late in the Soviet era that Western rock music was publicly played and enjoyed, although many artists, in particular Elvis Presley, the Beatles, the Rolling Stones, and others, had enjoyed widespread underground popularity since the 1960s.

The advent of glasnost in the late 1980s and the subsequent collapse of the Soviet system dramatically changed this situation. In a few short years, Central Asia was flooded with foreign entertainment, especially music and films. The majority of this influence came from the West, but Indian movies also penetrated the Uzbek market. Kiosks selling cassettes and CDs, many of them illegally copied, sprang up by the hundreds in all major urban areas, and although a much smaller percentage of the population had access to video or DVD players than in the West, stores selling these media may be found in most Uzbek cities. Television also began featuring Western films and programming, something unheard of during the Soviet period. At the same time, Uzbek performers, both traditional and modern, also enjoy a large following.

Traditional Music

Singing, instrumental music, and dance have been part of Uzbek culture for centuries and are important components of the many celebrations and ceremonies observed by Uzbeks and other Muslims of Central Asia. For example, a wedding, whether following traditional ritual or not, is unthinkable without music and dancing in Uzbekistan. The Uzbek musical tradition was greatly influenced by trends and innovations from both the Middle East and China. Influence from each of these regions can be observed in the musical instruments used, as well as in the musical terminology employed, much of which is borrowed from Arabic, Persian, or Turkish. Common instruments include the *dutar,* a two-stringed lute; the *surnay,* a reed instrument similar to the oboe; and the *daira,* a large tambourine that may be used in an ensemble as a percussion instrument or played solo (Spector 1989).

The vocal musical tradition of Central Asia has played an essential part in developing a sense of ethnic and national identity among various groups via the great epic poems, called *dastans.* These traditional folktales, typically featuring a hero and his legendary deeds, have once again become popular in the new countries of Central Asia. Among the Uzbeks, the most famous of the dastans is *Alpamish,* but many others exist. These now appear as literature, but traditionally they were sung by bards who were revered for their skill and creativity. Interest in the *dastanchi,* or traditional singers of epics, has seen a revival since the collapse of the USSR. Another style of traditional singing, still frequently performed in Uzbekistan, is *sozanda,* which consists of folk songs typically performed by a female soloist accompanied by a single stringed instrument or sometimes only by percussion instruments, especially the daira.

Modern Music and Music Video

Both foreign and local musical artists, representing a wide range of musical styles and tastes, are popular in today's Uzbekistan. The most popular foreign artists are from Western Europe and North America, and they range from soft rock musicians such as Whitney Huston, Celine Dion, Michael Jackson, and Britney Spears to rap and hip-hop performers

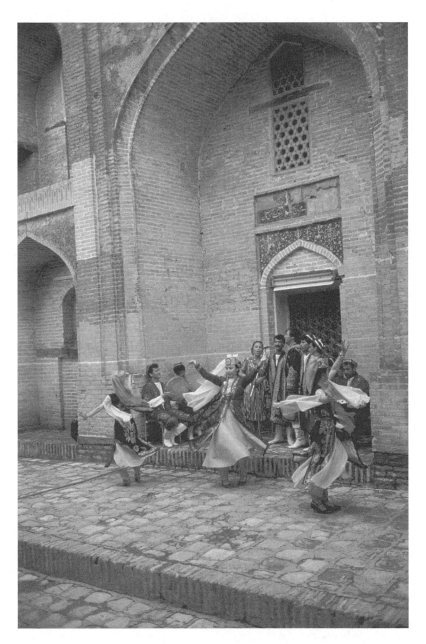

Folk dancers and musicians in Bukhara, Uzbekistan.
(K. M. Westermann/Corbis)

such as Eminem and others. Since independence, a large number of musicians from Uzbekistan have emerged who emulate the styles, and often the appearance, of more widely known international stars, although they remain basically unknown outside of Central Asia. Just as in the West, the popularity of such individuals and groups tends to rise and fade abruptly. Recent popular artists include the female trio Setora, female soloist Sevara Nazarkhan, and the male vocal group Shahzod. The music of these artists often features themes that emphasize the Uzbek national heritage. In addition, performers from Russia such as Alla Pugachova and her husband, Philip Kirkorov, are well known to music fans in Uzbekistan and remain popular with Russians and other ethnic groups.

A new phenomenon in musical culture in Uzbekistan is the advent of music video, produced both in Uzbekistan and abroad. Although there is no channel such as MTV or VH1 that is devoted to broadcasting hours of music videos per day, the popular television channel for young people, *Yoshlar* (Youth), offers several hours a week of such programming. Videos from foreign artists do not typically include those with overt sexual themes or scantily clad models, although many young people in Uzbekistan are familiar with these productions via satellite television or the Internet. Music videos from Uzbek performers are more constrained than those from abroad; female Uzbek performers appear modestly dressed and do not dance in a suggestive manner, reflecting the norms of Uzbek society. The emphasis of the typical video is more on the lyrics or message of the song, rather than on glitzy visual effects or sexuality. As in the West, music videos are quite popular among young people, and they represent a growing influence in local culture.

Television and Film

As with music, the collapse of the USSR brought about a revolution in accessibility and exposure to foreign broadcasting for citizens of Uzbekistan. Beginning in the early 1990s, a wide variety of foreign programming, dubbed in Russian or Uzbek, appeared on local channels in the country. Soap operas from the United States and Latin America were an instant hit with the Uzbek audience. One of the most popular in Uzbekistan was the U.S. program *Santa Barbara,* along with various shows from Mexico and Brazil, which provided many in Uzbekistan with their first exposure to Western television, and a glimpse, if rather artificial and inaccurate, of life in the West. In addition, programming from the BBC and other sources in Western Europe occasionally appeared on Uzbek TV, alongside popular shows from Russia.

U.S. films are now shown in Uzbekistan as well, both in movie theaters and on television, either on local channels or on network broadcasts from Moscow. The genre of film ranges from action movies featuring Steven Segal and Arnold Schwarzenegger to children's comedies, and many Uzbeks are familiar with major U.S. actors. Although rarely shown on television, movies from India are often shown in movie theaters, and Indian musicals are particularly popular with many people. There is also a burgeoning Uzbek movie industry, which produces feature films of all types, although since independence the emphasis appears to be on historical dramas, celebrating the country's long and storied heritage.

Sports

The Soviet government emphasized participation in sports, or "physical culture" as it is still termed, and this continues in independent Uzbekistan. The most popular team sport is soccer, and Uzbekistan's national team is followed with great fervor when engaging in international competition. In total, there are thirty-six official soccer teams in the country, forming two leagues. Boys will play soccer in any open field or even in side streets, and international soccer stars from Latin America and Europe, known only to a small percentage of

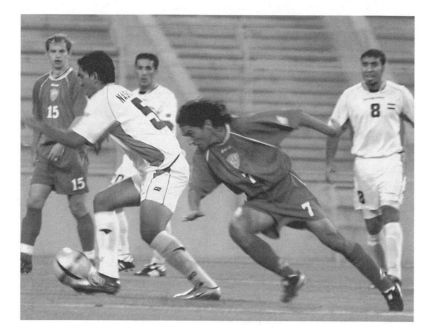

FIFA Soccer 2004, World Cup Qualifier, Iraq versus Uzbekistan. Soccer is quite popular in Uzbekistan, and Uzbeks avidly follow their national team. In this match, Uzbekistan prevailed, 2–1.
(Ali Jarekji/Reuters/Corbis)

Americans, are household names to Uzbek fans. Individual contests such as tennis, boxing, and cycling are popular, and Uzbekistan in recent years has produced world-class Olympic athletes in the latter two sports. A traditional martial art that has enjoyed a major revival since independence is *kurash,* a form of wrestling that allegedly developed over a thousand years ago in Central Asia. In 1998, Tashkent hosted an international kurash tournament, and subsequently the International Kurash Association was formed, with participating member organizations in forty countries.

Uzbekistan's mountainous terrain in the eastern portion of the country offers plentiful opportunities for outdoor recreation, and hiking, swimming, trekking, skiing, and mountain climbing are all enjoyed by natives and visitors alike, depending on the season. Several national parks provide the opportunity to view the region's natural flora and fauna, and the country's rivers and lakes frequently attract those who enjoy fishing. Tashkent is the home of a sizable water park and zoo, and many people enjoy simply strolling along city streets, especially after dark during the summer months, when temperatures on the street are often more comfortable than inside poorly ventilated Soviet-era apartment buildings. Taking a stroll also assists in the most popular recreational activity in Uzbekistan—socializing (and sometimes gossiping) with neighbors, relatives, and friends.

UZBEKISTAN AND THE WORLD

Uzbekistan's geographic position, wedged among Russia, China, South Asia, and the Middle East, bestows on the country, and the entire Central Asian region, a strategic importance that inevitably must increase with time. Just as the cities of medieval Transoxiana served as vital links along the Silk Road between imperial China and Rome, so, too, can modern Central Asia function as a conduit linking the emerging markets and powers that surround it. Lying at the core of Central Asia, Uzbekistan stands poised to play the leading role in this process and holds the key to the entire region's future. Uzbekistan borders all the remaining Central Asia countries, and a prosperous Central Asia is unimaginable without stability and sustained economic growth in Uzbekistan.

Ironically, it is not just the potential role of connector that provides Uzbekistan strategic significance, but also its possibilities as a buffer between the more moderate, Westernized Muslim communities of Russia and the former Soviet republics of Central Asia and the traditional—in some cases radicalized—Islamic societies of Iran, Pakistan, and Afghanistan, even with the removal of the Taliban. Russia and China, the latter holding a restive Uighur community that shares cultural and historical ties with the Uzbeks, view a temperate Uzbekistan, economically and politically integrated with the region and the global community, as essential to their efforts to prevent the radicalization of their own Muslim groups.

Since independence, Uzbekistan has developed relations with its neighbors and with countries further abroad, based on its strategic location and the ability to function as both bridge and barrier. When the Commonwealth of Independent States (CIS) was formed in December 1991, consisting of all of the former Soviet republics except the Baltic states, Uzbekistan readily accepted a role as a charter member. Through the 1990s, however, the Karimov government became increasingly skeptical of the functionality of the CIS and of what it viewed as Russian attempts to dominate the organization. At the same time, Uzbekistan quickly expanded its membership in international groups. In 1992, the country joined the United Nations and shortly thereafter was admitted to the Organization for Security and Cooperation in Europe. Subsequently, Uzbekistan became a participant in the Partnership for Peace program administered by NATO, providing a link to the West's most important security organization, and the Karimov regime has made no secret of the fact that Uzbekistan would welcome closer ties to the European Union.

Before the fall of 2001, Uzbekistan's relations with the United States had been occasionally rocky, as the U.S. government was a frequent critic of human rights abuses by the Uzbek administration throughout the 1990s. The terror attacks of September 11, 2001, changed the relationship of the two countries abruptly and dramatically, as the Bush administration sought allies in Central Asia in the conflict against the Taliban regime in Afghanistan. After brief negotiations, some of which were conducted personally by U.S. Secretary of Defense Donald Rumsfeld in Tashkent, Uzbekistan agreed to lease the former Soviet airbase of Khanabad, not far from the southern city of Karshi, to U.S. forces. Only minutes by air from the Afghan border, Khanabad played a key role in the invasion of Afghanistan and the elimination of the Taliban, a foreign policy goal both countries now had in common. In addition, in the wake of the Afghan war, American economic and military aid to Uzbekistan increased exponentially, as Washington sought to stabilize its new ally.

At the same time, Uzbekistan has strengthened its relationship with regional neighbors and with Russia and China, both of whom are wary of Uzbekistan's growing relationship with the United States. In 2001, Uzbekistan signed the charter of the Shanghai Cooperation Organization (SCO), a group consisting of all the new Central Asian states except Turkmenistan, along with China and Russia (Marketos 2001). The SCO was initially formed to promote stability and combat terrorism in the Central Asian region. Uzbekistan's status in the SCO was considerably enhanced when the location of an antiterrorist center was shifted from Bishkek, the capital of Kyrgyzstan, to Tashkent in late 2003. SCO members have pledged to cooperate on economic matters and development strategy as well as fighting terrorism, and although the viability of the new organization remains to be proven, Uzbekistan's participation mirrors its geopolitical position—straddling the divide between East and West and seeking the cooperation of both.

References

Akiner, Shirin. 1997. "Between Tradition and Modernity: The Dilemma Facing Contemporary Central Asian Women." In *Post-Soviet Women: From the Baltic to Central Asia,* edited by Mary Buckley. Cambridge: Cambridge University Press.

Allworth, Edward. 1990. *The Modern Uzbeks: From the Fourteenth Century to the Present.* Stanford, CA: Hoover Institution Press.

Gleason, Gregory. 1997. *The Central Asian States: Discovering Independence.* Boulder, CO: Westview Press.

Marketos, Thrassy. 2001. "Shanghai Cooperation Organization: A

Political/Military Coalition in the Making? *Journal of Central Asian Studies* VI (1), pp. 44–49.

Olcott, Martha. 1991. "Women and Society in Central Asia." In *Soviet Central Asia: The Failed Transformation,* edited by William Fierman. Boulder, CO: Westview Press.

Spector, Johanna. 1989. "Musical Tradition and Innovation." In *Central Asia: 120 Years of Russian Rule.* Durham, NC: Duke University Press.

PART TWO
REFERENCE SECTION

Key Events in Uzbek History

329 B.C.

Alexander the Great campaigns in Transoxiana, meeting stiff resistance from the Sogdians and their allies. He captures their main city, Marakanda (Samarkand), and also takes a wife, the incomparable Roxana. While encamped at Samarkand, Alexander kills his long-time advisor, Cleitus, in a drunken rage.

A.D. 700–800

Muslim conquest of major Silk Road cities. Over the course of the century, most of the population converts to Islam from Zoroastrianism and other faiths. In 751 Muslim forces turn back a Chinese army near Talas, thereby ensuring that Central Asia remain a part of the Muslim cultural realm.

1218–1223

Mongol conquest of Central Asia. In 1219, Genghis Khan destroys most of Bukhara, Samarkand, and other cities along the old Silk Road. Under his successors, trade routes are eventually reestablished, and Muslim civilization gradually recovers.

1370–1500

Era of the Timurids. Amir Timur (Tamerlane) creates the Timurid dynasty, making Samarkand his capital. Timur establishes an empire that stretches from India to Turkey and brings architects and artisans from the Middle East to beautify Samarkand, creating one of the most spectacular cities in the world. His grandson, Ulug Bek, adds to the grandeur of the city and makes significant additions to knowledge of astronomy.

1500–1700
Movement of Uzbek Tribal Confederation into Silk Road cities and establishment of Shabynid dynasties. From 1501 to 1510, Shabani Khan, leader of the Uzbeks, battles the Timurid prince Babur and eventually drives him from Central Asia. Shaybanid rulers add to glory of Bukhara, Samarkand, and other cities by constructing mosques, *medressehs*, and palaces, but Silk Road trade declines because of new water routes to the Orient.

1865
Tashkent falls to Russian forces. Russia pursues conquest of Central Asia as part of the Great Game with Great Britain. A decade after the fall of Tashkent, Russia absorbs the Khanate of Kokand, opening the way for complete Russian control of the Fergana Valley.

1898
Andijan Revolt.

1917–1921
The Bolshevik Revolution and Russian Civil War create turmoil and chaos in Central Asia. Many Jadids, young Muslim reformers, join the Bolsheviks. Mikhail Frunze conducts the military conquest of the region, eventually defeating the White forces and driving out the rulers in Bukhara and Khiva, with huge losses on both sides and among the civilian population. People's republics are set up in Bukhara and Khiva, closely aligned with the Bolshevik administration in Tashkent.

1920–1936
Basmachi Revolt. Bands of rebels challenge Soviet authority in the Fergana Valley and other regions of Central Asia. The

revolt reaches its height in 1921, but pockets of resistance continue for fifteen more years.

1924

Establishment of Uzbek Soviet Socialist Republic (SSR). For the first time in history, the ethnic identification "Uzbek" is associated with a definitive territory. Literary Uzbek is established, based on the Tashkent dialect. The Tajik Autonomous SSR is defined as a component of the new Uzbek SSR and is established as a separate SSR in 1929, but the predominantly Tajik cities of Samarkand and Bukhara remain within the Uzbek SSR.

1928

Josef Stalin initiates a policy of collectivization of agriculture in the Soviet Union. *Kolkhozi,* or collective farms, are created from individual holdings and land confiscated from Islamic authorities earlier. Soviet planners begin emphasizing the production of cotton at the expense of other crops, a trend that will continue for decades.

1936

The Karakalpak Autonomous Soviet Socialist Republic is detached from Kazakhstan and joined to the Uzbek SSR, nearly doubling the land area of Uzbekistan. This rearrangement of the region's political geography gives Uzbekistan a portion of the Aral Sea.

1938

The executions of Akmal Ikramov, Faizulla Khojaev, and other Uzbek leaders as a result of Stalinist purges take place.

1940

Uzbek is converted to Cyrillic script from the Latin alphabet. This represents the second change of alphabet in less than twenty years.

1941–1945

The German invasion of the Soviet Union in June 1941 results in the relocation of many factories and enterprises to Central Asia. The industrial importance of Tashkent is magnified as a result, as is the case with other cities in the region. In 1943, Stalin proposes the establishment of Muslim spiritual boards in the Islamic regions of the USSR, a de facto recognition that Islam remains a cultural influence in the Soviet Union. The largest such body is headquartered in Tashkent and administers the five Central Asian republics.

1959

Sharaf Rashidov is elected to the post of first party secretary of the Uzbek Communist Party. Rashidov will control the republic for almost a quarter of a century and preside over a tremendous expansion of the cotton monoculture.

1966

A massive earthquake strikes Tashkent, killing thousands and leaving more than 100,000 without shelter. Volunteers arrive from all over the USSR to help with reconstruction, which requires almost a decade.

1981

Mamadali Mahmudov's controversial novel *The Immortal Cliffs* is published and condemned by Soviet critics for its "nationalist" overtones.

1983

Investigation into the "cotton affair" is initiated. Rashidov is removed as first party secretary.

1988

Uzbek intellectuals form the opposition group known as Birlik.

1989

Bloody riots between Uzbeks and Meskhetian Turks result in approximately 100 deaths and widespread property damage. Islom Karimov replaces Rafik Nishanov as head of the Uzbek Communist Party. Uzbek is made an official language of the Uzbek SSR.

1990

A split in the Birlik leadership results in the formation of Erk, a second opposition group composed of Uzbek writers and academicians. The Uzbek Soviet Socialist Republic declares its sovereignty from the USSR.

1991–1993

In the wake of an attempted coup in Moscow, Islom Karimov declares Uzbekistan's independence from the USSR. In December, Karimov is elected president. His only opposition is Muhammad Solih, the leader of Erk, who garners almost 13 percent of the vote in the election, despite being denied access to the media. Karimov subsequently intimidates and drives into exile potential challengers, establishing an authoritarian regime.

1997–1998

The Uzbek regime initiates a crackdown on "unofficial" Muslim groups, especially alleged Wahhabis. In 1998, the Oliy Majlis, the Uzbek parliament, passes the Law on Freedom of Conscience and Religious Organizations, dramatically restricting the activities of religious believers.

1999

A series of car bombs rock Tashkent in February, killing more than fifteen people. In August, incursions by the Islamic Movement of Uzbekistan fail to reach Uzbek territory, but similar attempts the following year penetrate parts of southern Uzbekistan, although the invaders are quickly forced to withdraw.

2001

The Uzbek government agrees to allow U.S. forces to use its air space and a military base in the war against the Taliban regime in Afghanistan.

2004

In March, a series of shoot-outs and suicide bombings occur in Bukhara and Tashkent. The Uzbek government blames the violence on Islamic extremists. In July, suicide bombers strike the Israeli and U.S. Embassies, as well as an Uzbek government office, killing several people.

2005

In May, demonstrators in Andijan storm government buildings and free numerous prisoners, including several men charged with belonging to a radical Islamic organization. Uzbek security forces open fire on a large crowd, resulting in possibly hundreds of deaths. Nearby, the city of Karasu is briefly occupied by antigovernment dissidents.

Significant People, Places, and Events

Afandi, Nasriddin   Also known as Hoja Nasriddin, and several other variants across the Muslim world, it is unclear whether Nasriddin was an actual historical person or a composite folk figure, nor is it certain whether he was Turkish or Persian. Nevertheless, humorous anecdotes about this Islamic holy man are related throughout the Middle East and Central Asia and have become more popular in Uzbekistan since the decline of the USSR.

Ahmedov, Muhammad Ali (1942–)   One of Uzbekistan's best-known living writers and essayists, Muhammad Ali published his first novel in the late 1960s. Most of his works concern historical themes, and he has produced several works of the *dastan* genre. In the late 1980s, he published a number of essays critical of Soviet policy in Uzbekistan, which called for a greater awareness and respect for Uzbek culture and heritage. He has been a professor at Tashkent State University for many years, and in the 1990s, he taught Uzbek language at the University of Washington. He has been awarded numerous literary honors.

Andijan   A city located at the eastern end of Uzbekistan's portion of the Fergana Valley. Andijan is an ancient Silk Road city that has acquired new significance in recent years. For centuries, the city's main historical significance was its role as the birthplace of Babur, but it is also famous for its large main bazaar, second only to that of Osh, a few hours away in neighboring Kyrgyzstan. Near Andijan is the largest automobile plant in Central Asia, built by Daewoo Corporation of South Korea.

Ark (Bukhara)   The "ark" in Central Asian cities was a citadel that typically housed the most important buildings and facilities. A number of towns in Central Asia possessed arks, but the most impressive was that of Bukhara, one of the oldest and largest in the region. The palace of the emirs who ruled the city and surrounding region is located in the Ark, and some of the ruins may be more than a thousand years old. Today several museums occupy the buildings, and despite the poor repair of many of the structures, the power and influence that the leaders of Bukhara once enjoyed are still apparent.

Babur, Zahiriddin (1483–1530)   Babur was born in the city of Andijan, a descendant of both Genghis Khan and Amir Timur. In the early 1500s Babur struggled to reconstruct the glory of the Timurid empire and established himself at Samarkand for a while, but he was driven from the region by Shaybani Khan, the leader of the Uzbek tribal confederation. Babur took up residence in Kabul, the capital of modern Afghanistan, and from there launched an invasion of northern India. He is credited with establishing the Mogul dynasty, one of India's greatest periods of expansion and artistic achievement—one of Babur's descendants, Shah Jahan, built the Taj Mahal. Babur was not only a warrior, but also a man of letters—his epic work *Baburname* is an autobiographical account that provides crucial insights into the cultural and social systems of the time.

Basmachi Revolt   The rise of Bolshevik power in Central Asia at the conclusion of the Russian Revolution of 1917 led to widespread discontent among the local population. In response, an insurgency arose, composed of various elements who opposed the programs and policies of the new regime. Most of the Basmachi fighters operated in the Fergana Valley, and the movement at one time probably had the support of 10,000 soldiers. The movement proved difficult for the Soviet regime to eliminate—some accounts hold that Basmachi guerrillas were active in some parts of Central Asia well into the 1930s, more than ten years after the Communists took control of the region. Many Basmachi members fled into northern Afghanistan, where they found refuge among the local Uzbek population.

Berdakh (1827–1900) Berdakh is considered the national poet of the Karakalpaks, an ethnic group that lives in the Karakalpak Autonomous Region (Karakalpakstan) of western Uzbekistan. In Nukus, the capital of Karakalpakstan, tributes to Berdakh seem to be everywhere—one of the main streets of the city is named after him, as is the largest theater in town and a university, and several statues of the bard adorn the city. His best-known work is probably the poem "Akybet," although he wrote many others. Berdakh was honored on a postage stamp in Uzbekistan in 1998.

Bibi Khanym An enormous mosque complex located in the heart of Samarkand. A massive Koran stand of stone occupies part of the courtyard, and the structure has been under renovation since Uzbekistan's independence, an effort partially funded by UNESCO (United Nations Educational, Scientific, and Cultural Organization). The complex was built during the reign of Amir Timur and named for a beautiful wife from China. Legend holds that the builder was so taken by the gorgeous lady that he demanded a kiss for his efforts while Timur was absent from the city. Upon his return from campaigning, Timur learned of the illicit peck and had the man put to death for dishonoring his alluring spouse.

Conolly, Arthur. *See* **Stoddart, Charles, and Conolly, Arthur**

The Cotton Affair In 1983, the central administration in

Moscow sent a team of investigators to Uzbekistan to root out alleged corruption. The investigation lasted for several years, and many Uzbek officials were charged, including Yury Churbanov, the son-in-law of the late Soviet leader Leonid Brezhnev. The heart of the scandal involved misrepresentation of the amount of cotton that Uzbekistan was delivering to the central government—the difference allegedly amounting to a billion rubles, which was skimmed off by officials at various levels of authority in Uzbekistan. The fact that the main investigators were ethnically Russian and most of those accused and convicted were Uzbek led many in Uzbekistan to view the entire affair as an ethnic witch hunt. The image of pervasive corruption among the party cadre in Uzbekistan led to the dismissal of the republic's long-time leader, Sharaf Rashidov.

Fitrat, Abdulrauf (1886–1938) Fitrat was a poet and playwright who as a young man joined the reformist movement known as Jadidism. Fitrat was from Bukhara and had acquired an Islamic education in that city's famous medressehs, but by the early years of the twentieth century, he had become an outspoken critic of the backwardness and decadence of Central Asian society, especially the inefficient and corrupt educational system. He joined the Jadids and after the Bolshevik Revolution supported the new order for a time, only to be arrested during Stalin's purges in the 1930s. He was executed in 1938.

Frunze, Mikhail (1885–1925) Mikhail Frunze was born in what is today Bishkek but spent many of his formative years in Moscow and other parts of Russia. Arrested several times in his youth for revolutionary activity, Frunze proved his military leadership qualities in Moscow in 1917, when he commanded a unit of Bolshevik soldiers. During the Russian Civil War, Frunze was commissioned with the rank of general in the Red Army and sent to Central Asia to battle anti-

Communist forces there. In 1920, Frunze's army had seized most of the main cities of Central Asia, including Bukhara and Khiva, although many more years would pass before the Basmachi rebellion was quelled in the Fergana Valley. During much of the Soviet period, the capital city of Kyrgyzstan, called Bishkek today, was known as Frunze. Frunze died under mysterious circumstances during an operation at age forty.

Gur-i-Amir   A small mausoleum near the heart of Samarkand, featuring a magnificent turquoise ribbed dome. Gur-i-Amir is the final resting place of Amir Timur or, as he is known in the West, Tamerlane. In recent years, the building has been restored to much of its former glory, including the gold leaf that covers the interior of the huge dome. Inside lie stone sarcophagi marking the graves, but the actual bodies lie below the floor. The mausoleum holds the remains of Timur, two of his sons, his famous grandson Ulug Bek, another grandson, and two of Timur's most revered teachers and advisors.

Ikramov, Akmal (1898–1938)   Ikramov became the first ethnic Uzbek to lead the Uzbek Communist Party, being elected to that position in 1929. His tenure was tumultuous because he presided over the processes of collectivization and de-Islamization of Uzbek culture. In 1938, he, along with other leading Uzbek Communists, was executed during Stalin's purges. For several decades Ikramov became a nonentity, and his name disappeared nearly completely from Soviet sources. After Stalin's death, his memory was revived, and today he is seen by many in Uzbekistan as a tragic, if misguided, victim of Soviet oppression.

Islom-huja Medresseh   For centuries, the city of Khiva in western Uzbekistan was famous as a center of Islamic scholarship. Today the most famous *medresseh* (Islamic seminary) in that city is the Islom-huja, accompanied by the tallest and most colorful minaret in the city. The medresseh was established just before the Bolshevik Revolution by the Khan's vizier, a reform-minded official named Islom-huja. Islom-huja had worked to modernize the city, attempting to bring electricity to its residents and to restructure the educational system. The vizier made many enemies, who eventually managed to assassinate him. His medresseh and minaret remain the most distinctive buildings in Khiva.

Jadidist movement The Jadids represented an Muslim intellectual and social movement, heavily influenced by the Tatar reformer Ismail Bey Gaspirali. The Jadids sought a "new method" of teaching in Central Asia, and initially the Jadids were in fact seeking reforms in the educational system in Central Asia. By the end of the first decade of the twentieth century, however, the movement had acquired political dimensions, and many leading Central Asian Jadids had adopted a much broader agenda of social change. Some Jadidist intellectuals joined the Bolsheviks after 1917, while others rejected the new ideology. Some of the leading Jadidists in Uzbekistan were Mahmud Khoja, Munawwar Qari, Abdulhamid Cholpan, Hamza Niyaziy, and Abdalrauf Fitrat.

Kalon Minaret A massive tower that stands almost 150 feet high in the heart of Bukhara. For centuries the Kalon Minaret was the tallest structure in Central Asia. Legend holds that even Genghis Khan was awed by the structure and spared it on that basis, although he razed much of the remainder of the city. In the seventeenth and eighteenth centuries, the emirs of Bukhara used the minaret's great height for executions, having criminals flung from the top to the pavement below it. Although the region around Bukhara is prone to earthquakes, the Kalon Minaret has suffered only minor damage because of straw packed into its foundation, which cushions the tower.

Karimov, Islom (1938–)   Islom Karimov was born in the city of Samarkand in central Uzbekistan. He was raised in an orphanage, joined the Communist Party as a young man, and obtained a degree in economics. Rising through the ranks, by 1989 Karimov had become the first party secretary of the Uzbek Communist Party, the most powerful political position in Uzbekistan.

Karimov aggressively dealt with any political movements that might challenge his authority, and when the USSR dissolved in 1991, he was the only figure in a position to assume power in independent Uzbekistan. He was elected president in 1991, extended his term in 1995, and was reelected in 2000—in each of these contests, no serious challenge was allowed. In 2002, the Uzbek constitution was changed to extend his term in office to 2007.

Khanabad airbase   A former Soviet base built to defend the USSR during the Cold War. It is located a short drive from the city of Karshi in southern Uzbekistan. Ironically, in the aftermath of the terrorist attacks of September 11, 2001, the Uzbek government granted the United States rights to the facility, and in October of that year, Khanabad became the first location in the former USSR to host American troops. The leasing of the base to the United States solidified its military relations with Uzbekistan and increased Russian concerns over U.S. ambitions in the region.

Khojaev, Faizulla (1896–1938)   At the time of the Bolshevik Revolution in the city of Bukhara, Khojaev was a member of a reformist group known as the Young Bukharans, who styled themselves after the Young Turk movement in Turkey. Upon the abdication of the emir, Khojaev managed to form a government and became the president of the Bukharan People's Republic, which was absorbed by the Soviet government in 1924. Khojaev then in turn became the president of the newly formed Uzbek SSR, but by the 1930s he and other Uzbek leaders increasingly opposed the policies of Stalin in Central Asia. In 1938, Khojaev was tried and executed for treason, along with other prominent members of the Communist Party.

Mahmudov, Mamadali (1940–) One of the most controversial writers of the late Soviet period and today a prominent political prisoner in Uzbekistan. Mahmudov gained fame in 1981 with the publication of his novel *The Immortal Cliffs,* a work set in the nineteenth century that focuses on the violence and disruption created by the Russian conquest of Central Asia. The novel was widely seen as a critique of Soviet society and was denounced as "anti-Marxist" and "nationalist" by many Soviet critics. In the late 1990s, Mahmudov was detained by Uzbek authorities and has spent the last several years in prison.

Mir-i-Arab Medresseh A large medresseh, or Islamic seminary, constructed in Bukhara in the mid-1500s, which served for centuries as the largest such facility in Central Asia. Young Islamic scholars from every corner of the Muslim realm came to Bukhara to study at the Mir-i-Arab. In the 1920s, Soviet authorities closed the medresseh, but it was reopened during World War II and for most of the remainder of the Soviet era was one of two functioning medressehs in the USSR.

Muhammad Yusuf (1952–) Muhammad Yusuf is a controversial religious figure who has been active in the country's religious politics since the late 1980s. Yusuf was educated at the Mir-i-Arab medresseh in Bukhara, as well as in Libya. In 1989, he was elected mufti of the Central Asian Muslim Spiritual Board in Tashkent and quickly proved to be an outspoken critic of some aspects of Soviet policy toward Islam. After independence, Yusuf fell out of favor with the Karimov regime and fled the country in 1993, eventually taking up residence in Saudi Arabia. In 2000, he returned to Uzbekistan and has remained a muted but consistent critic of some of the regime's policies toward Muslim believers in Uzbekistan.

Naqshband, Baha al-Din (?–1389) Naqshband is the founder of the Naqshbandi *tariqa,* or Sufi order. The Naqshbandis are the most popular Sufi order in Uzbekistan, although it is difficult to determine exact numbers of adherents to the group. Naqshband's mausoleum is located a short distance from the city of Bukhara, and during the Soviet era when many Muslims could not make the hajj, his tomb became a site of pilgrimage. Since Uzbekistan's independence, interest in Sufism has increased among many Muslims, and visits to Naqshband's burial place remain an important ritual for many believers.

Nasrullah Khan (?–1860) A notoriously cruel and despotic ruler of Bukhara for more than thirty years, Nasrullah Khan became the archetypal Central Asian ruler in the minds of many Europeans in the nineteenth century. Nasrullah was the infamous dictator who imprisoned the British envoys Charles Stoddart and Arthur Conolly and eventually executed them. Nasrullah kept large numbers of slaves, had an immense harem of young women for his pleasure, and waged war on both neighboring Khiva and Kokand for much of his reign. When he captured Kokand in 1842, Nasrullah killed its leader, Madali Khan, and his mother, the famous poetess Nodira.

Navoi, Alisher (1441–1501) Navoi (sometimes spelled Nav'ai) is considered Central Asia's greatest scholar and writer of the Timurid period. The Uzbeks claim him as part of their heritage, although in reality he was not ethnically Uzbek—a technicality of little importance to most people in Uzbekistan. He lived most of his life in Herat, a city located today in Afghanistan. Navoi composed his works in both Chagatay, a Turkic language, and Persian, with the bulk appearing in the former. The fact that Navoi chose to write in Chagataai greatly assisted in its emergence as a literary language. Navoi has a city and region named in his honor in Uzbekistan, and many cities have numerous streets and parks named for him as well.

Nodira (1790–1842)   Nodira was the wife of Umar Khan and the mother of Madali Khan, both influential rulers of the Khanate of Kokand in the first half of the nineteenth century, when the Khanate rose to prominence in eastern Uzbekistan. Famed for her beauty, Nodira also was an accomplished writer and poet. The *ulema,* or community of Islamic scholars in Kokand, condemned both her poetry and her behavior as transgressing acceptable standards for a woman of her day. She was executed along with other members of her family when the Khanate was invaded by the emir of Bukhara. Nodira is viewed as a heroine and martyr in modern Uzbekistan.

Polatov, Abdurahim (194?–)   Polatov was one of the founding members of Birlik (Unity), a large opposition group in Uzbekistan in the early 1990s. The group was never allowed to register as a political party, however, and therefore Polatov was denied the opportunity to challenge Islom Karimov for the post of president. In June 1992, Pulatov was assaulted in broad daylight in Tashkent and beaten so badly that his skull was fractured. He subsequently fled Uzbekistan and in 2005 had lived in exile for most of the previous thirteen years.

Qadiry, Abdullah (1894–1939)   Qadiry was one of the most influential Uzbek men of letters of the twentieth century and is considered by many to be the first modern Uzbek novelist. In his youth, he supported the Jadidist movement and wrote for several reformist newspapers. It seems clear that Qadiry was sympathetic to the Bolshevik cause in Central Asia during the first years of the Russian Revolution, but the complex nature of his political philosophy also included support for Uzbek nationalism. His masterpiece is the novel *Days Gone By,* a disturbing work dealing with social and gender relations in traditional Uzbek society, among other themes. Qadiry was condemned by the Stalinist regime and executed in 1939.

Rashidov, Sharaf (1917–1983) Rashidov served as first party secretary of the Uzbek Communist Party from 1959 to 1983. During his long tenure at the pinnacle of the political structure in the Uzbek SSR, the republic became more economically dependent of the cotton "monoculture," and as a result tremendous environmental damage was inflicted on the Aral Sea. Rashidov was brought down by the so-called "cotton affair" and by charges of widespread corruption. He died of a heart attack in 1983. After Uzbekistan's independence, his reputation was revived, and one of Tashkent's central streets is named in his honor.

Registan (Sandy Place) The most famous site in Uzbekistan, and probably in Central Asia. Registan lies at the heart of Samarkand and is a complex of three spectacular medressehs, which enclose a central square. The oldest of the medressehs is the Ulug Bek, built by that Timurid prince in 1420. It is more than two centuries older than the remaining structures of the Registan. Directly across from the Ulug Bek medresseh is the Shir Dor medresseh, completed in 1636. The Shir Dor is an unusual example of Islamic architecture in that it features two large lions on the façade of the medresseh. The last medresseh, the Tilla Kari (Golden Medresseh), is located between the Ulug Bek and Shir Dor medressehs and has a stunning domed mosque inside its grounds.

Shahri Zinda An ancient necropolis in Samarkand, the name of which means "Tomb of the Living King." Legend holds that Shahri Zinda is the final resting place of Qasim Ibn Abbas, a cousin of the Prophet Muhammad who came to

Samarkand to spread the word of Islam. The entire complex consists of numerous mausoleums decorated with colorful tiles, most of which have withstood numerous earthquakes over the last 600 years. Most of those buried in the Shari Zinda are relatives of Amir Timur, who constructed several of the tombs for his many wives and daughters. During Soviet times, the tomb complex attracted pilgrims, and it continues to do so today.

Shakhimardan An Uzbek enclave inside Kyrgyzstan, about 30 miles south of the Uzbek city of Fergana. Shakhimardan is a picturesque, mountainous region famous for its fresh air and beautiful scenery. To reach it, one must travel through Kyrgyz territory, but oddly no visa is currently required, although in recent years the Uzbek government has attempted to obtain control of the strip of land that separates the enclave from Uzbekistan. The future status of Shakhimardan and two other enclaves nearby is unclear, and issues of control and access may lead to serious border disputes with Kyrgyzstan.

Shakhrisabz Amir Timur's birthplace, which was called Kesh in ancient times. Although Samarkand was officially his capital, there seems little doubt that Shakhrisabz was an important city to the conqueror, and it is likely that he intended for this small city, not Samarkand, to be his final resting place. Many of the buildings are in ruins, but even the ruins have a grandeur that is impressive. The central building in Timur's time would have been the Ak Saray palace, which must have been enormous before age and earthquakes brought about its collapse. Numerous tombs from the time of Timur can still be seen in the city, some of which hold the remains of two of his sons.

Solih, Muhammad (1949–) Solih is one of Uzbekistan's most outspoken dissidents and has the distinction of mounting the only legitimate challenge to Islom Karimov in a presidential election in Uzbekistan. Solih is a poet who rose to prominence in 1988 when he was elected secretary of the Uzbekistan Writer's Union, a platform he used to criticize Soviet policy in Central Asia. Solih was an early member of the opposition group Birlik but withdrew from that organization in 1990 and formed an alternative party, Erk. In the 1991 elections for president, Solih was allowed to run against Karimov but was given virtually no access to the media. Despite limited exposure, Solih still captured almost 13 percent of the vote. He later fled Uzbekistan and has lived in exile for most of the last decade. In recent years, the Karimov government has accused Solih of involvement in terrorist acts against Uzbekistan, although little evidence has been offered to support such claims.

Stoddart, Charles, and Conolly, Arthur   British Army officers who tragically fell into the clutches of Nasrullah Khan, the ruler of Bukhara. Charles Stoddart was sent on an embassy to the Khan in the late 1830s in an attempt to secure his support against the Russians. Stoddart made several fatal errors in protocol and behavior, however, and Nasrullah had him imprisoned. Arthur Conolly arrived two years later in an attempt to free Stoddart and reassure the Khan of British intentions in the region, all to no avail—Nasrullah imprisoned him as well, placing both men in the infamous "bug pit" located in Bukhara's Ark. Both men were publicly beheaded in 1842, an event that confirmed the despotic and barbaric character of Central Asia to many in the British government and public.

Ulug Bek (1394–1449)   The grandson of Amir Timur, Ulug Bek was an educator, patron of the arts, and scholar, as well as serving as an administrator in the Timurid Empire his famous forebear had created. As regent of Samarkand, Ulug Bek built the first of the three large structures that compose the Registan, the medresseh that bears his name, completed around 1420. According to legend, he taught mathematics there. A brilliant astronomer, Ulug Bek built an observatory on the outskirts of the city, centered on an enormous astrolabe that rotated along a track nearly 100 feet long. Lost for centuries, the observatory was unearthed in 1908. After a short reign as emperor, Ulug Bek was murdered on the orders of his own son.

Language, Food, and Etiquette in Uzbekistan

LANGUAGE

There are two official languages in Uzbekistan, Uzbek and Russian. Around 70 percent of the population is ethnically Uzbek, and most of that group is conversant in their own tongue. Among the Russians, however, who still account for about 6 percent of the population, only a small percentage is fluent in Uzbek, and certain other minorities such as Armenians and Koreans have low fluency in Uzbek as well. On the other hand, virtually all groups in Uzbekistan retain the ability to communicate in Russian, and thus Russian continues to serve as a language of interethnic communication. Since independence Uzbek has gradually displaced Russian in some official capacities, and the long-term aim of the Uzbek administration is for all citizens to eventually have fluency in Uzbek.

Uzbek is a member of the Turkic branch of the Uralic-Altaic language family and is derived from Chagatay (Turki). The Uzbek lexicon contains many words borrowed from Persian, Arabic, and Russian. From the 1940s until independence, Uzbek was written in a modified Cyrillic script, but since 1991 the Uzbek government has slowly but steadily introduced the Latin script, and public examples of Uzbek in this alphabet now abound. The shift to Latin script has been somewhat controversial but is seen by the current (2005) regime as necessary to the modernization of the new state, much in the same way that Latinization of Turkish in the Republic of Turkey was pursued in that country during Ataturk's time. The standardized spoken dialect is based on the Tashkent dialect, but numerous dialects may be encountered across the country.

Uzbek does not follow the rigid word order of English and, like other members of the Turkic languages, is an agglutinative language, meaning that words are formed by adding various suffixes, particles or other word elements to nouns or verbs to alter meaning. This allows for the formation of long words, and in some cases a single verb with its various additions may function as the equivalent of an entire sentence in English. Considerable meaning can therefore be conveyed in only a few words, and native speakers typically speak quickly, compared with English speakers. A common interjection, particularly when discussing plans for the future is *hudo holasa,* or "God willing."

Following are several useful and common phrases in Uzbek:

Salom alaikum	Hello, good day, greetings (literally, "Peace to you")
Yakshemisiz?	How are you?
Yakshi	Well, good
Siz chi?	And what about you?
Hayr	Goodbye
Hope	Okay, alright, yes
Rakmat	Thanks
Kaerda?	Where is . . .?
Marhamat	Please
Kechirasiz	Excuse me
Ha	Yes
Yok	No
Kancha?	How many, how much?
Soat nechada?	At what time?
Yemon emas	Not bad.

FOOD AND BEVERAGES

The consumption of food and beverages in Uzbek society is typically a social event, and food is a common part of any celebration. In fact, the production and consumption of huge quantities of both food and drink are expected activities at weddings, birthday parties, and various other occasions. It would be unthinkable to hold such festivities without providing a sumptuous feast, and it is a strong-willed guest indeed who departs the premises without having stuffed himself, or having been stuffed, with the provisions of his host.

Certain foods have a symbolic status that goes beyond simply serving as a source of nourishment. Bread, for example, is typically torn into pieces and distributed by the head of household at the beginning of a meal, and a piece of bread should never be placed upside down on the table. Similarly, if bread goes stale, it should not be thrown out, but broken into crumbs and left for birds or other animals. On the other hand, the Muslim prohibition against pork is widely observed among Uzbeks and other traditionally Islamic groups, although sausages containing pork, along with other meats, may be eaten by Muslims.

Common Uzbek Dishes

Plov. Without question, plov is the national dish of Uzbekistan. Usually made by men, it is served on important social occasions and at parties. The basic ingredient is rice, which is cooked in a large pot called a *kazan.* Usually carrots (either orange or yellow) are finely sliced and, along with cumin, are blended with the rice, which is then topped with meat, usually mutton, but beef may be substituted. The plov is placed on a large platter, a *lyagan,* from which everyone is served. Traditionally plov is eaten without utensils, using only the right hand. If a utensil is used, it is usually a large spoon. The basic differences in various styles of plov derive from the ingredients added to the rice in addition to the carrots: raisins, chickpeas, garlic, and quince may be added, depending on the region of Uzbekistan, and the preference of the preparer.

Samsa. Frequently eaten as a snack or quick meal, samsa are meat pastries baked in a traditional oven or *tandir,* or they may be cooked in a standard oven. The pastry shell is made from wheat dough, which is then stuffed with a mixture of ground meat and onion. The finished product is usually triangular in shape. In the autumn, the meat and onion mince may be replaced with chopped pumpkin, a delicacy that may be served as dessert or as an appetizer. Like plov, samsa are typically served at social gatherings or when guests are expected.

Manti. Manti are steamed dumplings, filled with a mince of ground meat and onions. The soft outer shell of the dumpling is made from wheat flour, and the meat used to stuff the interior may be mutton or beef. Manti are made using a *mantyshnitsa,* a special steamer designed for preparing this delicacy.

Non (Russian: Lepyoshka). One of the great delights of Uzbek cuisine is the traditional flatbread, called non in Uzbek. Fresh, warm non is available every morning in the local bazaar, where the round, flat disks of bread are kept wrapped in blankets to preserve their taste and texture—even in late afternoon, the bread may still be warm. Non is prepared by pressing the flattened dough against the interior of the *tandir,* a free-standing traditional oven—eventually, the entire inside of the tandir is covered, and the bread is allowed to bake. Various regions have their own unique styles of non (Samarkand is famous for its thicker, decorative bread), and special breads are prepared for weddings and other celebrations.

Shashlik. Called kabob outside of Central Asia, shashlik is the Central Asian equivalent of fast food. Stands selling shashlik are scattered throughout the larger cities, and one may find them along the main roadways as well. Chunks of meat, usually mutton but also beef, are impaled on sharp sticks or metal skewers, and then cooked over an open charcoal grille. If the meat is mutton, the chunks are often alternated with choice cuts of fat, taken from the tail of Central Asia's famous fat-tailed sheep. A variation is to tightly press spiced ground meat around the skewer, resulting in a kind of hamburger on a stick. Unlike elsewhere in the world, vegetables are not placed on the skewer when making traditional shashlik.

Shurpa. Various types of soups are a common component of Uzbek meals, and shurpa is probably the most popular. Similar to mutton stew, this soup is made when chopped potatoes and other vegetables are boiled in broth with large chunks of mutton. Served in a deep bowl, every ingredient is consumed except the bones, and it is not considered ill mannered in the least to raise the bowl to one's mouth and loudly slurp the remaining broth. Shurpa is typically served before the main course of a meal or alternatively may be served by itself as a snack or light supper.

Melons. The oasis settlements of Central Asia have for centuries been famous for the size and quality of their melons. In the late summer, many street corners and vacant lots in Tashkent and other large cities are covered with enormous piles of watermelons and the local favorite, *dinya,* which simply means "melon." The dinya is elongate in shape and the interior fruit is exceptionally sweet and succulent. During Soviet times, visitors from outside the region frequently carried these melons home as presents for friends or treats for themselves. Both the dinya and watermelon are typically served as dessert.

Common Uzbek Beverages

Tea. Tea is the most popular beverage in Uzbekistan among all ethnic groups. Tea is served at every meal and whenever guests arrive. Much social interaction occurs over tea, and the *chaikona,* or teahouse, is a common gathering place for Uzbek men where politics, religion, and other issues are discussed. Tea is always served hot, and black tea is the most common, although green tea is widely drunk as well.

Alcoholic Beverages. Over the last century and a half, the Muslim groups in Central Asia have widely adopted Slavic drinking customs, despite the Islamic ban on the consumption of alcoholic drinks. The most popular alcoholic beverage is vodka, drunk straight up with no mixer or dilution. Cognac, beer, wine, and champagne are also popular and widely available. Drunkenness is unfortunately a common result of the frequent celebrations and parties of Uzbek culture.

Soft Drinks. Soft drinks are frequently drunk at parties and are widely available. Street vendors offer chilled Western brands in the bazaars and in restaurants, and local brands are increasingly available in a range of flavors. Diet soda is also sold but is not as popular as regular varieties. Soft drinks are still rather expensive for the average person in Uzbekistan and are therefore considered a luxury.

ETIQUETTE

Overall, Uzbekistan is a traditional country, although social mores and practices vary considerably, depending on one's ethnic affiliation and socioeconomic status. As a general rule, Russians and other European-influenced groups tend to be less conservative and traditional, whereas Uzbeks and other Muslim groups usually are more tightly bound to traditional views and values. Within the Uzbek community, urban Uzbeks are the least traditional in terms of dress and behavior, whereas rural residents frequently adhere strongly to established customs and views. Although social practices are malleable over time, a number seem eternal and are common to all levels of society.

Taking Off Shoes. When entering a house, apartment, or mosque, it is standard practice to remove one's shoes. Frequently the host of a private residence will provide guests with house shoes to wear while enjoying his hospitality. Uzbekistan is a desert country, and by removing shoes at the entry, dust and dirt acquired in the street are left at the doorway. This practice is common across the Muslim world.

Use of Hands and Feet. In Muslim culture, the feet are considered to be a dirty part of the body, and the left hand is generally reserved for bodily functions. Therefore, among traditional Muslim groups, one should observe certain restrictions on the placement of feet and on the use of the left hand. One should not pass food using the left hand, nor use the left hand when eating plov by hand in the traditional manner. Similarly, one's feet should never approach the surface of a table or other area where food is being served, particularly if the meal is being served in the traditional style—that is, using a cloth on the floor.

Social Hierarchy and Respect. Elders in Uzbek society are granted respect and reverence, particularly those in positions of authority and leadership. Younger individuals will typically address an older acquaintance, or even a total stranger, as *aka* or "elder brother," signifying deference and humility. In addition, placing the right hand over one's heart when greeting an elder or superior signals respect and sincerity. At social gatherings, it is usually the eldest member of the group who is served food first and who makes the first toast, whatever the occasion. Showing open disrespect to an elder is considered antisocial and uncultured behavior.

Public Display of Affection between Opposite Sexes. Among Uzbeks and the other Muslim peoples of Uzbekistan, physical affection between sexes does not usually take place in public. This is particularly true for unmarried couples, and especially for unmarried females. On the other hand, among Russians, Armenians, and Koreans taboos on public affection are much less stringently observed. With these groups holding hands and kissing in public is not condemned, although if done too openly, it is considered to be in poor taste.

Sitting. It is common among traditional Uzbek families to take meals on the floor. Typically, Uzbeks will sit cross-legged or with the feet tucked underneath and behind the body. One should not allow one's feet to approach the food, nor should one touch the feet while the meal is in progress.

Nose Blowing. As in other Asian countries, one should not blow one's nose while taking a meal or in a public place. If it is necessary to use a handkerchief, one should seek out a private location to do so.

Bargaining. Bargaining for the price of an item is expected in the bazaars of Uzbekistan. A buyer is expected to negotiate the price, and the consumer is never expected to pay the initial asking price—doing so will instantly identify one as a foreigner. In the Western-style retail stores and kiosks, items have set prices, and the customer does not bargain in these venues. One is also expected to negotiate the price of private taxis, which are not equipped with meters.

Business Cards. Since independence, business cards have become more common in Central Asia, and many professionals and business people carry them. In formal situations, they are frequently exchanged.

Clothes. Styles of dress vary dramatically in Uzbekistan, according to economic status, social standing, and ethnic affiliation, especially in the case of women. Uzbek and Tajik women dress conservatively and generally do not wear short skirts, shorts, or dresses that display cleavage. In the countryside, women of all ages commonly wear a headscarf in public, and although much rarer in Uzbekistan than in Afghanistan or Pakistan, a few women since independence have donned the *paranja,* or veil. Slavic and other non-Muslim women do not abide by these restrictions, and dress in a fashion similar to their counterparts in Moscow, Paris, and New York. Men typically dress in slacks and a shirt, wearing sandals or loafers. Professionals and businessmen wear suits and ties to work, and one typically dresses up for parties and celebrations. In general, people of all ethnic groups in Uzbekistan take great pride in their appearance.

Uzbekistan-Related Organizations

BUSINESS AND ECONOMIC

The following is a short list of various organizations working to promote business in Uzbekistan. Many more may be found by searching the Internet. When calling locations in Uzbekistan from outside the country, one must dial the country code (998) and the respective city code. The city code for Tashkent is (71).

The American-Uzbekistan Chamber of Commerce
1717 N. Street, NW
Washington, DC 20036
Telephone: (202) 828-4111
E-mail: aucc@erois.com
Web site: http://www.aucconline.com/aucc/data/contact
   This organization is well known to business people in the United States, and its functions in Uzbekistan are similar to its U.S. counterpart—to promote honest and professional business practices and the development and expansion of business in Uzbekistan.

Business Information Service for the Newly Independent States
Telephone: (202) 482-4199
Web site: http://www.bisnis.doc.gov/bisnis/country/uzbekistan.cfm
   This Web site features more than 100 links to a wide variety of business-related information. There are sections linking to documents and Web sites on tenders and leads, events, trade show reports, legal and regulatory issues, industry

reports, general reports, market updates, reports on business and economic development in specific regions of Uzbekistan, and more. A valuable trove of information for the researcher or prospective investor in Uzbekistan.

Chamber of Commodity Producers and Entrepreneurs of Tashkent
Hospital Massiv 12
Tashkent, Uzbekistan 700015
Telephone: (998) 71-3327-07
Fax: (998) 71-5515-57
E-mail: chamber@tashtitp.bcc.com.uz

The focus of this grassroots organization is promoting and assisting the small business owner in Uzbekistan. Legal advice, consulting, and training are offered to members, and the chamber keeps a database on local business development. It also produces a monthly newsletter.

CULTURE, EDUCATION, AND EXCHANGE

ACTR/ACCELS
1776 Massachusetts Avenue, NW
Suite 700
Washington, DC 20036
Telephone: (202) 833-7522
Fax: (202) 833-7523
Web site: http://www.americancouncils.org

The American Councils for International Education works "to advance education, research and mutual understanding" between the United States and the countries of the former Soviet bloc. ACTR/ACCELS offers a number of programs that are designed to support educational initiatives in the region and scholarly research, which contributes to the emergence of civil society. Programs are available for both teachers and students.

Eurasia Foundation
1350 Connecticut Avenue, NW
Suite 1000
Washington, DC 20036
Telephone: (202) 234-7370
Fax: (202) 234-7377
E-mail: Eurasia@eurasia.org
Web site: http://www.eurasia.org

Eurasia Foundation works to promote democracy and the development of free markets in all the former states of the USSR except the three Baltic countries. The foundation makes grants from the United States and from the new states in Eurasia available to institutions, both public and private. It also funds programs developed on its own initiative. There are branch offices in most of the former Soviet countries, including Uzbekistan in the city of Tashkent.

Fulbright Association of Uzbekistan
54, Buyuk Ipak Yoli
Tashkent, Uzbekistan 700137
E-mail: lola@freenet.uz
Web site: http://fulbright.freenet.uz

The Fulbright Association provides exchange programs for teaching and research to U.S. scholars in Uzbekistan and funds scholars from Uzbekistan to work and teach in the United States. Those eligible include individuals from the private sector, scholars, teachers, and administrators at the secondary and postsecondary levels and advanced graduate students working on master's and doctoral degrees.

Uzbek Dance and Culture Society
PO Box 65195
Washington, DC 20035
E-mail: uzbekdance@aol.com
Web site: http://www.uzbekdance.org

This organization is one of a few in the United States that offers lessons in Uzbek dance and music. Besides providing lessons on a regular basis, it features special summer camps where one may learn the intricacies of Uzbek dance. Its Web site also offers information on dancers and musicians from Uzbekistan who are touring the United States and provides related links.

GOVERNMENT

Consulate General of Uzbekistan
801 Second Avenue, 20th Floor
New York, NY 10017
Telephone: (212) 754-6178
Fax: (212) 838-9812
E-mail: info@uzbekconsulny.org
Web site: http://www.uzbekconsul.org

Embassy of Uzbekistan
1746 Massachusetts Avenue, NW
Washington, DC 20036-1903
Telephone: (202) 887-5300
Fax: (202) 293-6804
E-mail: embassy@uzbekistan.org
Web site: http://www.uzbekistan.org

Republic of Uzbekistan—Portal of the State Authority
Web site: http://www.gov.uz
This Web site offers a wealth of information about the politics, economics, culture, and history of Uzbekistan and has numerous links to related sites.

TOURISM

Uzbekistan may seem to be a remote and somewhat forbidding land to the average Western traveler, but in fact the country presents an abundance of cultural experiences, magnificent historical sites, and stark, beautiful landscapes. A frugal tourist can find many bargains in accommodations and dining, and for those who seek top-quality facilities, there are numerous four- and five-star hotels in most major cities in the country. Regardless of where one stays, the culture, people, and land are well worth a visit.

Lonely Planet Publications
150 Linden Street
Oakland, CA 94607
Telephone: (800) 275-8555; (510) 893-8555
Fax: (510) 893-8563
E-mail: info@lonelyplanet.com
Web site: http://www.lonelyplanet.com
    Even if you do not invest in the Lonely Planet guidebook for Central Asia, a visit to the company's Web site will be time well spent for the prospective tourist. The site has information on a wide variety of topics, including when to go, costs, activities, history, culture, and current news and information. There are also many useful links provided, and one can order the guidebook directly from the site.

Travel Agencies

A number of companies conduct tours to Uzbekistan, and the choices have increased in recent years. The following two are based in the country, but many others may be found by searching the Internet.

Advantour LLC
Mirobod kochasi 116
Tashkent, Uzbekistan 700090
Telephone: (998) 71-152-4200
Fax: (998) 71-254-8612
E-mail: info@advantour.com

Web site: http://www.advantour.com

This company has been operating tours for several years and offers a number of itineraries of various length and costs. They also will customize tours for individuals and groups. The Web site has several important links, including how to get a visa for Uzbekistan.

Karamel Fur
Yusuf Hos-Khojib Street
Building 46-12
Tashkent, Uzbekistan
Telephone: (998) 71-134-6581
Fax: (998) 71-152-1162
E-mail: admin@uzbektravco.com
Web site: http://www.uzbektravco.com

Annotated Bibliography of Recommended Works on Uzbekistan

The written sources and Web sites described in this section provide additional information for those who wish to learn more about Uzbekistan. For convenience, the listing is organized in the same fashion as the narrative section, although some of the sources of information could fall under more than one of the headings used, especially general references and Internet sites.

THE GEOGRAPHY AND HISTORY OF UZBEKISTAN

Allworth, Edward. 1990. *The Modern Uzbeks: From the Fourteenth Century to the Present.* Stanford, CA: Hoover Institution.

The most comprehensive single volume work on Uzbek cultural history available in English. The coverage of literary figures and their role in shaping Uzbek identity is particularly enlightening and is required reading for anyone seeking an in-depth knowledge of this topic. The book's main shortcoming is the author's indirect and circuitous style.

Carlisle, Donald. 1994. "Soviet Uzbekistan: State and Nation in Historical Perspective." In *Central Asia in Historical Perspective,* edited by Beatrice F. Manz. Boulder, CO: Westview Press.

Carlisle sketches out the process of state formation in Uzbekistan, focusing on the actions and approaches of Uzbekistan's native elite. He makes a persuasive case that the key figure in the formation of the Uzbek Soviet Socialist Republic was Faizulla Khojaev, who more than anyone else shaped the boundaries of the Uzbek state.

Lentz, Thomas, and Glenn Lowry. 1989. *Timur and the Princely Vision: Persian Art and Culture in the Fifteenth Century.* Washington, DC: Smithsonian Institution.
    A glossy coffee-table volume that brims with stunning photographs of art and architecture from the Timurid period. The book was written to accompany an exhibition of some of these treasures that toured the United States in the 1980s. The text is informative and written in an engaging style.

McChesney, R. D. 1996. *Central Asia: Foundations of Change.* Princeton, NJ: Darwin Press.
    This contribution is an interesting and innovative approach to Central Asian history. The organization of the discussion differs from many standard texts in the field, and the author's writing style is lively and captivating. The discussion of religious shrines in the region is not found in most other books on Central Asia in English.

Sinnott, Peter. 1992. "The Physical Geography of Soviet Central Asia and the Aral Sea Problem." In *Geographic Perspectives on Soviet Central Asia,* edited by Robert A. Lewis. New York and London: Routledge.
    Sinnott offers a solid introduction to the region's physical geography. His discussion of the Aral Sea issue is now a bit dated but is still useful to a reader encountering the problem for the first time. A good deal of statistical information is presented, along with some rather mundane maps.

Soucek, Svat. 2000. *A History of Inner Asia.* Cambridge: Cambridge University Press.
    An extremely useful single-volume history of this complex

region. For a general introduction to Uzbek and Central Asian history, this work is perhaps the most readable available.

THE ECONOMY OF UZBEKISTAN

Bearingpoint.uz
http://www.bearingpoint.uz
This Web site features frequent economic reports on Uzbekistan's economy, as well as a sizable amount of statistical data.

Craumer, Peter. 1995. *Rural and Agricultural Development in Uzbekistan.* London: Royal Institute of International Affairs.

This is an important summary of the agricultural dilemmas Uzbekistan faces, along with an assessment of the variety of imbalances brought on by the overdependence on cotton. Many tables and maps are featured.

Dosumov, Rustam. 1996. "Uzbekistan: A National Path to the Market." In *Central Asia in Transition,* edited by Boris Rumer. Armonk, NY: M.E. Sharpe.

An in-depth discussion of the challenges facing the Uzbek economy during the transition from a command-style economy to a market-oriented structure. Dosumov is brutally frank about the employment problems in the country and the near collapse of the country's aged and inefficient industrial sector.

Ilkhamov, Alisher. 2001. "Impoverishment of the Masses in the Transition Period: Signs of an Emerging 'New Poor' Identity in Uzbekistan." *Central Asian Survey* 20(1), pp. 33–54.

An interesting piece on what Ilkhamov terms the "new poor" in Uzbekistan. The discussion is directed at the attitudes and economic conditions affecting the life of Husain

Jurayev, a resident of the Fergana Valley, who has become dismayed at the decline of the Uzbek economy.

Karimov, Islom. 1995. *Uzbekistan: Along the Road of Deepening Economic Reform.* Tashkent: Uzbekiston.
Here is President Islom Karimov's economic philosophy in his own words, as well as his plans for shifting the country's economic structure to a free market basis. A worthwhile read for both those who agree with the policies promoted in the book and those who view the strategy as misguided.

UZBEK INSTITUTIONS

Bohr, Annette. 1998. *Uzbekistan: Politics and Foreign Policy.* London: Royal Institute of International Affairs.
An excellent complement to Critchlow's work on politics in Uzbekistan during the Soviet era (see following entry). Bohr offers a thoughtful critique of the political landscape of Uzbekistan in the post-Soviet years.

Critchlow, James. 1991. *Nationalism in Uzbekistan.* Boulder, CO: Westview Press.
This is the most complete summary of the political development of Uzbekistan during the Soviet era available. Published the year Uzbekistan gained independence, this study provides important groundwork for understanding Uzbek politics in the post-Soviet era.

Gleason, Gregory. 1997. *The Central Asian States: Discovering Independence.* Boulder, CO: Westview Press.
An enlightening study of Central Asia's history, political and cultural development, and geopolitics. Gleason provides an essential introduction to the region and skillfully places each of the new countries of Central Asia in regional and global context.

Hanks, Reuel. 2004. "Religion and Law in Uzbekistan: Renaissance and Repression in an Authoritarian Context." In *Regulating Religion: Case Studies from Around the Globe,* edited by James T. Richardson. New York: Kluwer Academic.

A discussion of the Uzbek regime's campaign against manifestations of "unofficial" Islam and the repressive character of recent Uzbek law governing religion.

March, Andrew. 2002. "The Use and Abuse of History: 'National Ideology' as Transcendental Object in Islam Karimov's 'Ideology of National Independence.'" *Central Asian Survey* 21(4), pp. 371–384.

A thoughtful critique of the Uzbek regime's employment of history and national symbols to create a national identity in Uzbekistan. March provides insight on the process of constructing a national ideology for Uzbekistan via the use of historical figures to justify authoritarianism.

Melvin, Neil. 2000. *Uzbekistan: Transition to Authoritarianism on the Silk Road.* Amsterdam: Harwood Academic.

A general introduction to Uzbekistan. This work gives background on the history, culture, and economic development of Uzbekistan with the focus on events since the collapse of the Soviet Union.

UZBEK SOCIETY AND CONTEMPORARY ISSUES

Akiner, Shirin. 1997. "Between Tradition and Modernity: The Dilemma Facing Contemporary Central Asian Women." In *Post-Soviet Women: From the Baltic to Central Asia,* edited by Mary Buckley. Cambridge: Cambridge University Press.

A summary and analysis of the trials and dilemmas facing Central Asian women. Much of the discussion is focused on women in Uzbekistan. This work offers a view of the role that

Islam played traditionally in society and describes the balance that many women in independent Uzbekistan are seeking between recovering their traditions and integrating into the global community.

Bissell, Tom. 2003. *Chasing the Sea: Lost among the Ghosts of Empire in Central Asia.* New York: Pantheon.

An entertaining and somewhat depressing account of Bissell's experiences in Uzbekistan, first as a Peace Corps volunteer and later as a journalist researching the Aral Sea disaster. Also provides an indictment of both Soviet and current policy in the region.

Dadabaev, Timur. 2004. "Post-Soviet Realities of Society in Uzbekistan." *Central Asian Survey* 23(2), pp. 141–166.

A survey of contemporary economic conditions and attitudes among the Uzbek population. This piece contains numerous tables and survey data on social attitudes generally unavailable in other sources.

Fathi, Habiba. 1997. "Otines: The Unknown Women Clerics of Central Asian Islam." *Central Asian Survey* 16(1), pp. 27–43.

An interesting and informative article dealing with the female mullahs of Central Asia, a subject rarely investigated even within the region itself. For readers eager for a deeper understanding of women's role in Islam in Uzbekistan, this piece will prove both useful and stimulating.

Mayhew, Bradley, Paul Clammer, and Michael Kohn. 2004. *Lonely Planet Guide to Central Asia.* Oakland, CA: Lonely Planet.

Like all the Lonely Planet guidebooks, this work offers historical summaries, practical advice, and entertaining vignettes. An absolute necessity for anyone considering a visit to Uzbekistan or its neighbors and a valuable general introduction to the Central Asian states.

Polat, Abdumannob. 1999. "Can Uzbekistan Build Democracy and Civil Society?" In *Civil Society in Central Asia,* edited by M. Holt Ruffin and Daniel Waugh. Seattle: University of Washington Press.

Abdumannob Pulatov is the brother of Abdurahim Pulatov, the exiled leader of the opposition group Birlik. In this chapter, he outlines the political situation in his homeland and offers an assessment of Uzbekistan's chances of developing institutions that support a more open and democratic society.

Uzbekistan—World News. http://cgi.wn.com/?template=uzbek istan/

This is a highly useful site featuring current news from Uzbekistan, as well as a multitude of links to other Web sites that offer information and commentary about the country.

KAZAKHSTAN

PART ONE
NARRATIVE SECTION

The Geography and History of Kazakhstan

Kazakhstan is a land of contrasts, both physical and symbolic. The dominant geographic feature of the Kazakh landscape is the steppe, an expansive, rolling grassland that covers most of the country. The steppe is not merely a physical zone; rather, it also represents an essential component of the Kazakh national character and identity, as for centuries the Kazakhs were a nomadic people, moving their herds of livestock across this "sea of grass," drawing their sustenance and livelihood from it. The steppe, simultaneously foreboding and inviting, continues to be both benefactor and barrier to the modern Kazakh nation and is representative of the perils and potential facing this enormous country. As the Central Asian writer Chingiz Aitmatov notes in his masterful novel *The Day Lasts More Than a Hundred Years,* "The steppe is vast and man is small. The steppe takes no sides; it doesn't care if you are in trouble or if all is well with you; you have to take the steppe as it is" (Aitmatov 1988).

The steppe holds the riches of Kazakhstan. Utilized for centuries as prime grazing land, the plains now produce enormous yields of wheat, cotton, and other crops. Beneath its surface, particularly in the western portion of the country, the steppe conceals huge deposits of petroleum and significant pockets of natural gas, which have only recently begun to be exploited and carry the potential to make Kazakhstan a wealthy country indeed. The steppe lands also contain the bulk of Kazakhstan's considerable industrial capacity, especially the northern and eastern sections of the country, lying adjacent to the huge markets of Russia and China. Combined with a location directly between Europe and Asia, this abun-

A group of horses graze on steppe grasslands near Lugovoy, Kazakhstan. (Wolfgang Kaehler/Corbis)

dance of resources and economic development stands to make Kazakhstan not only a vital regional power, but also to magnify the country's significance as a global player.

Accompanying the great promise and potential of Kazakhstan come daunting challenges. These include massive environmental damage from the Soviet era, particularly in the eastern reaches of the country and in the southwest around the Aral Sea; serious friction between the two largest ethnic groups, the Kazakhs and the Russians; and continuing difficulties in making the transition to a free-market economy and a pluralistic political system. Compounding these problems is the country's landlocked geography and distance from current major markets, although these issues have been partially addressed via the planned construction of pipelines that will carry Kazakh oil to the global marketplace. How successfully these challenges are addressed will determine whether Kazakhstan merely survives or instead thrives and emerges as

Peak in the Tien Shan Mountains. (Dean Conger/Corbis)

an example of successful political and economic transition in the post-Soviet world.

PHYSICAL AND HUMAN GEOGRAPHY

In describing Kazakhstan's physical setting, the massive size of this young country is an obvious starting point. Kazakhstan is the ninth largest country in the world, accounting for 1,052,100 square miles of territory; it stretches for more than 1,800 miles at its greatest east-west extent. In other words, superimposed on the United States, Kazakhstan would extend westward from New York City to near El Paso, Texas; and from New York southward to Jacksonville, Florida, covering virtually the entire eastern half of the United States. Yet this enormous state contains only about 16 million people, just about the same population as Florida, giving Kazakhstan one of the lowest population densities in the world at around sixteen people per square mile.

Such a large territory is bound to contain significant geographic variety. Despite the uniformity of the steppe, contrasts abound in Kazakhstan's physical geography. The Tien Shan (Mandarin: Heavenly Mountains) impinge on the southeastern border and hold the country's highest peak, Khan Tengri, standing just short of 23,000 feet. Several subranges split away from the Tien Shan and penetrate Central Asia, including the Ala Tau mountains, which lie just to the south of the capital city of Almaty and separate southeastern Kazakhstan from the basin of Lake Issyk Kul in Kyrgyzstan.

To the north of this rugged corner a huge upland stretches toward the Russian border, occupying nearly the entire eastern third of the country. Contained within this plateau are a number of significant lakes, including the largest body of water in eastern Kazakhstan, Lake Balkhash. The lake extends over an area of more than 7,000 square miles and is approximately 376 miles long. Fed by three rivers—the Ili, the Karatal, and the Aqsu—Balkhash has no outlet yet has the curious characteristic of being part salt water, part fresh water. The flow of the Ili River, which enters the lake in the southwestern corner, introduces enough fresh water to make the western half of the lake fresh and usable for irrigation. A dam built on the Ili River in the early 1970s restricted some of that stream's flow into Balkhash, and losses of water to human use and to evaporation and seepage take a heavy toll on Lake Balkhash in an average year. Recent studies indicate that the lake's volume has declined steadily over the last several decades, leading to concerns over the future of the lake and possible ecological problems.

The eastern extreme of the Kazakh Plateau contains another sizable lake, Lake Zaysan, which lies along the course of the Irtyush River. The Irtyush enters the lake from the south and flows along the eastern margin of the country, serving as the main source of water for the important industrial cities of Semey (Russian: Semipalatinsk) and Pavlodar. North of the latter the Irtyush crosses the border between Kazakhstan and Russia, finally joining the Ob River in western Siberia and eventually flowing into the Arctic Ocean. Unlike Balkhash, the level of Lake Zaysan has actually been rising in recent years, after the construction of the Bukhtarma dam north of the lake, which created a large reservoir of the same name.

In the northwest, the Ural River enters the country from Russia and drains almost directly southward into the Caspian Sea, a huge body of salt water that forms most of Kazakhstan's western border. The Caspian is also fed by another river flowing from Kazakhstan, the Emba, which originates in the uplands of west-central Kazakhstan, although in dry years the Emba fails to reach the Caspian and ends in a series of marshes and swamps near its shore. Although relatively sparsely populated on its Kazakh coast, the Caspian and its environs are an enormously important region to the country because of the abundance of resources found there, including large deposits of petroleum and natural gas. Serious exploitation of this hydrocarbon wealth has only begun in the last decade, and the income from oil alone could make Kazakhstan one of the richest countries in the region. Most of the oil and gas lies to the northeast of the Caspian Sea, in a large surface depression of the same name. To the southeast the topography rises slightly in elevation, resulting in the Ustyurt Plateau, a desolate land of stony desert, interspersed with salt marshes and sand dunes.

Eastward of the Ustyurt Plateau is yet another topographical depression, occupied by yet another inland, international sea—the Aral. The border between Kazakhstan and Uzbekistan cuts almost directly through the heart of the Aral, giving both countries a stake in the survival of this threatened body of water. A body of salt water like its cousin the Caspian, the Aral was historically replenished by two streams, the Amu Darya and the Syr Darya. Although the larger Amu Darya does not flow within the boundaries of Kazakhstan, its smaller counterpart, the Syr Darya, enters the country from Uzbekistan and flows almost directly northwestward, eventually ending near the former port of Aralsk, in central Kazakhstan. The Aral Sea is surrounded by deserts: to the south, the Kara Kum (Black Sand) desert, to the east the Kyzyl Kum (Red Sand), to the north the Greater Barsuki Desert, and to the west the parched hills of the Ustyurt Plateau. This arid setting has provided the stage for one of history's greatest ecological disasters (see the following section on climate and ecology).

Lying directly between the Aral Sea and Lake Balkhash, in the heart of Kazakhstan, lies the country's largest desert, the Betpak Dala, which gradually melds into the drier steppe zone in the north. To the south of this huge clay desert is the Muyunkum, stretching to the highlands along the border with Kyrgyzstan. Taken together, the deserts of Kazakhstan account for slightly more than 40 percent of the country's area, yet only 14 percent of the land can produce crops. Still, this amounts to an enormous area in such a large country, and when the prime grazing lands of the steppe are added in, it is little wonder that Kazakhstan is a significant producer and exporter of grain, cotton, meat, and other agricultural products.

Climate and Ecology

Kazakhstan is the largest landlocked country in the world, and its distance from the planet's oceans greatly affects the climate. Because of the lack of moderating influences provided by an adjacent ocean, Kazakhstan's climate indicates marked continentality, expressed most vividly in wide seasonal temperature extremes. In the northeastern reaches of the country, near western Siberia, temperatures in winter may drop to –60 degrees Fahrenheit, whereas at the height of summer in the southern deserts readings well above 100 degrees are common. In general, winters are colder in the northern half of the country, although summers tend to be somewhat milder. A climatic characteristic common to the entire country, however, is aridity. Even the relatively well-watered north and extreme eastern regions receive no more than about 15 inches of precipitation in an average year, but this is sufficient to support the steppe grasses that are crucial to the country's livestock herds, as well as providing enough moisture to support the cultivation of grains like wheat and barley. In the south, crop production is mostly dependent on irrigation, with intensive production of cotton concentrated along nearly the entire length of the Syr Darya, after that stream enters the country from Uzbekistan.

Like Uzbekistan, Kazakhstan sustained widespread ecological damage during the Soviet era. The Kazakh SSR (Soviet Socialist Republic), as the region was called then, was the main site for the testing of Soviet nuclear weapons for several decades, especially in the vicinity of the city of Semipalatinsk (Semey). According to one Western specialist, during the last four decades of Soviet control, 468 nuclear tests were carried out near Semipalatinsk, with 26 of those occurring above ground (Olcott 2002). The main area for testing lay to the west of the city, and because of prevailing westerly winds, radioactive fallout was sometimes carried directly over the city. The first detonation in 1949, an above-ground test, may have exposed 25,000 people to dangerously high levels of radiation. The impact on the health of residents of Semipalatinsk has been catastrophic, with a doubling of the rate of stillbirths between 1960 and 1988 (Olcott 2002) and significant increases in the rates of numerous types of cancer, especially leukemia and lung cancer. Testing was halted in 1989, due mostly to the efforts of a grassroots organization, the Nevada-Semipalatinsk Antinuclear Movement, founded by the famous writer and activist Olzhas Suleimenov.

In addition to the ecological damage near Semipalatinsk, Kazakhstan, like its neighbor, Uzbekistan, has been forced to confront the catastrophic decline of the Aral Sea, since the international boundary between them cuts directly across the Aral. The decline of the sea was brought about by disastrous

Four signs declare the dangers of radioactivity October 13, 2000, at a site near Semey. (AFP/Getty Images)

Soviet policies, a legacy both countries have struggled to address. The collapse of the entire Aral ecosystem in only three decades, between 1960 and 1990, is unprecedented in human history and has wrought serious environmental, economic, and social problems for the entire region. Residents around the Aral in Kazakhstan have experienced a general decline in health in recent decades, with the incidence of blood disorders and certain cancers rising alarmingly. The fishing industry that once supported the local economy of the city of Aralsk, near the mouth of the Syr Darya, is gone, because the fish have vanished. There is little hope the Aral will ever regain its former shores, and current efforts on the Kazakh side are directed at preventing any further losses. The sea is now divided into two sections, and authorities in Kazakhstan believe that the northern remnant, lying entirely within Kazakhstan, may be successfully stabilized in the next few years.

Political Geography

In the aftermath of the Bolshevik Revolution, what is today the state of Kazakhstan was split into two political units. The southern portion of the country was included as part of the Turkestan ASSR (Autonomous Soviet Socialist Republic), while the northern section, where Russians predominated, was assigned separate administrative status. Gradually over the next decade, as Soviet Socialist Republics were created first for the Uzbeks, and then the Tajiks from the Turkistan ASSR, some Kazakh-populated territories were added to the Russian-dominated ASSR. In the 1920s, the capital of this unit was shifted from Orenburg in the north to the south, first to Kyzyl Orda and then to Alma Ata (Almaty). In 1936, the Kazakh SSR was established, along with the Kyrgyz SSR—the last two ethnically based republics created in Central Asia under the Soviet government. In 1991, independent Kazakhstan inherited these boundaries, which had been only slight modified during the Soviet period.

The borders drawn up by Soviet administrators in Central Asia, establishing political units based on majority ethnic groups, did not in fact precisely match the actual ethnic landscape, and the imprecision of this process is reflected in simmering boundary disputes between some Central Asian countries, as well as by the presence of ethnic minorities along the margins of all of the new Central Asian states. Kazakhstan has had an extended border dispute with Uzbekistan since independence, and several cities in the southern portion of the country probably contain a majority Uzbek population, such as Shymkent and Turkistan. Political tensions over borders and pockets of ethnic minorities continue to fester, and the legacy of Soviet administration in Central Asia casts a long shadow over the region's chances for long-term stability.

Kazakhstan's large Russian minority has also compounded relations with its giant neighbor to the north. In the first years of independence, some Russian leaders and commentators, including the Nobel Prize winner Alexander Solzhenitsyn, suggested that those oblasts (provinces) in Kazakhstan that held a majority of Russians should be joined to the Russian Federation, while at the same time Cossack communities in the northern oblasts were agitating for autonomy or integration with Russia. Such talk alarmed Kazakh authorities, and even before the collapse of the USSR they pressed Boris Yeltsin, then president of the Russian Federated Soviet Socialist Republic, for guarantees that the border between the two countries would continue to be observed. These were granted, but Russia's continuing concerns over ethnic Russians living in what it calls the "near abroad" has ensured that Kazakh president Nursultan Nazarbayev and his government have been careful not to antagonize their Russian minority, thereby giving Russian nationalists in both countries reason to call for intervention from the Russian Federation.

Population Characteristics

Ethnic and Religious Geography

Like the other former Soviet Socialist Republics of Central Asia, the Kazakh SSR was the homeland of numerous ethnic groups, or "nationalities" as the Soviet regime referred to them. Kazakhstan was rather unusual in that, unlike almost all other SSRs, the Kazakhs themselves did not constitute a majority in the republic carrying their name for much of the Soviet era, although they were the most numerous group. Until the 1990s, Russians were almost as numerous as Kazakhs in the republic. This curious situation was created by historical events of the last two centuries, when several large waves of Slavic settlers entered northern Kazakhstan, and also by tragic losses among the Kazakh population during the years Josef Stalin ruled the USSR. The details of these demographic changes are covered in the section on Kazakh history later in this chapter.

The Kazakh people are a mixture of many genetic strains, but they are most closely related to surrounding Turkic groups, particularly the Kyrgyz and the Karakalpaks of western Uzbekistan, and additionally have much in common with the Mongolians. Historically the Kazakhs were separated into three hordes (*juz*), based on the geographic territory each controlled. These were led by a *khan* and were usually referred to as the Greater, Middle, and Lesser hordes. In addition to these three divisions, within the hordes distinctive clans were identified, as well as the *aul,* a social grouping generally consisting of several related families who migrated together as a single unit. Much of this social structure remains intact today, and many if not most Kazakhs are aware of the juz they belong to, as well as the clan relationships that form an important part of their heritage.

Russians represent the second-largest group in the country, although their numbers have dropped steadily and precipitously over the past three decades. The Russian population are largely city dwellers and are collected in the northern oblasts of Kazakhstan, making many of the cities of those regions, such as Pavlodar, Semipalatinsk, Karaganda (Qaraghandy), and others predominantly Russian in character. This is also the region of the country that contains most of the industrial capacity, and thus the Russian population plays a vital role in the Kazakh economy, supplying much of the labor to Kazakhstan's factories. The impact of the Russian population extends beyond economics, because many aspects of Russian culture continue to influence Kazakh society, especially the Russian language, which remains the most widely used tongue, even among Kazakhs and other non-Slavic groups.

The Kazakhs and Russians together represent more than 80 percent of the country's population, and no other ethnic group in Kazakhstan reaches even 5 percent of the population. Ukrainians are about 4 percent of the population, and both Germans and Uzbeks make up around 2.5 percent each.

The Germans once held a much greater share in the population, but large numbers began emigrating in the 1980s and continued to do so well into the 1990s. The Uzbeks tend to be concentrated in the southern reaches of Kazakhstan, along the border with Uzbekistan. A number of the cities in this part of the country hold large communities of Uzbeks, such as Shymkent and Turkistan, and it is possible the Uzbeks hold a majority in these locations.

As is the case in other Central Asian countries, significant clusters of Koreans and Armenians are located in Kazakhstan's larger urban areas, adding yet another layer of variety to the existing cultural diversity found in the region's cities. The Koreans were brought to Kazakhstan and the larger region by Josef Stalin, who had several hundred thousand deported from the Soviet Far East when he ruled the USSR. Many have adopted Russian culture to a large degree, speak Russian as a first language, use Russian given names, and follow Russian customs, but other elements of Korean culture survive, especially cuisine. In the larger bazaars of Almaty and other cities, one may encounter a section featuring traditional Korean foods and spices, some ready to eat and others requiring preparation. Many in the Korean community are successful in business and education and are important contributors to the Kazakh economy.

The nomadic Kazakhs were converted to Islam much later than the sedentary communities living in the Silk Road cities, lying along the southern margin of the steppe. For the most part, adherence to Islam was a gradual process that slowly seeped into Kazakh culture over several centuries, rather than a mass conversion in a few decades. This measured adoption of the faith ensured that much of the Kazakh pre-Islamic traditional belief system was retained, resulting in a kind of hybridized Islam, or what specialists often term "folk Islam." Kazakhs certainly did not engage in the construction of grand mosques and *medressehs* (Islamic seminaries) like their settled neighbors and probably were less devoted to the regular rituals of the faith. Eventually all three hordes were converted to Sunni Islam, with a significant influence from various Sufi orders (a mystical form of Islam), whose followers were active among the steppe nomads. For this reason, it is often suggested by scholars that Kazakhs are "less Islamic" than most other Central Asian peoples, although many Kazakhs absolutely consider themselves part of the Muslim realm.

With the decline of Soviet control and eventually independence, Kazakhstan experienced an Islamic revival akin to that in the other Central Asian republics, as many Kazakhs sought to reinforce their identity, particularly vis-à-vis the Russian population. The fervor and extent of the Islamic renaissance in Kazakhstan was not as intense as that seen in Uzbekistan or Tajikistan, however. Nevertheless, in the last years of the Soviet administration, the number of mosques in the Kazakh SSR increased by a factor of five, a medresseh was opened in Alma Ata, and the first newspaper directed at Kazakh Muslims was launched (Olcott 1995, 262) . In general, the rise of interest in Islam in Kazakhstan has not been viewed with alarm by the government, and the Nazarbayev regime has not crushed unofficial Muslim with the ferocity displayed next door in Uzbekistan. By the same token, Kazakhstan has been spared the violence allegedly instigated by radical Islamic groups that has plagued Uzbekistan in recent years.

The Kazakh language has taken a more central role than Islam in the formation of a distinctive Kazakh identity, both before and in the wake of Soviet collapse. In 1989, the new first secretary of the Kazakh Communist Party, Nursultan Nazarbayev (who two years later became Kazakhstan's first president), introduced legislation to establish Kazakh as the official language of the republic. This development was immediately challenged by representatives of the Russian population, because less than 1 percent of the Russians living in Kazakhstan had a knowledge of Kazakh, and in fact many Kazakhs themselves had little ability to speak the language, instead using Russian. Kazakh is a Turkic language, closely related to Kyrgyz, Karakalpak, Uzbek, and other Turkic languages in the region. Although Kazakh has utilized the Cyrillic alphabet since the 1940s and has borrowed many words from Russian, it is not closely related to the Slavic tongues in terms of grammar and syntax and is a difficult language for native Russian speakers to master. Despite government-sponsored efforts to promote the use of Kazakh, Russian remains the most widely used language in the country, even among Kazakhs.

Distribution and Growth

As noted earlier, Kazakhstan has one of the lowest population densities in the world, at just slightly more than 6 persons per square kilometer, or just under 16 people per square mile. As might be expected, population densities in Kazakhstan are highest in the urbanized, industrialized regions in the northern section of the country and lowest in the southern and western desert zones, although the 1990s witnessed a clear shift of population to the southern oblasts. This shift is transpiring due to several demographic changes, including higher birthrates among Kazakhs and the continued emigration of the Russian population.

According to census data released in 1999, Kazakhs accounted for approximately 53 percent of the total population of slightly less than 15 million, although they had made up only about 40 percent just a decade earlier. During the same period, the percentage for the Russians living in Kazakhstan fell from just over 37 percent to 30 percent, (Rowland 2001). The remarkable gains for the Kazakhs during the 1990s may be explained by several factors. First, birthrates among the Kazakhs were significantly higher (and had been for several decades prior to the 1990s), resulting in a faster population growth rate for Kazakhs. Second, following independence the pace of out-migration by ethnic Russians remained high, a continuation of a trend that had been initiated as early as the 1970s. In addition, the average age of the Russian population was significantly higher than that for the Kazakhs, and birth rates for the Russians were lower. Finally, after 1991 the Kazakh government undertook a campaign to attract ethnic Kazakhs who had been dispersed to surrounding countries in previous decades back to Kazakhstan. Known as the *oralmandar,* these returnees number in the several hundred thousands and in some cases had been living in Mongolia, Turkey, western China, and Afghanistan for several generations.

Migration and Urbanization

As previously mentioned, at least three significant migrations across the borders of Kazakhstan have occurred during the last thirty years, and all three continue to some degree today. The first of these involves the movement of Slavic peoples out of Kazakhstan into Russia, Ukraine, and other locations in the region. Slavs began to leave the Kazakh SSR in the 1970s, and this trend accelerated during the 1990s. The Slavic out-migration not only has demographic ramifications, but also carries significant economic and social consequences because many of those leaving are trained in technical fields and work in industry and education.

The second migration also began in the 1970s, and like Slavic emigration, picked up steam during the next two decades. This has been the departure of large numbers of Germans, whose population in Kazakhstan has effectively collapsed: in 1989, almost 950,000 Germans lived in the Kazakh SSR; by 1999, that figure had dropped to just over 353,000, and the decline has continued. Both the Slavs and the Germans have left for the same reasons: the displacement of the Russian language by Kazakh to some degree, a perceived rise in the influence of Islam, and the allure of what many believe are better economic opportunities abroad. The third significant movement of people across Kazakhstan's borders is more recent and involves the return, at the encouragement of the Kazakh government, of Kazakhs living abroad, the so-called Oralmandar. The government promotion of the Oralmandar, along with the shift of the capital from Almaty to Astana in the mid-1990s, is widely seen as an effort to strengthen the position of what has become the Kazakh majority.

There is a marked contrast in urbanization among major ethnic groups in Kazakhstan. Slavs and the remaining Germans are heavily urbanized, although the share of these groups in the urban population has declined in recent decades, an expected trend given their out-migration. On the other hand, although Kazakhs did not make up a majority of the urban population according to the 1999 census, their share of the urban population has been steadily increasing in recent years. Although Kazakhs still do not represent a majority of the urban population of either Almaty, the largest city, or Astana, the capital city, their percentage in both locations greatly increased in the 1990s. In 1999, the percentage of the total population living in urban areas was 56 percent, representing a slight drop of less than a percentage point from 1989, but this decline was likely due to the loss of Russian population, which is heavily urbanized (Rowland 2001).

HISTORY
Early History

Considerable archaeological evidence indicates that groups of migratory humans were living on the plains of Kazakhstan by the second millennium before the time of Christ. Probably influenced by the Cimmerian culture of the southern Russian steppe region, these peoples left behind numerous rock drawings and other artifacts that show they possessed some technological skill, including at least rudimentary abilities to work metallic ores. In particular, this group was able to work bronze and produced axes and blades for weapons of a sophis-

This warrior's costume, also known as the "Golden Man," is Kazakhstan's most notable archaeological treasure, Almaty. (David Samuel Robbins/Corbis)

ticated nature, as well as bronze utensils (Grouset 1970, 5). Although they may have occasionally raised crops, their lifestyle was apparently primarily a nomadic one, adapted to the spacious grasslands of the steppe. Contact with those living in permanent agricultural settlements lying along the river systems of southern Central Asia no doubt occurred but was sporadic and had limited impact on the culture of the nomads, who probably had a loose-knit social structure with no centralized authority and traveled in relatively small groups.

Around 750 B.C., a warlike civilization suddenly burst forth from the Central Asian steppe lands, a people who are known in the West as the Scythians but whom the Persians, who had frequent and often violent contact with them, called the Saka. Famed for their prowess with the bow and arrow, especially from horseback, the Saka were also master goldsmiths and left behind magnificent and intricate works of jewelry, as well as weapons and armor wrought from this precious metal. One of the greatest discoveries of Saka artifacts occurred in southern Kazakhstan in 1969, when a Saka *kurgan,* or burial mound, was found to hold thousands of gold platelets forming an armor suit, resulting in the so-called Golden Man, a replica of which is on display in the Central State Museum in Almaty. Although the relationship in reality is tenuous, many in Kazakhstan currently view the Saka as the first manifestation of a Kazakh nation. Symbolically, this notion is reinforced by a statue of the Golden Man, which crowns a towering column in Almaty's central square.

Beginning in the second century B.C., a new people arrived in what is today eastern Kazakhstan and began to displace the Saka, driving them westward. These invaders, described by Chinese sources as having red hair and blue eyes, are called the Wusun, or in some sources, Usun. Ruling from their capital on Lake Issyk Kul in modern Kyrgyzstan, the Wusun controlled eastern and southern Kazakhstan for several centuries, until they, too, were overrun by invaders from the east, the

Huns. Various groups of Hunnic peoples had been known to the Chinese for centuries, but in the first century B.C., a western branch of these Turkic peoples moved across the Tien Shan and onto the Central Asian steppe. For several centuries they apparently roamed the plains east and north of the Aral Sea, and then around A.D. 375 abruptly drove to the west, ultimately threatening the Roman Empire under their great leader, Attila. This migration had the effect of weakening the power of the Huns in Central Asia, however, and opened the door for yet another wave of invaders from the east.

Around the middle of the sixth century, a powerful Turkic people pushed westward from Mongolia into the valley of the Ili River, driving the remnants of the Huns out and establishing a loose confederation of tribes that would more or less control the region for the next three centuries. Known as the Western Turkic Khanate, this empire would finally fall to the Persians, but they would in turn yield to yet another Turkic power, the Karakhanids, around the turn of the millennium. The Karakhanid Turks were devout Muslims, and during this era Islam flourished in the eastern Silk Road cities of Central Asia. Islamic scholarship thrived under the patronage of the Karakhanid rulers, and it was under their protection that the great Muslim philosopher al-Farabi produced works on political philosophy that had a profound influence across the Muslim realm. In the early 1200s the eastern part of the Karakhanid empire fell to Buddhist invaders, the Khitans, and in the west the Shah of Khorezm incorporated portions of their territory into his realm. These new conquerors would have only a century to enjoy their victory, however, for the most devastating nomadic army in history would soon arrive on their borders—the Mongols, under Genghis Khan.

The Mongols captured all of Central Asia, and in those areas where resistance was offered, laid waste to the cities and countryside alike. After the death of Genghis Khan in 1227, his empire was divided among his sons. Most of present-day eastern and central Kazakhstan became the land of the Chagatai Khanate, named for the son who initially possessed it. Ultimately, the Mongol conquest brought some positive changes to Central Asia, including political consolidation, increased trade, and religious tolerance. At the end of the 1300s, one of Genghis Khan's descendants, Amir Timur (or Tamerlane in the West), fashioned an empire that encompassed nearly all of the steppe lands and oasis cities of Central Asia. A patron of the arts and a Muslim, Timur built several monuments in the region, including a magnificent mausoleum dedicated to the Sufi saint Ahmed Yassavi, in the southern Kazakh city of Turkestan. The decline of the Timurid Empire would bring a dispersal of administrative authority and political instability for half a century, from which would emerge an informal confederation of nomadic tribes who would come to rule the steppes of Central Asia—the Kazakh Khanate.

Qasim Khan, the leader of the Kazakhs in the early 1500s, is generally credited with forming the Kazakh Khanate and initiating an identity for his people that distinguished them from other Central Asians. According to Olcott, after the time of Qasim, the Kazakhs saw themselves as distinct from the Uzbeks, a people they lived in close proximity to and who had much in common with Kazakh culture (Olcott 1995, 9). It was roughly during this period that the Kazakh tribes divided into three separate but closely related hordes, the juz. The juz were not based on common bloodlines, and exactly why they were formed is a question open to debate. Because it is still somewhat unclear exactly when the juz system was created, the rationale for its formation is also difficult to identify precisely.

By the end of the 1600s, each of these divisions controlled a specific portion of the steppe, in what would eventually evolve into the Kazakh SSR under the Soviets. The Lesser Juz (sometimes referred to as the Little or Junior Juz) occupied the western half of modern Kazakhstan, from the upper valley of the Syr Darya westward of the shores of the Caspian Sea.

The Middle Juz controlled the vast steppe lands from Lake Balkhash northward to the edge of Siberia, which was falling under the control of the Russians. In the southeast, the Greater Juz roamed the rich grasslands and river valleys south of Lake Balkhash to the foothills of the Tien Shan, and westward to the central portion of the Syr Darya valley. This was known as the Jeti-su, or "land of seven rivers" to the Kazakhs and as Semireche to the Russians.

The Imperial Russian Period

Russian contact with the Kazakhs was sporadic and indirect before the 1500s, when Russian penetration and eventual conquest of Siberia brought Russian trading outposts into more consistent interaction with the nomads of the steppe region, which lay along the southern margin of Russia's newly acquired lands.

In the 1500s, the Kazakh Khanate and the Russian Empire attempted to form an alliance, but after unsuccessful negotiations, contact between the two diminished. Had an agreement with the tsar been forthcoming, it likely would have spared the Kazakhs one of the most calamitous periods of their history, as control of the steppe was about to be wrested from them by an aggressive people migrating into Central Asia from the east—the Kalmyks.

The Kalmyk invasion began around 1600, as this warlike confederation of mostly Buddhist nomadic herdsmen moved from their traditional homeland in western China into southern Siberia and eventually toward the Caspian Sea. As they shifted toward the west, the Kalmyks raided both fellow nomads, including the Kazakhs, as well as Russian forts lying along the northern edge of the Kazakh grazing lands. By the 1630s, the Kalmyks were established as far west as the Emba River, and within a century were in control of much of the territory that today makes up northwestern Kazakhstan (Khodarkovsky 1992). The most disastrous event of this period for the Kazakhs occurred in 1723, when a large Kalmyk force invaded the territory of the Greater Juz and drove them from their traditional lands, killing thousands. Among Kazakhs this series of terrible defeats and chaotic retreat is referred to as the *Aktaban Shubyryndy,* or Great Catastrophe.

In 1731, the Lesser Juz had accepted the jurisdiction of the Russian tsar, becoming the first of the Kazakh groups to fall under Russian domination. The pressure exerted by Kalmyk aggression for the first half of the 1700s forced Kazakh leaders to seek support from the tsarist government, which in turn meant surrendering much of Kazakh independence to the Russians, as well as allowing for an increased Russian presence in the steppe. Two events would slow but not stop this process in the second half of the century. The first took place in 1759, when Chinese forces absorbed the Jungarian state in western China, effectively separating those Kalmyks living in the western steppe regions from a vital base of support. The second was the rise of an effective and shrewd leader among the divisive Kazakhs, Abylai Khan. A famous *batyr,* or warrior, of the Middle Juz, Abylai Khan was responsible for reestablishing Kazakh unity after a century of turmoil and also balancing Kazakh interests between those of his two expansionist neighbors, Russia and China. Abylai's death in 1781 opened the door for increased Slavic expansion into the steppe, as the Russian Empire pushed its borders southward.

By the 1760s, Russia had constructed a string of forts along the northern margin of the steppe, garrisoned mostly by Cossacks. Abylai Khan's passing at the end of the century signaled an opening that the Russian court was determined to exploit, as the era of the Great Game, Russia's century-long rivalry with the British in Central Asia, was dawning. By the beginning of the nineteenth century, increasing numbers of Slavic immigrants were appearing in the northern steppe, putting the rich earth there to the plow. Tsarist administration was imposed, with the levying of taxes and restrictions on the movement of the nomads, who were steadily encouraged to abandon their lifestyle. The Kazakh reaction was a series of revolts, especially from the Lesser Juz and Middle Juz, culminating in 1837 in a rebellion led by Kenesary Khan, a grandson of Abylai Khan. Kenesary Khan would eventually swear allegiance to the Russian crown, but several smaller revolts would plague the Russian authorities for the next several decades. The Tsarist regime continued to build forts in the Kazakh lands, one of the most important of which was Verny, a settlement that would eventually become Kazakhstan's largest city, Almaty. By 1865, Tashkent, a key city lying along the southern margin of the lands of the Great Juz, had fallen to Russian troops.

The last decades of the nineteenth century witnessed the consolidation of Russian control of the Kazakhs and their grazing lands. Although the traditional Kazakh way of life was undermined by Russian policy, waves of Russian and Ukrainian migrants were settled in the northern steppes, and when available land there became scarce, settlers were directed into southern Kazakhstan. As the twentieth century opened, the tide of migration surged to even larger numbers—by 1910, well over 700,000 Slavic immigrants had staked a claim to a portion of the steppe, and that figure would double in only six more years, as hundreds of thousands of settlers from Russia and Ukraine poured into Central Asia. The Kazakhs, decimated by two centuries of warfare with the Kalmyks and then the Russians, could do nothing to stem the flow of migration or protect their grazing lands from confiscation.

Although the majority of the Kazakh people resisted these changes, sometimes violently, some Kazakhs embraced Russian culture and rule, among them arguably the first Kazakh man of letters, Cholkan Valikhanov. A remarkably talented and courageous individual, Valikhanov entered the Russian army and served as both an officer and spy for the tsar.

Valikhanov's military exploits were not his only achievements, for he was a careful scholar who observed and recorded the characteristics of Kazakhstan's natural environment and native culture while carrying out his missions and was a friend of the exiled Russian writer Fyodor Dostoyevsky while the latter was living in Central Asia. Valikhanov died before his thirtieth birthday and today is a revered figure in Kazakhstan. Although he favored the incorporation of his people into the Russian realm, he also was not afraid to criticize the harsh policies employed against Central Asians by the conquering Russian military. Another Russophile Kazakh intellectual of the nineteenth century was Abai Kunanbayev, who unabashedly promoted the adoption of Russian language and culture among his people.

The tensions of a century of conquest and settlement in Kazakhstan came to a head on the eve of the Bolshevik Revolution, while the Russian administration was embroiled in World War I. In the summer of 1916, the tsar's government issued an *ukase,* or edict, calling for the conscription of thousands of draft-age Central Asian men, who were to be organized into noncombat brigades to assist on the German Front. For the Kazakhs and other Central Asian peoples, this order was simply too much to bear, and armed resistance erupted across the region, starting first in the south in the oasis cities and spreading rapidly to the northern steppes. By the fall the rebel army had swelled to 20,000 men, and Central Asian forces were laying siege to a number of Russian-held cities. Russian commanders were forced to commit a sizable number of troops and supplies to quell this revolt in their hinterland, and it seems likely that the uprising played a part in destabilizing the tsarist regime and bringing on the abdication of Tsar Nicholas II in February 1917. It would also spark the fires of self-determination among the Kazakh elite, who that same year would initiate an independent government in the steppe, the Alash Orda.

The Soviet Period

The political turmoil in Russia in 1917 presented the emerging Kazakh elite, some of whom had served in the Russian Duma, or parliament, with an opportunity to form a Kazakh-led government. In early December 1917, a congress of representatives tentatively established a provisional government for the steppe region of Central Asia, called Alash Orda, based on democratic principles, including freedom of the press, freedom of speech, and separation of church and state. A month later, the government was officially formed but found itself immediately at odds with the Bolshevik forces in the region. The Alash Orda formed an alliance with local anti-Communist forces (the so-called Whites), and for a few months held several towns and cities. By December 1919, however, the momentum shifted to the Bolsheviks, and Alash Orda was forced to integrate with the Bolshevik Party. Most of the leadership was eventually purged and either executed or imprisoned, and by 1922, the Communists had solidified control over the steppe.

The early 1920s were a time of political chaos and famine for the Kazakhs. As the Soviet administration rapidly moved to reshape society, it destroyed the existing economic and social order and was not sufficiently prepared to create a system to replace it. Grain production and numbers of livestock both collapsed, as the Soviets continued the tsarist policy of settling the remaining nomadic Kazakhs. Throughout the decade, the regime undertook a concentrated program to industrialize Kazakhstan, focused especially on the development of heavy industries such as smelting and production of iron and steel. Some Kazakhs reacted by fleeing to China or other surrounding countries, and others joined an armed resistance movement, the *Basmachi,* a loosely knit organization of disaffected landowners, intellectuals, Islamic officials and others. By far the greatest damage to the Kazakh people and way of life would come at the end of the decade, however, with Stalin's policy designed to absorb privately owned farmland.

Collectivization and Its Consequences

No aspect of policy from the Soviet period had as devastating an effect as the drive to collectivize the agricultural holdings of the Kazakh people. The Bolsheviks, once they had consolidated power, had pursued a policy of nationalizing property, but had backed away from this drive in the 1920s. By the late 1920s, however, Josef Stalin, now the unchallenged leader of the Soviet Union, was once again determined to confiscate privately owned land and convert this property into communal agricultural collectives, controlled by the Soviet state. This plan was complicated in the case of the Kazakh steppe lands because a considerable number of Kazakhs living there still followed a nomadic lifestyle, following their herds of livestock, and had not settled into permanent farming communities. Soviet authorities set out to dismantle this traditional Kazakh way of life, confiscate private-owned livestock, and forcibly place the Kazakh herders and farmers on state-controlled collective farms, or *kolkhozi*.

The Kazakhs reacted with fierce resistance to the Soviet effort to destroy their lifestyle and seize their animals. Rather than voluntarily turn over their vast herds of sheep, cattle, camels, and other property, Kazakh herders slaughtered the animals where they stood. Those animals that could not be immediately eaten were simply left where they had fallen, leaving the steppe littered with thousands of rotting carcasses. Estimates of the number of animals lost are inexact, but all agree that the destruction was catastrophic, with possibly 12 million sheep and cattle killed just in 1930 alone, and millions more over the next several years. The number of livestock on the Kazakh steppe did not recover to its precollectivization figure until the 1960s, and then only after several decades of intensive effort by Soviet planners to rebuild the herd. At the same time, the majority of Kazakh nomads were forced onto the agricultural collectives—during the 1930s, some 400,000 Kazakh herders were settled.

More catastrophic than the loss of livestock was the concurrent human tragedy, as famine swept the steppe lands of Kazakhstan. Not only was there a massive loss of livestock, but Soviet planners failed to supply the newly established kolkhozi with adequate machinery, seed, fertilizer, and other necessities to produce grain in sufficient amounts for the population. Food shortages were commonplace in the Kazakh SSR during the 1930s, and mass starvation claimed the lives of possibly a million and a half people during that decade just in Kazakhstan (Conquest 1986, 190). While some Western journalists and politicians were extolling the industrial achievements of Stalin's USSR during this time, millions died across the Soviet Union from famine brought on by the misguided and inept attempt to collectivize agricultural production. The Kazakh population did not recover from this disaster for decades, and the destruction visited on their traditions and people remain in the minds of many contemporary Kazakhs.

The era of Stalinism not only transfigured the economic landscape of Kazakhstan, but also fundamentally changed the ethnic makeup of the Kazakh SSR, which was formed in 1936. Various tsarist regimes had utilized the remote Kazakh steppe as a place of internal exile for dissidents and criminals, but Stalin enlarged on this policy, dumping tens of thousands of politically "suspect" people from across the Soviet Union into the republic's cities and farming collectives. Among the larger groups were Germans from the Volga basin, Koreans from eastern Siberia, Chechens and Ingush from the Caucasus, and Tatars from both the Crimea and lower Volga basin. In addition, the Soviet prison system known as the Gulag was extensive in Kazakhstan, a fact later publicized by a one-time resident, Nobel Prize winner Alexander Solzhenitsyn. At its greatest extent, the Kazakhstan Gulag may have held 200,000 prisoners.

The last years of the Stalin regime also brought the first nuclear tests conducted on Kazakhstan's territory, most of them near the city of Semey (Semipalatinsk), in eastern Kazakhstan. The first Soviet atomic weapon was successfully exploded in 1949, and testing above ground and later below would continue in the Semipalatinsk Polygon, a zone of approximately 10,000 square miles, until the late 1980s. In total, nearly 500 nuclear weapons were exploded in the area, with tragic environmental consequences. Perhaps more than any other issue, it was the Soviet policy of turning this corner of Kazakhstan into a nuclear wasteland that galvanized opposition to the Soviet administration in the late 1980s. Before the era of glasnost (openness) in that decade, however, the people of Kazakhstan (many of those adversely affected by the testing were ethnic Russians) had little recourse but to live in a region contaminated by nuclear fallout.

The 1950s heralded a time of change, as a new Soviet leadership assumed control of the country. Nikita Khrushchev, the new Soviet leader, denounced some of the excesses committed by Stalin, yet he, too, would profoundly modify the ethnic makeup of the republic via his policies. In 1958, Khrushchev set in motion what he termed the Virgin Lands Program, a grandiose scheme to convert much of the remaining grazing land in Kazakhstan into collective farms, producing mostly wheat. To establish the kolkhozi, hundreds of thousands of young Russians and Ukrainians "volunteered" to migrate to Kazakhstan and work the new farms. Overall, the program met with limited success, but many of the new arrivals stayed on. Thus, as had happened at the beginning of the century, a large influx of Slavic settlers shifted the republic's demographic and ethnic character, ensuring that the ethnic Kazakhs would fail to hold a majority in the Kazakh SSR for the remainder of the Soviet period.

The 1960s and 1970s witnessed a strengthening of Kazakhstan's industrial base, as well as the solidification of the republic's role as a major grain supplier to the rest of the USSR. The northern oblasts contributed mightily to the Soviet Union's output of steel, petrochemicals, and other industrial products, and the southern and central sections of the Kazakh SSR produced huge amounts of wheat, sugar beets, cotton, and additional crops. The republic gained fame in the 1960s for being the home of Baikonur, the Soviet space launch complex, which blasted Yuri Gagarin, the first human in space, into orbit in 1961. At the same time, the ethnic Kazakhs were becoming thoroughly Russianized, with many of the younger generation learning Russian as their first, and often their only, language. Islamic religiosity, never as prevalent among the Kazakhs as among the Uzbeks and Tajiks, was also undermined, as the physical suppression and propaganda directed against the faith by the authorities had a significant effect among the Kazakh population. At the same time, during the 1970s Slavs and Germans began to leave the Kazakh SSR, a trend that would accelerate over the next two decades.

The Alma Ata Riots

A reasonable argument might be made that the visible decline of Soviet power began in Alma Ata (Almaty) in December 1986. Mikhail Gorbachev had already begun a purge of the Communist Party leadership in most of the Central Asian republics upon his rise to power in March 1985, and by December 1986, he had succeeded in ousting the first party secretary in the Kazakh SSR, Dinmukhamed Kunaev, as well. Kunaev was a Kazakh and was replaced by an ethnic Russian, Gennady Kolbin, who had only recently arrived in the republic. Gorbachev badly underestimated the reaction this move would incite among the Kazakhs, many of whom were already taking his promises of glasnost to heart. Within twenty-four hours, crowds assembled in Alma Ata, and the capital was shaken for several days by rioting. Even nearly twenty years in the wake of these events, no clear figure for the number of killed and injured has been provided by the Kazakh government, although some estimates run as high as several hundred, many of them university students. News of the riots was reported widely in the Soviet and international media, publicizing an episode of mass resistance to the regime by Soviet citizens for the first time in decades.

Few in the USSR or elsewhere could have imagined that, almost five years to the day after the Alma Ata riots, the Soviet Union would simply disintegrate, and Kazakhstan, along with the remaining constituent republics, would suddenly emerge as an independent country. In the case of Kazakhstan, as with the other Central Asian republics, there was no historical experience of functioning as a sovereign state. The collapse of Soviet power was not wholly unexpected, however, and in fact Kazakhstan's republican government, controlled by the republic's Communist Party, issued a statement of "sovereignty" in September 1990 claiming the precedence of the republic's laws over those of the union, more than a year before the formal disassociation of the USSR. Nevertheless, First Party Secretary Nazarbayev suddenly found himself, in late December 1991, the leader of one of the world's largest countries, a state equipped with nuclear weapons and a space launch facility but lacking a standing army, a national currency, and membership in a single international organization. Ready or not, Kazakhstan entered the world stage.

Independent Kazakhstan

The formal bonds of empire may be dissolved with the stroke of a pen, but the actual linkages between states emerging from a larger political and economic union are not so easily broken. This was a lesson that all the new countries coming out of the USSR's demise learned quickly, and Kazakhstan was no exception. Geography alone meant that Kazakhstan, sharing a border with Russia more than 2,000 miles long, would continue to be tightly connected to her giant neighbor. Indeed, because of the large number of ethnic Russians living in Kazakhstan, President Narzarbayev recognized that his new state's relationship with Russia was of paramount importance, if political and economic stability were to follow the collapse.

Initially, Kazakhstan stayed within the "ruble zone," continuing the use of the Soviet and later Russian currency. By late 1993, however, Russia's increasingly strict demands for remaining in the zone led Kazakhstan to introduce a national currency, the *tenge*. This allowed for more economic autonomy for the country and helped to propel the decidedly pro-business, pro-investment agenda Nazarbayev had pursued from the first months of independence. Specifically, the Nazarbayev regime sought foreign investors, especially in the lucrative oil and gas sectors. Even before independence, the Chevron oil company and other foreign firms had been negotiating for concessions in the enormous Tengiz field in western Kazakhstan, and other minerals resources, including gold, were also attractive to outside investors. Compared with other Central Asian states, Kazakhstan was hugely successful in this effort, landing approximately $10 billion of FDI (foreign direct investment) during the 1990s, the majority of which was funneled into the energy sector (Olcott 2002, 145).

The first constitution for independent Kazakhstan was produced in 1993, establishing a strong executive branch, but this document was replaced in 1995 by a second constitution that gave even greater powers to the president and weakened the legislative branch to such a degree that the bicameral legislature created, consisting of a senate and a *Majlis,* or lower house, was for all intents and purposes an advisory body to the president. In the early 1990s, opposition parties and a critical press had been allowed to function in Kazakhstan, but as the decade wore on, the Nazarbayev regime became increasingly authoritarian, following the general pattern for the new Central Asian states as a whole.

Corruption scandals, some involving Nazarbayev's family, became a common characteristic of Kazakh politics, and Nazarbayev consistently eliminated any in his government who appeared as a potential rival to his monopoly on political power. By the late 1990s, the Kazakh media was under strong pressure to conform to the government position, and open criticism of Nazabayev's policies and behavior became rare. In 1998, Nazarbayev's supporters in the legislature called for early elections for both the presidency and the legislature and passed legislation extending the presidential term and eliminating term limitations, effectively allowing him to remain in office without restrictions. The next year, Nazarbayev was reelected to the presidency with virtually no opposition because the early date of the elections did not allow the weakened and disorganized opposition to mount a serious challenge. The Kazakh government had become, and remains, the personal domain of Nursultan Nazarbayev.

At the time of the collapse of Soviet power, Kazakhstan was one of only four SSRs that contained portions of the Soviet nuclear arsenal, the others being Russia, Ukraine, and Belarus. Kazakhstan was of special concern to the United States, however, because of its proximity to the Middle East and the fact that the Kazakhs are at least nominally Muslim, facts feeding U.S. fears that either weapons or technology for manufacturing them could be transferred to radical Islamic groups or governments. In December 1991, Secretary of State James Baker traveled to Kazakhstan to consult with Nazarbayev and articulate U.S. concerns and policy toward the new Central Asian countries. Both the Bush and Clinton administrations admonished the Kazakh government to abandon its nuclear weapons and strategic capabilities, and although some in Kazakhstan saw the possession of such armaments as enhancing the country's status, by 1995 Nazarbayev had relinquished the weapons with the aid of considerable U.S. technical and financial assistance, netting some $400 million for his country in the process (Meyer 2003, 175).

Although he enjoyed considerable success in handling the issues of both dismantling his nuclear stockpile and attracting foreign investors, Nazarbayev's most formidable challenge has been managing the tense relations between Kazakhstan's two largest ethnic groups, the Russians and the Kazakhs. Balancing the interests of both groups has been compounded by the looming presence of Russia next door, which has at times since the USSR's disintegration regarded itself as the champion of displaced Russians in the "near abroad." The Kazakh government has the difficult task of promoting Kazakh culture, history, and language while avoiding alienating the large and economically vital Russian community. In 1995, Nazarbayev decreed that the national capital would be shifted from Almaty, the country's largest city and capital for most of the Soviet period, to Akmola (later renamed Astana), in the north central section of Kazakhstan. The motivation for this move has been much debated, with at least one specialist suggesting that it strengthened the government's ability to "supervise" the country's Russian-dominated oblasts (Olcott 2002, 194).

CONCLUSION

The thirteen years of Kazakhstan's independence have highlighted both the potential and the failures of this giant country. A high level of urbanization and a relatively well-educated workforce, along with vast and valuable resources, all make Kazakhstan's economic future brighter than that of most of its neighbors. At the same time, the Nazarbayev regime has drifted from its commitment to human rights and the structures of a civil society, including a pluralistic and democratic political system. Simmering below the surface of Kazakh society are serious ethnic tensions, which the regime thus far has been able to control but ultimately may erupt to the surface and complicate both the domestic politics and the society of Kazakhstan, as well as the country's relations with Russia.

Without stability, both internally and externally, it will be much more difficult for Kazakhstan's people to reap the benefits of their nation's massive resources.

References

Aitmatov, Chingiz. 1988. *The Day Lasts More Than a Hundred Years.* Bloomington: Indiana University Press.

Conquest, Robert. 1986. *The Harvest of Sorrow.* New York: Oxford University Press.

Grousset, Rene. 1970. *The Empire of the Steppes.* New Brunswick, NJ: Rutgers University Press.

Khodarkovsky, Michael. 1992. *Where Two Worlds Met: The Russian State and the Kalmyk Nomads, 1600–1771.* Ithaca, NY: Cornell University Press.

Meyer, Karl. 2003. *The Dust of Empire.* New York: Public Affairs.

Olcott, Martha Brill. 1995. *The Kazakhs.* 2d ed. Stanford, CA: Hoover Institution Press.

———. 2002. *Kazakhstan: Unfulfilled Promise.* Washington, DC: Carnegie Endowment for International Peace.

Rowland, Richard. 2001. "Regional Population Change in Kazakhstan during the 1990s and the Impact of Nationality Population Patterns: Results from the Recent Census of Kazakhstan." *Post-Soviet Geography and Economics* 42(8), pp. 571–614.

The Economy of Kazakhstan

Kazakhstan is a country gifted with enormous economic resources and potential. More industrialized under the Soviet regime than any of the other Central Asian states, Kazakhstan holds huge expanses of productive farmland; has apparently substantial, and possibly enormous, reserves of petroleum and natural gas; and mines a variety of valuable and rare minerals. The population is relatively small, but well educated and skilled. All these advantages have not meant that the wholesale shift from the command system of the Soviet era to a market economy has been easier or faster than elsewhere in the region, however. Completely overhauling a country's economic structure requires skill and patience, qualities that were in short supply in the early years of independence, when the Kazakh economy went into freefall, suffering a nearly 50 percent decline in gross domestic product (GDP) in only a few years. Yet despite these difficulties, the government moved forward with the introduction of a new currency, the *tenge,* as well as with fundamental reforms in both the agricultural and industrial sectors.

By the late 1990s, conditions in the Kazakh economy appeared to improve significantly. The economy was growing at a robust rate, poverty and unemployment rates, although still too high, were falling, and foreign investment in the country remained high, especially in the oil and gas industries. Fundamental challenges to future business and economic growth remain, however. A serious and pervasive problem is corruption and cronyism at all levels, a problem that undermines the public's faith in the system and inhibits entrepreneurship. In 2003, after years of negotiations, the problematical issue of how to transport Kazakh oil from the Caspian basin to the world market appeared resolved, but the pathway

185

chosen, through Azerbaijan and Georgia to Turkey, remains fraught with peril. Political turmoil in the volatile Caucasus region could endanger the financial bonanza that many in Kazakhstan expect to enjoy by emerging as an "oil nation." In this respect, geography continues to both bless and curse Kazakhstan, as the country strives to raise the living standards of its people and enter the global arena.

AGRICULTURE

Agriculture accounts for a much smaller share of the GDP in Kazakhstan than in other Central Asian countries. In 2003, agriculture made up only 7.8 percent of the GDP by value, and that figure had declined steadily since the 1990s (World Bank 2005). During the difficult transition to a market economy in the 1990s, the agricultural sector experienced serious disruption, and the productivity of most crops, and especially livestock, dropped. Oddly, employment in agriculture leapt almost 10 percent from 1999 to 2000 and has held steady at slightly more than one-third of the workforce since then (International Monetary Fund [IMF] 2004, 8). Although future exports are expected to shift significantly toward petroleum and natural gas, wheat and other agricultural products remain important contributors to export earnings as well, and with increased mechanization and productivity, Kazakhstan could become a major supplier of wheat to world markets.

Cropping Pattern

The steppes of Kazakhstan represent one of the world's most productive agricultural regions. The northern quarter of the country receives enough rainfall in an average year to produce many types of crops without irrigation, whereas in the southern tier of oblasts access to irrigation water is essential. Several streams in the south supply the fields with this pre-

Grain harvest in Kazakhstan. The country is a major producer and exporter of wheat. (Yevgeny Khaldei/Corbis)

cious commodity, including the Syr Darya, the Chu, and the Ili Rivers. The northern part of the country is blessed with highly productive *chernozem* soils, a soil type rich in humus and nutrients, and wheat and other grains dominate most of the acreage there. Along the river valleys of the south, much of the land is planted in cotton and rice, with additional areas of wheat production as well. In some areas of the south, soil degradation has occurred because of overirrigation and the exhaustive practice of repeatedly growing cotton without rotation with other crops. Animal husbandry, the traditional livelihood of the Kazakhs, is still widely practiced, and the country is home to large herds of sheep, horses, and goats.

One measure of the volume of wheat production in Kazakhstan is the fact that in most years, Kazakhstan grows more wheat per capita than any other country. About a quarter of that production is exported, mostly to surrounding countries, although a significant proportion winds up on the world market. Wheat production has declined since independence, however, because of a combination of factors, including disruptions in past trading relationships, a decline in investment in the agricultural sector, problems associated with the dismantling of the collectivized system of landholding, and losses in the labor force (Esentugelov 1996, 206). Should these problems be overcome, the potential for impressive increases in production exist, and Kazakhstan could become a supplier of grain to the world market on the scale of Australia or Argentina. A much smaller percentage of the country's agricultural land is devoted to rice production, and virtually all the rice produced is consumed within Kazakhstan. Irrigated cotton provides some additional exports earnings in many years and helps to supply the domestic textile industry. Cottonseed oil is an important by-product from the harvesting of the cotton fiber, and eastern Kazakhstan has enormous fields of sunflowers, grown primarily for oil. The southern portion of Kazakhstan also generates a bounty of fruits, nuts, melons, and vegetables, and potatoes and beets are planted across the country.

Centuries before the rich soils of Kazakhstan were broken by the plow, Kazakh nomads were guiding vast herds of animals across the plains, deriving their livelihood and measuring their wealth from the livestock they controlled. The two animals that made up most of the herds before the twentieth century were sheep and horses, although camels and goats also were often included. Today some cattle have joined the mix, although sheep continue to make up the majority of live-

Livestock are a major part of Kazakhstan's agricultural production. These sheep provide both wool and meat. (Library of Congress)

stock in Kazakhstan. Sheep are valued for their meat, which is eaten much more commonly in Central Asia than in the United States, and also for their wool. The soft high-quality wool known as *karakul,* shorn from the lambs of certain sheep, is used to make expensive hats and sweaters, and the wool brings top prices for those producing it. Horses, although not as numerous as sheep, have been vital to the Kazakhs for centuries, both as beasts of burden and as sources of food. Kazakhs do not share the aversion to horseflesh that most Americans hold, and horse meat is considered a special treat at any feast. Mares provide *kumiss,* or fermented mare's milk, a traditional alcoholic beverage widely consumed at social gatherings. Kazakh herdsmen often carried a *kookor,* a leather flagon containing kumiss, to fortify them during long rides.

Land Ownership and Reform

Before the arrival of Russian administration, land tenure among the nomadic Kazakhs was informal. The three *juz* (or hordes; see previous chapter) occupied their various geographic locations, and individual clans and tribes possessed specific grazing lands, in the sense that their animals had fed and watered there for many years, frequently for generations. These distinctions were fluid, however, and such lands were not marked by formal, legally recognized boundaries. The arrival of settlers from Russia in the nineteenth century changed the concept of land "ownership" entirely, in that the new immigrants—who were farmers, not nomads—demanded surveys, land deeds, and clearly marked boundaries to distinguish their holdings from those of their neighbors. During this time, there were many clashes between the nomadic Kazakhs and the Slavic farmers over access to grazing land and water. Both sides viewed the lifestyle of the other as inferior and backward, but from the late 1800s, it was the Kazakhs and their herds who were systematically displaced.

The changes resulting from the incursion of Russian agriculturalists and the tsarist government paled in comparison to the transformation brought on by Soviet administration, particularly after 1928. That year Josef Stalin's scheme of collectivizing agricultural holdings across the USSR was implemented, a policy that would result in what historian Robert Conquest has called the Kazakh Tragedy (Conquest 1986). Collectivization met with strong resistance in many corners of the Soviet Union, but in Kazakhstan the opposition was especially fierce and dramatic. Collectivization meant that the Soviet government required the Kazakhs to turn over their animals to state control, a process that robbed most Kazakhs of their main source of income and wealth. The Kazakh herders responded by slaughtering millions of animals rather than allowing the Soviet state to confiscate them. Conquest reports that between 1929 and 1933, the number of sheep in Kazakhstan fell by more than 20 million head (Conquest 1986, 190). This did not deter the Soviet authorities, and by the late 1930s, almost all the Russian farmers and Kazakh pastoralists had been forced onto collective farms (*kolkhozi*), or state farms (*sovkhozi*), and the great majority of agricultural land became the property of the government.

The collapse of the Soviet system brought fundamental change to the nature of land ownership in Kazakhstan, although several years passed before many of the changes took effect. The privatization of agricultural land was an early goal of the independent Kazakh government, and by 1996 the collectivized system had been dismantled, with the creation of more than 44,000 peasant farms, as well as cooperatives and other forms of private ownership (Kasenov 1998, 36). These new owners held rights to the land in the form of leases and did not own the land outright initially because there was almost no way to accurately determine land values at the time. Kazakhstan made more rapid progress toward privatizing this key sector of its economy than did any of the remaining Central Asian states, although many obstacles beset the process of returning the collectivized holdings to private hands. For example, many small-scale farmers found it difficult to obtain commercial loans to buy badly needed equipment, upgrade facilities, or even purchase seed, fertilizer, or other necessary supplies. Because of these and related problems, agricultural production declined significantly in the first half of the 1990s, and many new land owners found it impossible to make a living from the land.

In 2003, the Kazakh government passed legislation that allowed individuals to legally own their land, but this new law revealed new problems. The market value of the land is determined by the government, but in some regions of the country land prices fixed in this manner are far too high for most farmers to afford. In addition, basic structural problems plague the rural areas, reducing productivity. A serious short-coming is the underdeveloped transportation infrastructure found throughout the countryside, a problem that limits the ability of farmers to market their crops. There are insufficient storage facilities in most of the country, which results in considerable loss to spoilage. In 2004, the Kazakh government committed more than $200 million over the course of three years to improve infrastructure and living conditions in the countryside and possibly to relocate farmers from regions where the local economy has stagnated (Nurskenova 2004). Although it is clear that Kazakhstan's agricultural sector continues to struggle, if the legacy of the Soviet period can be overcome, the country could emerge as a major food exporter.

INDUSTRY

From the first decades of Russian penetration of Central Asia, northern Kazakhstan was the most industrialized part of the region, and this remains true today. Geography played a great role in this development, as the northern steppes were endowed with extensive and valuable mineral deposits, and in addition the northern plains were closer to the markets of Russia than were any other section of Central Asia. The wealth of mineral resources ranged from metallic ores like iron, copper, and zinc to hydrocarbons, principally coal and petroleum. The Soviets developed industry further, expanding the smelting plants in the Kazakh SSR and building a large iron and steel plant at Karaganda, drawing on large quantities of high-grade coal located nearby. The relocation of much of Soviet industrial capacity to Central Asia during World War II further stimulated Kazakhstan's manufacturing industries, and by the eve of Soviet disintegration, Kazakhstan had developed into one of the USSR's most important industrial regions.

Oil exploration and exploitation in Tengiz, Kazakhstan. Aerial view over oil field exploration site, 1990. (Bernard Bisson/Corbis Sygma)

Since independence, the resource in Kazakhstan that has generated the most discussion has been the country's oil reserves. Although a modest petroleum industry in Kazakhstan had emerged during the Soviet period, in 1979 a large oil deposit was identified in western Kazakhstan near the Caspian Sea, the Tengiz field. Even before independence, Kazakh authorities were negotiating an arrangement with the U.S. oil firm Chevron to extract the Tenghiz oil, and by the early 1990s, other major oil companies from abroad were showing their eagerness to invest in the Kazakh oil industry. Kazakhstan's role as a future supplier of petroleum to the global market received yet another huge boost in 1997, when the Kashagan field, lying below the northern Caspian Sea, was discovered. The Kashagan deposit is estimated to be significantly larger than the Tenghiz field but will be more difficult to exploit because of its depth and location under water. If the most optimistic estimates for the total capacity of petroleum deposits in Kazakhstan are accurate, the country may well hold larger reserves than Russia and might become a major petroleum exporter in coming decades. Significant pockets of natural gas have been found in conjunction with the new oil reserves.

The discovery of Kazakhstan's oil and gas wealth has brought large amounts of foreign investment, and Kazakhstan has been the most successful of the Central Asian countries at attracting capital from abroad. The structure of FDI in the country has been heavily skewed toward the burgeoning hydrocarbon industries, however. In 1998, the oil and gas sector accounted for more than two-thirds of all FDI, and the following year that percentage rose to almost 85 percent (IMF 2001, 74). The United States has provided the largest amount of investment, contributing about $1.5 billion between 1993 and 1998 (Olcott 2002, 150). China, facing an impending energy shortage, has also shown a willingness to invest in the Kazakh petroleum industry and in constructing a pipeline that would move oil eastward, but the billions of dollars required for such a project have not materialized. As is the case with its agricultural potential, if Kazakhstan can solve the many difficulties associated with the petroleum and gas industries, the country could well become one of the most important exporters of hydrocarbon fuels in the twenty-first century and simultaneously raise the standard of living for all its citizens.

Oil and gas may represent the brightest prospects for the future of industry in Kazakhstan, but other industries could contribute to the country's economic growth as well, if leftover problems from the Soviet era can be overcome. Gross industrial output more than doubled between 1999 and 2002, a heartening sign that industries across the board are recovering (IMF 2004, 8). Metallurgical manufacturing has tremendous potential given the rich ore deposits found in many regions. Foreign investors have sought out opportunities in these industries as well, and companies from India, Japan, Korea, and elsewhere have pumped money into revitalizing the production of iron and steel, copper, chromium, and other metals. More modest investment has flowed toward the consumer goods industry and food processing, as well as into enterprises such as hotels and office buildings. Turkish investors, who share many common cultural characteristics with the Kazakhs, have been the source of much of this capital. Certain key industries, such as the production of food-processing and textile manufacturing equipment, as well as agricultural machinery, remain woefully underdeveloped, a situation that forces the country to import costly equipment necessary to basic industries. On the whole, Kazakhstan's prospects to advance its industrial development appear bright, if inadequacies such as these can be addressed in coming years.

SERVICES

Services represent the most diversified segment of the economy in any country and range from a simple haircut to legal advice and representation. A basic service sector was in place under the Soviet regime in Kazakhstan, but more sophisticated services, including insurance, consulting services, banking, real estate services, database management, and a wide array of others, were completely lacking at independence and had to be organized with little experience. Between 1999 and 2003, the service sector accounted for more than 50 percent of the employment in Kazakhstan (IMF 2004, 8), and this percentage will almost certainly increase as the shift to a market-based economy continues, with demand for many of the new services rising.

After 1991, the Kazakh government had to create a number of institutional services, which had developed in the West over many decades, virtually overnight. For example, there was no independent banking system to provide loans to new businesses, no stock exchange for raising badly needed investment capital, no insurance industry to protect against losses, and so on. To stimulate banking services the government created the National Bank of Kazakhstan, which quickly became the dominant financial institution in the country, but both domestic and foreign competitors have been allowed to enter the market since the early 1990s. Initially, many people were reluctant to place their savings in a bank because they lacked trust in the system, and relatively few applied for loans. Over time, the role and function of banks have become apparent to a growing number of people, however, and the banking system in Kazakhstan is the best developed in Central Asia.

Other lending agencies have supplemented the banking system in making loans to entrepreneurs wishing to begin a business. Both the United States Agency for International Development and the European Bank for Reconstruction and Development have provided help to those interested in starting a business, even on a small scale. Some loans total only a few hundred dollars, but even amounts this small have helped to stimulate business development in Kazakhstan. Other services, such as insurance, investment advisement, consulting, and other activities that figure prominently in developed economies are nearly absent in Kazakhstan, but as the economy continues on the path to privatization and the country's vast natural resources are further exploited, specialized, sophisticated services such as these are quite likely to play a larger role in the Kazakh economy.

POVERTY

One of the most disturbing side effects of the economic transition in Kazakhstan has been the rise of poverty. This is not to suggest that poverty did not exist in the Soviet Union; by any definition of the term, many Soviet people were "poor," and the USSR was far from being the classless society its propaganda organs claimed it to be. Poverty in independent Kazakhstan is more apparent and public than during the Soviet period, however, when homelessness and public begging were rarely encountered. Poverty levels in Kazakhstan have increased since independence, primarily because of the economic disruptions brought about by the collapse of the USSR and the subsequent effort to convert to an economy directed by market forces. In addition, poverty levels vary significantly by ethnic group, age, gender, and geographic region.

According to the United Nations Development Program (UNDP) in Kazakhstan, in 2002 those earning less than 4,751 *tenge* (the local currency, equal to about $31) a month lived below the "subsistence minimum," meaning they lived in poverty in comparison with the remaining population (UNDP Kazakhstan 2004, 22). Nearly a quarter of the population fell below this minimum standard in 2002, but in fact this represents the lowest percentage living in poverty since the early 1990s, and a significant decline from the peak year, 1998, when 39 percent of the population did not have incomes that met the subsistence minimum. Thus, although the percentage of those living in poverty remains high, there has been a dramatic drop in poverty since the late 1990s in Kazakhstan, a heartening sign that perhaps the economic transition has turned a corner. Overall the trend is positive, but some aspects of poverty continue to give cause for concern.

The geographic differentials of poverty in Kazakhstan are one such cause for concern. In general, those regions that are more urbanized and industrialized experience a lower incidence of poverty than do regions that are mostly rural and agrarian. The poor appear to be clustered in the eastern and southern portions of Kazakhstan (IMF 2001, 14), where other factors such as large family size and low levels of education contribute to a higher rate of poverty. The divide between conditions in the urban areas and those in the countryside are starkly illustrated when comparing the city of Almaty, the country's former capital and largest city, to its surrounding oblast (province). In the city of Almaty, only around 4 percent of the population had an income below the minimum subsistence level defined by the UNDP in 2002, but in the oblast the figure soared to 36 percent, the second-highest rate in the country (UNDP 2004, 58). In the new capital of Astana, the percentage of those failing to make the subsistence minimum was only 2.2 percent. A clear spatial division of poverty between north and south is also evident in Kazakhstan. Almost all of the oblasts in the southern half of the country had at least 30 percent of their populations living in poverty, whereas in northern Kazakhstan, adjacent to the Russian border, only 14 percent failed to reach the subsistence minimum.

In addition to its geographic dimensions, poverty in Kazakhstan disproportionately affects certain groups. Those at highest risk are the elderly, new immigrants, and families with multiple children. The elderly in Kazakhstan are almost universally dependent on state pensions, which have been eroded during the period of independence by inflation. In addition, the government in the late 1990s fell behind in making payments to pensioners, a situation that was rectified only after some time. Another group at high risk of falling into poverty are the *oralmandar,* ethnic Kazakhs who have returned to Kazakhstan since independence and who have frequently encountered difficulties finding well-paying jobs and integrating into a society where many of their fellow Kazakhs do not speak Kazakh fluently. Most of these new immigrants do not speak Russian.

Families with numerous children are more common in the rural areas than in the cities and are also much more likely to be Kazakh or Uzbek than Russian. Such families tend to be poor for a number of reasons, but perhaps the foremost cause is the reduction of social services in the 1990s.

TRANSPORTATION AND COMMUNICATION

Like its Central Asian neighbors, Kazakhstan is landlocked, and the distance from the country to the world's oceans pres-

Tanker cars line up on the tracks for a freight train, near Kul'Sary, Kazakhstan. (Wolfgang Kaehler/Corbis)

ents considerable disadvantage to economic development. Finding a suitable path to world markets for the country's rich assortment of resources, most important of which are its oil and natural gas, has been a vital objective of the government since independence. Although the Russian and Soviet governments oversaw the development of an extensive railroad system and other transport links in Kazakhstan, most of those lines connect to Russia and run north and south—east to west roads and railways are underdeveloped. The quality of many of the roadways is poor, especially in the south and west, and both the railroads and rolling stock (cars and locomotives) have degraded since the Soviet period. The antiquated telephone system is frequently unreliable even in the cities, but many well-to-do residents of the country are switching to cellular phones, bypassing the old system altogether. The construction of new transport and communications infrastructure in the next decade is vital to the economic advancement of the country, a fact the regime appears to recognize.

The transport issue that currently seems to be the concern of nearly every official in Kazakhstan, and perhaps for good reason, is the construction of a pipeline to carry the country's oil wealth to the world market. Since independence, Kazakhstan has been forced to rely on transport lines through Russia, a situation the Kazakh government quickly came to view as counter to long-term interests. The Kazakh administration considered alternative routes, one of which would carry Kazakh oil southward to Iranian ports, but both economic and political difficulties rendered such a plan unmanageable. In 2003, an agreement was reached that would allow Kazakh oil to be carried by ship to the Caspian port of Baku and from there piped through Georgia to the Turkish port of Ceyhan using a new pipeline. This pathway has its critics, who have pointed out possible damage to the environment, as well as the unstable political situation in the Caucasus, yet it is likely this will be the route whereby the preponderance of Kazakh oil will reach international markets in the future.

Since 1991, transport connections to the rest of the world have expanded. During the Soviet era one could not fly directly from an international location into Kazakhstan; the only route was by flying first to Moscow or Leningrad (St. Petersburg). Shortly after independence, a national airline, Kazakhstan Airlines, began to operate and now reaches many cities internationally as well as domestically, and a number of major foreign airlines provide flights to Almaty several times a week from Europe, Turkey, and the former USSR. Rail connections to Russia, China, and surrounding Central Asian states are well developed, and internally most goods and resources are moved via rail. There is some river transport as well, but many of the streams in the country are not suitable for moving freight long distances. Paved highways connect the country's major cities, but the quality of these roads is considerably below the highways of North America or western Europe, and off the major thoroughfares, many roads—especially in the southern oblasts—are in an alarming state of disrepair. Some efforts to upgrade and expand the existing road networks have been initiated with the help of international donors, and the World Bank is rebuilding the main highway between Almaty and Astana (World Bank Group, 2002). Improvement of the transport systems must become a priority if Kazakhstan is to reach its economic potential in coming decades.

TOURISM: POSSIBILITIES AND PROSPECTS

Because of its distance from countries that produce sizable numbers of international travelers, Kazakhstan's geographic position inhibits efforts to attract large numbers of tourists. A flight to Almaty from London, Paris, or Frankfurt requires approximately seven hours of flying time, and tourists traveling from North America or Japan must endure trips almost three times that length or longer.

The great majority of tourists who visit the country are from Russia and other neighboring states. Yet despite these disadvantages, the beginnings of a tourist infrastructure have emerged, in the form of new hotels, a considerable number of tour operators, and direct flights between Almaty and major cities in western Europe and North America. This development, however, has not been balanced in either a geographic sense or in terms of selection and choice. For example, most of the new hotels have been constructed in Almaty, Astana, and a few other large cities, and quality accommodations elsewhere are often difficult to find. In addition, those hotels that have appeared typically are five-star facilities that cater to a wealthy clientele. Although less expensive hotels that service the average tourist are in short supply, some moderately priced facilities are gradually appearing in locations with major tourist attractions.

The majority of Kazakhstan is steppe or desert, but some parts of the country feature magnificent scenery, particularly the north-central, eastern, and southeastern regions. The potential of these areas to attract tourists is substantial. Opportunities abound in the southeastern mountains, only a short distance from Almaty, for downhill and cross-country skiing in the winter and trekking, climbing, hiking, bird watching, hunting, and fishing in the summer. The Chimbulak ski resort and Medeo ice-skating rink, the latter being the largest such facility in the world, are located only a few minutes' drive outside of Almaty. In the north-central stretch of the country, the Kokshetau Mountains offer a spectacular landscape of pine forests and lakes, centered on Lake Borovoye, a famous resort and health spa.

Kazakhstan does not have the abundance of historical and cultural sites found in Uzbekistan, but the southern oblasts adjacent to Uzbekistan contain several monuments that would be of interest to visitors. The most impressive of these is the mausoleum of Sheik Ahmed Yassavi in the southern town of Turkestan. Yassavi was the founder of a Sufi order in the tenth century, and nearly three centuries after his death, Amir Timur (Tamerlane) built a magnificent mausoleum enclosing Yassavi's original, and rather modest, tomb to honor the sheik. The natural and historical wonders of Kazakhstan have the potential to draw many more visitors than heretofore has been the case, but this is unlikely to occur without a serious commitment from the government and investors.

ECONOMIC PERFORMANCE AND BARRIERS TO GROWTH

In recent years much of the economic news from Kazakhstan has been positive, as memories of the difficult years of the 1990s fade. Economic growth is up, poverty and unemployment rates have declined, productivity is increasing, and all signs indicate that the day is near when Kazakh oil will begin reaching the world market in ever-larger quantities. Indeed, given the country's generous endowment of resources, its highly skilled labor force, and its small population, economic conditions in the country may well improve dramatically over the next decade. This will only be the case, however, if the entrenched corruption, cronyism, and inefficiency that characterize much of the economy are reduced and meaningful progress is made toward democratization and the building of a civil society. These goals may represent the most serious challenges to advancement Kazakhstan has yet faced.

Kazakhstan's economic future is, in some ways, beyond its control, as varying world prices of commodities such as oil and wheat may bring either a windfall of profits or disappointingly short returns on investment. Powerful neighbors such as Russia and China also represent both promise and peril, in that the success or failure of economic policies pursued in these larger markets bordering on the country will affect the success of Kazakhstan's policies to a considerable degree. Recent trends away from democracy and toward authoritarianism by the Nazarbayev regime have raised concern among many commentators, who view political liberalization as inextricably linked to economic improvement. Nevertheless, if the country can remain internally stable and at peace with its neighbors, the generous flow of foreign investment it has enjoyed since independence is almost certain to continue, stimulating further economic development in this massive country.

CONCLUSION

Of the five Central Asian states to emerge from the Soviet Union, Kazakhstan has the greatest potential for rapid economic advancement. A host of factors support this assessment of the country: it possesses huge stretches of productive farmland and pasture; the west holds potentially enormous deposits of oil and natural gas, and recently solutions for transporting those riches to the global marketplace have been found; there are sizable quantities of other valuable, high-demand minerals; Kazakhstan inherited an aging but well-developed industrial base from the Soviet era; and finally, the Kazakh government has been more successful at attracting foreign investors than any of its Central Asian neighbors. To secure a stable future for the country, however, the Kazakh regime must work to eliminate the culture of graft, nepotism, and inefficiency that has surfaced since the country's independence and strive to set in place a pluralistic society based on the rule of law. Only then will the people of Kazakhstan be able to reach their full potential.

References

Conquest, Robert. 1986. *The Harvest of Sorrow.* New York: Oxford University Press.

Esentugelov, Arystan. 1996. "Kazakhstan: Problems and Prospects of Reform and Development." In *Central Asia in Transition: Dilemmas of Political and Economic Development,* edited by Boris Rumer. Armonk, NY: M.E. Sharpe.

International Monetary Fund. 2001, January. "Republic of Kazakhstan: Selected Issues and Statistical Appendix." IMF Country Report No. 01/20.

————. 2004, November. "Republic of Kazakhstan: Selected Issues." IMF Country Report No. 04/362.

Kasenov, Umirserik. 1998. "Post-Soviet Modernization in Central Asia: Realities and Prospects." In *Central Asia: The Challenges of Independence,* edited by Boris Rumer and Stanislav Zhukov. Armonk, NY: M.E. Sharpe.

Nurskenova, Assel. 2004, January 29. "Kazakhstan Has High Hopes for Agricultural Reform," *Eurasianet.* Available at http://www .eurasianet.org/departments/business/articles/eav012904_pr.shtml. Accessed January 16, 2005.

Olcott, Martha Brill. 2002. *Kazakhstan: Unfulfilled Promise.* Washington, DC: Carnegie Endowment for International Peace.

UNDP Kazakhstan. 2004. *Poverty in Kazakhstan: Causes and Cures.* No. UNDPKAZ 08.

World Bank Group. "Kazakhstan Data Profile." Available at http:// devdata.worldbank.org/external/CPProfile.asp?SelectedCountry= KAZ&CCODE=KAZ&CNAME=Kazakhstan&PTYPE=CP. Accessed January 21, 2005.

World Bank Group. 2002. "Rebuilding the Crossroads of Central Asia." Available at http://Inweb18.worldbank.org/ . . . /E4FF952CBAD26 51985256BF7006623ED?OpenDocumen. Accessed January 26, 2005.

Kazakhstan Institutions

The Kazakhs were the most "Russified" ethnic group in Central Asia, and perhaps in the entire USSR. The residue of this partial assimilation is clear today in the fact that a majority of Kazakhs speak Russian as a first language, and many cannot speak Kazakh. Creating a Kazakh nation since 1991 has been challenging because of the loss of Kazakh identity as well as the presence of the largest Slavic minority in Central Asia. Indeed, many Russians look askance at the efforts of the Kazakh president, Nursultan Nazarbayev, to implement a policy of "Kazakhification," a program they view as designed to demote them to the status of second-class citizens (Surucu 2002). The division between the two groups has also been widened somewhat by an increased visibility for Islam in the new Kazakhstan, a development that some Slavs and other non-Muslims receive with concern, although President Nazarbayev has gone to considerable lengths to reassure the Slavic minority that he will not brook any expressions of Islamic "radicalism" in his country.

Kazakhstan today has been deeply shaped by the will and personality of Nazarbayev, the former Communist boss and, since 1991, president of Kazakhstan. Nazarbayev has managed to hold his new state together despite a serious ethnic split, while at the same time encouraging the revival of Kazakh culture and heritage. He has accomplished this at a high price, however: democracy has given ground to authoritarianism, as Nazarbayev has created a governing apparatus that he can control at every stratum of administration and that has suppressed those who challenge its legitimacy. The purpose of the discussion here is to describe recent changes in some of the basic systems of Kazakh society—that is, government, religion, and education—with the hope that the information provided will enable the reader to gain an understanding of the complexities of each in this new country.

GOVERNMENT AND POLITICS

The personalities and attitudes of all the major players in Kazakh politics today were forged under the Soviet system, and an understanding of the current political environment in Kazakhstan must begin with an examination of the later Soviet period. President Nazarbayev rose through the ranks of the Communist Party eventually to become the head of the Kazakh republican Communist Party and subsequently the leader of independent Kazakhstan. Nazarbayev and his rivals all emerged from a tradition of totalitarian rule, a background that continues to shape the political landscape in their enormous country. In addition, most of the political challenges now facing the country result at least partially from Soviet policies of earlier decades. The following section is designed to provide a brief overview of governance and politics from the 1950s to the present, organized chronologically and focused on the central political figures of each era, with emphasis on the major events that ultimately led to Kazakhstan's appearance on the world stage and its development since 1991.

Khrushchev and the Virgin Lands Program

Nikita Khrushchev became chairman of the Communist Party of the Soviet Union in 1953 upon the death of Josef Stalin. His predecessor's policy of collectivization of agriculture had devastated much of Kazakhstan (see the previous chapter, Geography and History of Kazakhstan), and Khrushchev was intent on increasing agricultural production in the USSR. Early in his tenure, Khrushchev initiated the Virgin and Idle Lands program, designed to increase the volume of grain being raised in northern Kazakhstan and several other regions

Kazakh president Nursultan Nazarbayev listens to the national anthem as he stands during an inauguration ceremony in January 1999. (Reuters/Corbis)

(Dmytryshyn 1984, 281). Khrushchev's policies proved controversial and were resisted by many in the Kazakh branch of the Communist Party. Between 1954 and 1962, seven first party secretaries served at the helm of the Kazakh Communist Party, including Leonid Brezhnev, who was the only one of the seven who was subsequently promoted. Ironically, Brezhnev would eventually replace Khrushchev as the leader of the entire Soviet Union in 1964. It was precisely during this era of turmoil in the Kazakh CP that a young steelworker, Nursultan Nazarbayev, joined the organization and began to attract the attention of his superiors because of his capabilities as an organizer and leader.

The Kunaev Era (1964–1986)

Leonid Brezhnev ascended to the position of first secretary (later designated general secretary) of the Communist Party of the USSR in 1964 (Dmytryshyn 1984, 335) and immediately set out to consolidate his position by appointing supporters to lead the respective republican branches of the party. In the Kazakh Soviet Socialist Republic (SSR), Brezhnev installed Dinmukhamed Kunaev, an old ally, as first party secretary. Kunaev had been previously disgraced and removed by Khrushchev, but his loyalty to Brezhnev remained unquestioned over more than twenty years. Kunaev's influence during the Brezhnev years is amply illustrated by the fact that he eventually rose to membership in the Politburo, the most powerful political organization in the USSR, and was the only Kazakh ever to serve in that capacity.

Kunaev's long stay at the top of the party apparatus in Kazakhstan allowed him to build an extensive power base, with virtually every position of authority in the government filled with a friend or relative. The participation of ethnic Kazakhs in the CP increased under Kunaev's leadership, whereas before the 1960s the majority of the party elite had been Russian and Ukrainian. He did not alienate the ethnic

Slavs, however, and shrewdly worked both groups for support and patronage. For the first decade of Kunaev's term, economic conditions improved in Kazakhstan, as productivity increased in both the agricultural and industrial sectors. Many Kazakhs came to view him as something of a "protector," who would champion their interests. It was in this atmosphere that a young Nursultan Nazarbayev began his rise through the party ranks and, by the early 1980s, acquired an impressive portfolio in the republic's party structure, becoming a protégé of Kunaev himself.

Brezhnev's death in 1982 set in motion the decline of Kunaev's political fortunes, although his removal was not immediate. Despite occasional criticism of the Kazakh Communist Party from Moscow and the removal of a number of his political allies from posts within and outside of Kazakhstan, Kunaev skillfully stayed in his post until 1986, when he was replaced by an ethnic Russian, Gennady Kolbin. The architect of Kunaev's demise was the new general secretary of the Communist Party of the USSR, Mikhail Gorbachev, who had taken office a year and a half earlier. Gorbachev was intent on reforming the Soviet system, which he believed was approaching economic crisis. To implement his sweeping programs of reform, Gorbachev sought to remove officials who had become entrenched and who would likely resist any effort to change the nature of the Soviet system. Kunaev was surely such a figure, and Gorbachev was able finally to pry him from the Kazakh Communist Party helm in December 1986.

The Kolbin-Nazarbayev Interlude (1986–1991)

Gorbachev could not have imagined the furor that his removal of Kunaev would instigate, but it was quickly apparent that the new general secretary had underestimated Kunaev's popularity. Kunaev's successor, Gennady Kolbin, was not only from outside the Kazakh SSR, but was also an ethnic Russian, and the dismissal of Kunaev helped fan the flames of an emerging Kazakh nationalism. The morning after word reached the public that Kunaev had been replaced by an ethnic Russian, crowds of demonstrators began to gather in Alma Ata's (Almaty's) central square, protesting the move. There are conflicting accounts of the size and nature of the demonstration, but at some point security forces attacked those assembled with sharpened shovels. Violent rioting followed for several days, with the result of perhaps several hundred deaths, mostly of demonstrators. It appears that most of the crowd consisted of ethnic Kazakhs, whereas many if not most of the security forces were Russian. Thus began Gennady Kolbin's brief reign as Gorbachev's man in Kazakhstan.

Kolbin appears to have been ill equipped to deal with the multitude of changes that were occurring in Kazakh society. Although he successfully purged many of Kunaev's supporters from the ranks of the Kazakh Communist Party and at least initially backed Gorbachev's reformist policies, he was unable to stem a tide of rising Kazakh nationalism. A particularly sensitive issue was the status of the Kazakh language, and by the late 1980s, many ethnic Kazakhs, even members of the Communist Party, were demanding that Kazakh be made the official language of the Kazakh SSR. Kolbin paid lip service to this notion but lost credibility after he failed to implement any concrete reforms to elevate Kazakh to equal status with Russian. After another episode of interethnic violence erupted in western Kazakhstan in the summer of 1989, Kolbin was recalled to Moscow and replaced by Nursultan Nazarbayev.

The new first secretary understood the significance of the language issue and moved immediately to place Kazakh, at least legally, on an equal footing with Russian in his republic. Within two months, a new law making Kazakh the "state language" was passed, although many among the Russian population complained that the timetable for implementing the new requirements was too short, because virtually none of the Russians in Kazakhstan was conversant in Kazakh. Nazarbayev also took control of the Islamic revival that was sweeping Kazakh society, removing Kazakhstan from the Muslim Spiritual Board for Central Asia located in Tashkent and establishing a separate authority specifically for Kazakhstan. The Kazakh leader was already acting with considerable autonomy when a cabal of antireformist conspirators attempted to wrest control of the USSR away from Gorbachev in August 1991.

Independence (1991–)

Nearly a year before the August 1991 coup, the Kazakh republican government had passed a resolution declaring Kazakhstan's "sovereignty," indicating that laws established by the republic's government would supersede those imposed from Moscow. The establishment of "sovereignty" simply reinforced the political autonomy Nursultan Nazarbayev had exercised, with increasing boldness, since his assumption of the post of first secretary. However, Nazarbayev made clear by his public pronouncements and by his efforts to preserve some sort of union among the constituent republics of the USSR that he did not believe Kazakhstan was prepared to survive as an independent country. Nevertheless, Kazakhstan declared independence on December 16, 1991, the final Soviet Socialist Republic to do so. It was Nazarbayev, more so than any other former Soviet leader, who promoted the creation of the Commonwealth of Independent States in the aftermath of the dissolution of the USSR, since he felt it would be virtually impossible for many of the republics to survive without some political organization facilitating their economic integration and cooperation (Olcott 2002, 36–38).

Just two weeks before becoming an independent country, the Kazakh electorate had voted Nazarbayev into the new office of president on December 1, 1991. The election was reminiscent of Soviet elections, in that Nazarbayev ran unopposed and had absolute control of the media in Kazakhstan. According to the official tally, Narzarbayev won 99 percent of

The birth of the Commonwealth of Independent States, Alma Ata,
December 21, 1991. (Epix/Corbis Sygma)

the vote. With this "mandate," he moved swiftly to create an
independent Kazakhstan, and by the end of 1993 Kazakhstan
had a new constitution and a new currency, the *tenge*. The
country had continued to use the Russian ruble as legal tender for the first two years of independence, but this had
placed the Kazakh economy at the mercy of Russian macro-
economic policy. By leaving the "ruble zone," Nazarbayev
made clear that he did not intend for his new country to serve
as a vassal to its powerful neighbor to the north. He also
openly courted a close relationship with the United States,
allowing the Americans to disassemble and remove a large
number of nuclear weapons positioned in Kazakhstan.

The constitution of 1993 granted the Kazakh president
sweeping powers. He has the authority to appoint the prime
minister and the chairman of the Constitutional Council, the
body that adjudicates questions of the constitutionality of
statutes and legitimacy of presidential elections. In addition,

a new constitution adopted in 1995 gave Nazarbayev nearly complete control of the country's courts by establishing the president as the head of the High Judicial Council, the body that recommends judges to the Supreme Court, and allowed him to appoint regional and district court judges—thus, effectively every judge in the entire legal system in Kazakhstan is a presidential appointee. Nazarbayev also appoints each of the oblast governors, or *akims*, in the country, giving him control over every region and ensuring that these regional leaders are loyal to him (Nowicki 1997, 24). Thus, the powers awarded to the president by the 1995 constitution allow him to place his supporters into positions at all levels of both the judicial and executive branches of government.

According to the constitution of 1995, the legislative branch of the government or Parliament consists of two bodies, the Senate and the Majlis. The Majlis is roughly equivalent in function to the U.S. House of Representatives but is smaller, with only 77 members, whereas the Senate has 47 senators who serve six-year terms. Even in the Senate, the president exercises unusual powers; he has the authority to appoint seven of the senators directly. In theory, the Majlis has the authority to impeach the president, but because almost all the representatives in that body are from parties that support Nazarbayev and opposition parties are unable to gain much access to the major media in the country, the Majlis has rarely objected or challenged any of Nazarbayev's policies or programs.

Since the mid-1990s there has been an erosion of human rights and civil society in Kazakhstan, as the Nazarbayev administration has slipped further toward authoritarianism. In the early years of independence, there was a lively opposition press that on occasion even dared to challenge Nazarbayev publicly, but restrictions on the media have become increasingly heavy in recent years (George 2001; Katsiev 1999). Opposition parties have been mostly excluded from the political process, although they are tolerated more so than in neighboring Uzbekistan. The 1993 and 1995 constitutions allowed Nazarbayev to construct a political environment where he controlled virtually all aspects of power. In 1999, President Nazarbayev was reelected with 82 percent of the vote in an election that many observers believe was severely flawed and corrupt. Although authoritarian rule is efficient and predictable when compared with democracy, Nazarbayev's failure to establish solid democratic institutions and traditions has perhaps set the stage for political chaos, once time or circumstances force him to exit the political arena.

RELIGION AND SOCIETY

The majority of residents of Kazakhstan follow one of the two major faiths found there: Christianity or Islam. Most of the Christians adhere to the Russian Orthodox Church or some other variant of Orthodox Christianity, although there is a sizable minority of Roman Catholics (mostly Poles), Baptists, and other Christian sects scattered across the country. Religious affiliation and ethnicity are clearly linked in Kazakh society, as most of those who are Orthodox are Russian or Slavic, whereas the majority who are Muslim are Kazakh, Uzbek, Uighur, or other historically Islamic groups. The various Orthodox churches emerged from the church of the Byzantine Empire, evolving distinct structures of governance in several eastern European countries, as well as in Russia and Ukraine (Ware 1991), and it was not until the nineteenth century that significant numbers of Orthodox believers appeared in Kazakhstan. Since Kazakhstan gained independence, many evangelical Christian groups have been active in the country, attracting new followers from both the Orthodox Christian and Muslim peoples.

Islam was the last of the three great monotheistic traditions to arise in the Middle East, having been preceded by Judaism and Christianity. Around A.D. 610, an Arabic merchant working in the caravan trade named Muhammad began receiving visitations from the archangel Jibril (Gabriel in the Christian tradition), who brought to him the direct message of God. Muhammad became recognized by many around him as the messenger of God, and from these nightly communications the faith of Islam emerged in the southern Arabian peninsula. Eventually, the messages that God revealed to Muhammad were recorded in the book of scripture, the Koran. In slightly over a century, Islam would spread across the Middle East to North Africa, southern Spain, and into Asia Minor.

During his lifetime, Muhammad identified five actions in which all Muslims must engage, some requiring daily activity and some observed only once a year or in a lifetime. These are often referred to as the Five Pillars of Islam, and although many sects have emerged over the centuries, all Muslims have these five behaviors in common. The first pillar is the profession of faith, which in English is "There is but one God, Allah, and Muhammad is his prophet." Stated with sincerity and passion, this is all that is required for one to become a Muslim, and this profession of faith will be repeated by most Muslims many times over during their lives. The second pillar calls for daily prayers, conducted five times a day and recited while facing Islam's holiest city, Mecca.

The final three pillars are observed more infrequently but nevertheless are essential to being a devout Muslim. All Muslims are expected to be generous toward those less fortunate, and the third pillar of Islam requires that Muslims contribute a portion of their income to the poor, usually by giving to a local mosque that then distributes the money to those in need. Ramadan, the month-long fast, is the fourth pillar. During Ramadan, all true Muslims are expected to avoid food, beverages, and sexual activity between dawn and sunset. Ramadan is observed during the ninth month of the Islamic lunar calendar and so does not occur at the same time of year in relation to the Gregorian calendar. The fifth pillar is the pil-

Built by Amir Timur, the mausoleum of Sheik Ahmed Yassavi in Turkestan stands as one of the great Islamic monuments of Central Asia. Many Muslims consider it a site of pilgrimage, and one of the holiest places in Kazakhstan. (Photo courtesy of Reuel Hanks)

grimage to the holy city of Mecca, or the *hajj* in Arabic. The hajj transpires during the twelfth month of the Islamic calendar, and every Muslim must make this journey at least once during his or her lifetime, as long as he or she is in good health and can afford to do so.

Islam took hold in Central Asia in the eighth century, when Muslim forces advanced from eastern Persia into the valleys of the Amu Darya and Syr Darya rivers. The Muslims aggressively promoted their new faith among the people they found in Central Asia living in urban settlements, who at the time followed a diverse spectrum of religions: Zoroastrianism, Manichaeism, Buddhism, Judaism, and Nestorian Christianity. These faiths were displaced by Islam over the next century or so, and Islam became firmly entrenched as the major belief system in the Silk Road cities of Central Asia. Over the centuries numerous invaders came to Central Asia, and many were converted to Islam by those they conquered. Islam took much longer to penetrate the societies of the nonsedentary peoples of the region, however, who moved across the great grasslands with their livestock.

The nomadic Turkic ancestors of the modern Kazakhs followed a worldview that some Kazakh scholars refer to as *Tengrism*. Tengri was a powerful deity connected with the sky, and the religion was a complex mixture of ancestor and nature worship along with shamanism, all influenced by Buddhism. Tengrism was common to many Turkic and Mongol peoples of Inner Asia, who encountered the forces of nature on a daily basis and whose survival depended on the number and viability of their animals. Islam seeped into this society relatively slowly, and much of the old system of belief was retained and integrated with Islamic practice, resulting in what some have characterized as "folk Islam." The great mass of Central Asians, both urbanized and nomadic, have followed the Sunni tradition since the arrival of Islam in Central Asia, and among the nomads of Central Asia, Shia Islam never gained a following.

The activity of Sufi adepts was important in the gradual conversion of the Kazakhs and other nomadic peoples, and oddly enough, so were the policies of tsarist Russia. Sufism is frequently referred to as Islamic mysticism, and over the centuries a number of *tariqa*, or Sufi brotherhoods, developed. Sufis seek an intensely devotional, individualized relationship with God and carried their message to the tribes roaming the steppes of Central Asia. Ahmad Yassavi, whose magnificent tomb is located in the southern Kazakh city of Turkestan, founded an influential tariqa in the twelfth century. Despite the efforts of Sufi missionaries, as late as the eighteenth century, many Kazakhs remained only marginally connected to Islam, when Catherine the Great, empress of Russia, directed Muslim Tatars to convert more of the Kazakh population. Catherine believed that Islam would work as a "civilizing force" on the Kazakhs, meaning that they would become more loyal allies to Russia, but it is doubtful this policy achieved its goal (Olcott 1995, 46–47).

Islam did gain greater credence among the Kazakh hordes during the eighteenth and nineteenth centuries, but nevertheless the faith did not manifest itself in rigid, doctrinal observance. Rather, most Kazakhs melded the precepts of Islam with those to which they already held, resulting in the folk Islam mentioned earlier. For example, the use of the veil among Kazakh women was never widespread and in fact appears to have been relatively rare, whereas among the Uzbeks and Tajiks living in the oasis cities to the south, the veil was required of Muslim women appearing in public until the twentieth century. *Baksy,* or shamans, remained a part of Kazakh culture, and their powers of spirituality and healing became partially identified with Islamic fealty and devotion.

The establishment of Marxism-Leninism as a state ideology under the Soviet regime wrought enormous changes to the religious culture of Central Asia. Karl Marx's famous dictum that "religion is the opiate of the masses" in a capitalist society meant that under Communism, religious belief was superfluous. When religious dedication did not fade quickly, the Soviet regime took steps to ensure the fulfillment of Marx's predictions, confiscating religious property; closing churches, mosques, and synagogues; imprisoning religious leaders; and limiting access to religious education and literature. All faiths suffered repression under the Soviets, but efforts to eliminate Islam were especially forceful, as Muslim traditions were viewed as feudal and backward. During certain periods, circumstances forced the Soviet authorities to seek accommodation with religious believers, as when Germany attacked the USSR in 1941. Facing a powerful and ruthless invader, the Stalinist government garnered the support of Muslims by creating four spiritual boards in the country's Islamic regions. Every board was controlled by an Islamic official, a mufti, each of whom became the representative of "official Islam" in the Soviet Union. There were only occasional lulls in the repressive stance toward believers, and the goal of destroying religion in the USSR remained until the late 1980s.

The majority of Kazakhs today recognize that Islam is a part of their heritage and identity, and since Kazakhstan's independence, there has been an effort to reinstate Islam in Kazakh culture. New mosques have been constructed, and many people are attempting to become reacquainted with the teaching and requirements of the faith. Some regions are more devout, especially in the south, where the Uzbek population is concentrated, but by and large Kazakhs avoid rigid, absolutist interpretations of Islam, leading some to label them the "least Islamic" of Central Asia's main indigenous groups. More fundamentalist variants of Islam fail to resonate with most Kazakhs for a number of reasons: the relatively late conversion to Islam, compared with most other Central Asians; the retention of much of their previous religious identity in the form of shamanism and animistic beliefs; and the absorption of many Russian cultural norms, including the occasional consumption of prodigious amounts of alcohol, as well as eating pork.

The actions of the Nazarbayev administration even before independence highlight the unique attitude toward Islam. In 1990, a year before Kazakhstan became independent, the administration created a Muslim spiritual board exclusively for Kazakhstan, rejecting the authority of the mufti in Tashkent and reinforcing the division between the Kazakhs and the more pious Muslims of Uzbekistan and Tajikistan. In addition, the Kazakh constitutions written in 1993 and 1995 are the only such documents among the Central Asian states that do not recognize a unique role for Islam in Kazakh society (Olcott 1995, 276). Religious political parties have not been allowed to participate in the country's elections or to legally register, and although Nazarbayev approved the establishment of an Islamic university, he has been careful to stress repeatedly in his public statements that Kazakhstan is a secular country (Altoma 1994, 176).

Unlike Uzbekistan, Tajikistan, or Kyrgyzstan, Kazakhstan has experienced little violence at the hands of Muslim extremists since independence. Radical Islamist calls to action have failed to find much reception among young Kazakhs, although some claim that Hizb-ut-Tahrir (HT), a radical, anti-Western organization headquartered in London, is gaining in popularity in parts of Kazakhstan. Although the positions and rhetoric are certainly extreme, the group has not been conclusively linked to any specific act of violence in Central Asia, and in fact HT proclaims its commitment to change via nonviolent means. The central goal of HT is the resurrection of the Islamic caliphate and the unification of the Muslim world. Given the Kazakhs' marginal historical connection to the realm of Islam, it is difficult to envision HT gaining much traction as a mass movement among young people there. It seems more likely that the Kazakh people will continue along the path they have followed since the late 1980s—a rediscovery and reaffirmation of their Islamic identity marked by moderation and tolerance. Indeed, given Kazakhstan's ethnic composition, such a path appears to be the only way to ensure continued peace and stability.

EDUCATION

Before the twentieth century, education in Kazakhstan in even the most basic form was available only to a small segment of society, mostly ethnic Slavs living in the region's cities. The small percentage of Kazakhs who received an education were almost exclusively male, and the learning provided was religiously based. The Soviet educational system established in the 1920s, although ideologically biased in favor of Marxism-Leninism, provided universal education for both genders for the first time in the region's history, resulting in a spectacular rise in literacy rates in only a generation.

Since 1991, the educational system in Kazakhstan has attempted reform from the primary to postsecondary levels, but many challenges persist in the areas of funding, curriculum restructuring, the production of textbooks and other materials, and improving and expanding facilities.

Educational System

The Soviet system of education was heavily influenced by Marxist ideology, and independent Kazakhstan has struggled to reform most aspects of education since 1991. Textbooks in many instances are outdated, teachers are poorly trained or are not fluent in Kazakh, which now is displacing Russian as the main language of instruction, and students often do not have access to the technology they require to be completely educated in the twenty-first century. For example, few schools in rural areas are equipped with computers, and even fewer provide access to the Internet, although the Kazakh government has initiated programs to increase computer education. Many times the schools themselves are poorly maintained—broken windows, crumbling masonry, and worn-out furniture are commonplace in many schools. The Ministry of Education is the government agency responsible for educational standards and for funding the system from the primary level to university. In 1999, after eight years of independence, the Kazakh parliament passed the Law on Education, which established standards for the country.

Standards of classroom etiquette have been carried over from the Soviet system at all levels of education, and emphasis is placed on respect for the teacher and administrators. It is customary for all students to stand immediately when the teacher enters the classroom; students are taught this procedure from the primary grades on. Problems with student discipline are much less common than in U.S. schools, as a student who openly disobeys or disrespects an instructor is considered to bring shame on the entire class, and peer pres-

Schoolteacher holding puppet, Astana. (Liba Taylor/Corbis)

sure against such misconduct is considerable. Greater emphasis on group learning and cooperation is also more common than in the U.S. system, and the same group of students typically remains together throughout the entire span of their primary and secondary schooling years.

The typical student in Kazakhstan starts his or her education at age six and continues to age seventeen or eighteen. Slightly more than 3 million students are enrolled in primary and secondary grades, with the great majority of schools located in the countryside. Both primary and secondary education is compulsory by Kazakh law, and almost 100 percent of those children of eligible age for primary education are enrolled (United Nations Development Program 2004, 34). Instruction is offered mostly in Kazakh and Russian, although there are schools teaching in Uzbek, Uighur, Tajik, and several other languages. During the last decade, Kazakh administrators have attempted to shift curricula from an emphasis on scientific and technical subjects favored under the former system to a more balanced program of coursework including subjects in the humanities and social sciences. Besides the public schools, there are a limited number of private schools, but tuition costs at these institutions are typically too expensive for most families, although the quality of education they provide is generally held to be greater than that of the public system.

The nature and structure of higher education in Kazakhstan has undergone a substantial overhaul since the collapse of Soviet authority. As was the case at lower levels of the system, the curriculum at postsecondary institutions was heavily tilted toward technical subjects. The humanities and social sciences were deeply invested in the state ideology of Marxism-Leninism, and all teaching and scholarship in these disciplines was presented in the context of this philosophy. Since independence, the presentation of history, especially that of the Kazakh people, along with political science, sociology, and other related subjects, has witnessed a complete revision, although a shortage of new textbooks and teaching materials greatly hindered this process until the late 1990s. Before 1991, there were no programs in Kazakhstan devoted to business and public administration, and entirely new curricula featuring courses in accounting, management, and marketing have been developed at numerous institutions. In some cases, schools or colleges of business have been established. In total, 170 institutions of higher learning exist in Kazakhstan, ranging from comprehensive universities to vocational schools. The majority of these are privately owned and administered, and many have been founded in the last fifteen years.

Much has been accomplished in the educational sphere in Kazakhstan since the country's independence, but many serious problems remain. A disturbing trend through the 1990s was the steady erosion of state funding for education. The percentage of the government budget devoted to education declined by more than half in the first five years of independence and remained at an all-time low as of 2001. Moreover, the preschool system essentially collapsed in the 1990s. This was primarily because, prior to independence, most kindergartens in the USSR were provided by large, state-run farms and factories, and difficult economic times in the early 1990s forced the closure of more than 80 percent of the country's kindergartens. In 2003, only 18 percent of the country's preschoolers were attending kindergartens, although this figure had improved from the late 1990s, and one year of preschool is now compulsory by law (United Nations 2004). Teachers' salaries remain low, and a chronic shortage of textbooks, supplies, and teaching materials besets schools in many parts of the country, but especially in the countryside. The improvements in the Kazakh economy since 2000 may lead to increases in funding and better facilities, but more attention must be directed to the shortcomings in rural areas, where the majority of the country's children live.

Literacy

The Soviet system was devastating to the people of Central Asia in a number of ways, but there is no argument that one of the great achievements of Soviet administration was a phenomenal increase in literacy among all groups. In 1915, on the eve of the Bolshevik Revolution, literacy rates in more than half of the Russian-administered regions failed to reach even 5 percent and barely exceeded 10 percent in those areas that held a large Slavic population; by 1959 more than 50 percent of all the major indigenous groups in the region were literate (see tables in Allworth 1989). Literacy continued to increase through the succeeding decades so that by the time of the collapse of the Soviet state in 1991, the ability to read was nearly universal, although much of the Kazakh population was literate in Russian, but not in Kazakh.

The Kazakh government reports a literacy rate of nearly

100 percent, but disruptions and imbalances in the educational framework since independence may reduce this figure somewhat, at least temporarily. Many smaller settlements in the countryside lack primary schools, and this shortcoming will be difficult to rectify as the proportion of the state budget devoted to education continues to shrink. The high literacy rate of its population is one of Kazakhstan's great economic and social advantages, and the financial support must be found to protect this achievement.

Religious Education

Religious education in Kazakhstan is less commonplace than in Uzbekistan or Tajikistan because of the historically weaker foundation of Islam and the broader secularization of Kazakh society. Under the Soviet regime, some Kazakhs studied in the two officially approved Islamic seminaries, or *medressehs*, in Uzbekistan, but in 1990 the government in Kazakhstan withdrew from the Islamic religious board headquartered in Tashkent and established a separate administrative structure exclusively for Muslims in Kazakhstan. Although this move granted Islamic believers in Kazakhstan greater autonomy, it also meant that complementary religious training centers were necessary for the education of Kazakh scholars.

Already by 1991, a medresseh had been opened in Kazakhstan, housing sixty students; by the late 1990s, the Islamic University of Kazakhstan was functioning, training new Islamic scholars using a four-year program of coursework. Some students have been allowed to attend medressehs and other Islamic educational institutions abroad in the Middle East and southeast Asia, and some Islamic organizations from outside Kazakhstan have been permitted to set up shop in Kazakhstan. An example are the Turkish lyceums, which are privately sponsored schools inspired by the teachings of Said Nursi, a Turkish philosopher and educator. These institutions provide courses in Islamic studies and some secular training as well, but the total number of students attending these schools in Kazakhstan is relatively small.

CONCLUSION

The road to constructing a civil society in Kazakhstan has proven to be bumpy and winding, as the country works to reform its social, political, and economic systems. The Nazarbayev administration is certainly less authoritarian than some neighboring regimes, yet some of its characteristics are troubling. Since leading the country to independence, Nursultan Nazarbayev has maneuvered to concentrate much of the government's power in his hands, becoming increasingly dictatorial and authoritarian. Widespread corruption and nepotism, intimidation of independent media, and harassment of political opponents have all combined to undermine the public's faith in the government and led to cynicism regarding the "democratization" of the political system. If the country's vast wealth is to benefit the majority of its people, greater progress must be achieved toward creating an open and democratic society.

References

Allworth, Edward. 1989. "The Changing Intellectual and Literary Community." In *Central Asia: 120 Years of Russian Rule.* Durham, NC: Duke University Press.

Altoma, Reef. 1994. "The Influence of Islam in Post-Soviet Kazakhstan." In *Central Asia in Historical Perspective,* edited by Beatrice F. Manz. Boulder, CO: Westview Press.

Dmytryshyn, Basil. 1984. *USSR: A Concise History.* 4th ed. New York: Scribner.

George, Alexandra. 2001. *Journey into Kazakhstan: The True Face of the Nazarbayev Regime.* New York: University Press of America.

Katsiev, Oleg. 1999. "Prospects for Development of an Independent Media in Kazakhstan." In *Civil Society in Central Asia,* edited by M. Holt Ruffin and Daniel Waugh. Seattle: University of Washington Press.

Nowicki, Marvin. 1997. "Local Government Reform in Kazakhstan." *Journal of Central Asian Studies* 1(2), pp. 21–34.

Olcott, Martha Brill. 1995. *The Kazakhs.* 2d ed. Stanford, CA: Hoover Institution Press.

———. 2002. *Kazakhstan: Unfulfilled Promise.* Washington, DC: Carnegie Endowment for International Peace.

Surucu, Cengiz. 2002. "Modernity, Nationalism, Resistance: Identity Politics in Post-Soviet Kazakhstan." *Central Asia Survey* 21(4), pp. 385–402.

UNDP Kazakhstan. 2004. *Poverty in Kazakhstan: Causes and Cures.* No. UNDPKAZ 08.

United Nations. 2004, January 1. *Kazakhstan: Achievements, Issues and Prospects (A Perspective by the United Nations).* Available at http://www.undp.kz/library_of_publications. Accessed January 25, 2005.

Ware, Timothy. 1991. *The Orthodox Church.* London: Penguin Books.

Kazakh Society and Contemporary Issues

The steppe nomads of Central Asia are famous for their epic poetry, and the Kazakhs are no exception. Among the Kazakhs, Koblandy is a legendary hero who achieves greatness because he remains true to his traditions and ancestors. Koblandy represents a fitting ideal for today's Kazakhs, who find themselves in a time of trial and transition, and who must hold fast to their traditions while stepping boldly into the globalized world of the twenty-first century. Koblandy's battles and adventures to establish his identity and position in the turbulent society of the steppe nomads parallel the struggle of modern Kazakh society to find a bridge between the past and the future. The transition from Marxist-Leninist principles to those emphasizing freedom, capitalism, and individuality is not complete, but considerable progress has been made in only fifteen years of independence.

As in all multiethnic states, tensions exist between groups, and these stresses are frequently magnified during times of social change. This is the case in Kazakhstan, where members of the country's largest minority, the Russians, now find themselves living in an alien culture. Only fifteen years ago, it was the Russians who represented the dominant culture in Kazakhstan, and the loss of status and influence has increased friction between them and the Kazakhs, who have seized the opportunity presented by independence to create a Kazakh state.

Accompanying the ethnic divisions are daunting economic challenges, issues connected to political transition and building a civil society, and increases in crime, suicide, drug and alcohol abuse, and other wrinkles in the social fabric.

The path to a harmonious, stable social order has proven to be neither easy nor clear, yet a measure of progress has been achieved, illustrated by the fact that Kazakhstan has not suffered an outbreak of tragic ethnic violence like those seen in Uzbekistan in 1989 or Kyrgyzstan in 1990.

Like all societies, Kazakh society experiences constant evolution and transition, but these processes in Kazakhstan are occurring at multiple scales and dimensions. At one level is the shift to the consumerism, choice, and glitz of modern capitalist society from the drab, monotonous conformity of Soviet life. The current generation of young people encounter a radically different culture than even their older brothers and sisters experienced in the waning years of the USSR, as the information revolution and global connectivity penetrate Kazakh society. Listening to foreign music, watching foreign movies, and dressing in foreign clothing were all considered antisocial behavior not so long ago, but in today's Kazakhstan, these are routine activities for youth. Superimposed on these changes is the effort among many to rediscover the past and to use that rediscovery as a pathway to the future. The purpose of the discussion that follows is to frame, discuss, and detail some of the multidimensional patterns of transition in Kazakh society.

ETHNICITY AND SOCIAL SYSTEM
Ethnic Groups

Kazakhstan, like the other Central Asian states, is a multiethnic country holding nearly 100 different groups. Nevertheless, the ethnic geography of Kazakhstan in Central Asia is unique. Whereas in the remaining four states in Central Asia, the titular ethnic group has held a majority for decades, the Kazakhs only recently obtained majority status in Kazakhstan. The census of 1999 in Kazakhstan indicated that for the first time since the 1920s, Kazakhs accounted for more than 50

A group of university students in Almaty. The ethnic diversity of Kazakhstan society is evident even in this small class, which features students who are Kazakh, Russian, and Armenian. (Photo courtesy of Reuel Hanks)

percent of the population—precisely 53.4 percent (Rowland 2001, 579). This fact alone highlights two important aspects of the country's ethnic composition: Kazakhstan is and has been for two centuries a multiethnic territory; and the ethnic contours of the country are undergoing rapid change, particularly since Kazakhstan's independence. This change carries considerable implication for Kazakhstan's political and economic development, social stability, and relations with its powerful neighbor, Russia.

The Kazakhs are the most Russified indigenous people in Central Asia, in the sense that during the Soviet era most Kazakhs abandoned their native language for Russian. Both Kazakh and Russian are official languages, but only around 40 percent of the ethnic Kazakh population actually speaks Kazakh. Kazakh is a Turkic language related to the other Turkic tongues of the region and is most closely related to Kyrgyz and Karakalpak, all of which contain linguistic elements from Mongolian. There are three main dialects of Kazakh that correspond roughly to the three hordes (see the following discussion), but all are similar in structure and vocabulary. Kazakh has used several scripts over the last century. When a written form was first developed for Kazakh in the mid-1800s, the Arabic script was used, but under the Soviet regime the script was changed first to the Latin alphabet, and then in the 1940s to the Cyrillic alphabet.

The Kazakhs are divided into clans and tribes, and these join to form the three great hordes (Russia: *orda;* Kazakh: *juz*) that composed traditional nomadic society. The hordes are the Lesser, Middle, and Great, each of which controlled a distinct geographic area of the steppe. The Lesser juz occupied the steppe regions to the east and northeast of the Caspian Sea and was the first group to fall under the colonial control of the Russian Empire. The Middle horde ranged across what is today northern and central Kazakhstan, and the Great horde's lands were in the southeastern part of the country. A typical Kazakh will know his clan, tribal, and horde affiliation and usually will be aware of his *jeti ata,* or seven ancestors, meaning that he is expected to know the names of his ancestors back seven generations.

Kazakhs have abandoned their traditional attire more than most other Central Asian peoples, adopting Russian and European garments and styles. Most Kazakh men will wear a fur hat during the cold winters, with a heavy overcoat and knee-length boots. Winter clothing for both men and women is usually trimmed or lined with fur, to add to its warmth. Outside the larger cities one may still encounter men wearing a heavy quilted *chapan* during the coldest months, a woolen robe that is tied at the waist with a sash. Some chapans are worn only for ceremonial occasions and are beautifully embroidered with designs in gold or silver thread. Women's traditional dress consists of a decorative sleeveless vest, paired with a *beldemshe,* a skirt fastened with a broad belt. Women often wear a shawl or scarf over their hair, tied in a variety of fashions. A bride traditionally wears a *soukele,* a brightly colored conical headdress with a fringe and flaps that extend to her shoulders.

Russian (the largest minority group in Kazakhstan) and other Slavic settlers arrived on the Kazakh steppes in a succession of waves, beginning in the nineteenth century. By the dawn of the Bolshevik revolution, 1.5 million Russian settlers had reached Kazakhstan, accounting for more than 40 percent of the region's population. This massive migration generated cultural and economic conflict with the indigenous Kazakhs, whose nomadic lifestyle was undermined by the huge influx of Russian farmers. A second large migration occurred in the 1950s, under the Virgin Lands Program (see the previous chapter, Geography and History of Kazakhstan). The Russian population is concentrated in the northern oblasts (provinces) of the country and is more urbanized than the Kazakhs. Few Russians learned the Kazakh language during the Soviet period, and since independence a large percentage of the Russian population, along with other Slavs (Ukrainians and Belorussians), have departed Kazakhstan. Russians now make up 30 percent of Kazakhstan's population, a figure that is certain to decline over the next decade. Those leaving give various reasons for emigrating. A combination of economic factors, along with feelings of alienation due to the emphasis on recovering the Kazakh language and culture, likely play a central role in driving Russian out-migration.

Numerous smaller ethnic minorities are present in Kazakhstan, part of the legacy of the Russian and Soviet eras, when many peoples were invited or deported to the region. Since the 1970s, large numbers of the German community have left, but according to the 1999 census, more than 350,000 remain. Many Germans migrated from the lower Volga region in Russia to Kazakhstan during the nineteenth century, and others were deported by Stalin during World War II. Most of the German population lives in northern Kazakhstan. The Germans suffered a huge loss of numbers during the 1990s, with the total population falling from almost 950,000 to only about 350,000. Most of this decline was due to high rates of emigration to Germany, Russia, and other countries.

The Uzbeks, at 370,000, are slightly more numerous than the Germans now in Kazakhstan, and their numbers have been increasing due to fairly high birthrates and a relatively low rate of emigration. The Uzbeks are concentrated in southern Kazakhstan, near the border with Uzbekistan, especially in the cities of Chimkent, Taraz (Zhambyl), and Turkestan. Like the Kazakhs, they are Muslims whose native language belongs to the Turkic family. The Uzbek language is quite distinct from Kazakh, however, in that there is less Mongolian influence and far more borrowing from Persian (Tajik). Uzbek men are distinguished by their skullcap, or *doppa,* and the Uzbeks tend to hold more strongly to Islamic tradition and observance.

In the 1920s, the Soviet administration encouraged the migration of Korean families from eastern Siberia to Central Asia to develop rice farming in the region. A decade later, these migrants were joined by large numbers of Koreans exiled from Siberia because of Josef Stalin's fear that the Korean community there was in league with the Japanese government, and therefore a threat to Soviet security. The Koreans in Kazakhstan today number about 100,000 and are not only farmers but professionals and businessmen as well. Despite suppression of their culture during the Soviet era, the Koreans have retained their language and customs. Unlike the Slavs and Germans, Kazakhstan's Koreans are not leaving in sizable numbers, and their connections to South Korea have facilitated investment from that country into Kazakhstan (George 2001, 155).

Social System

The social structure in Kazakhstan differs significantly between ethnic groups and between rural and urban settings.

Kazakh elders pray before a Navruz celebration meal. Navruz, the ancient holiday of vernal equinox, or the first day of spring, is widely celebrated across Central Asia. (Shamil Zhumatov/Reuters/Corbis)

The discussion here focuses on the Kazakhs because they compose the majority of the population, and Kazakh culture is acquiring a dominant role in the country. The majority of Kazakhs live in rural areas, in small villages, or *auls.* As previously described, family, clan, and tribal connections remain important in Kazakh society. The nuclear and extended families remain the basic units of Kazakh society. In both, respect for elders is emphasized, and the advice of elders is sought by younger members of the family when making important decisions. At the family dinner table, the eldest person is accorded the tradition of *batas,* or the responsibility to lead the conversation. Respect for those older or in higher social position extends to society at large—to be disrespectful to such people is considered to be bad behavior indeed.

Kinship ties play an important role in the lives of Kazakhs, as with other Central Asian peoples. These connections, built by marriages and blood relationships, provide a network of social and financial support. Such networks are complex, because the array of relatives is usually broad—the kin of one's father, mother, and spouse may all be recruited for assistance at various times. Such assistance may take the form of a financial loan or some other favor, such as securing a job or a place in the university. These traditions of kinship assistance reach far back into Kazakh society and are called *sybaga.*

For example, according to sybaga tradition, when poorer relations visited a more prosperous family, the wealthier family was expected to slaughter a sheep and prepare a feast to honor their guests and even to present them with a gift of livestock, if necessary. Of course, in Kazakhstan today, social ties constructed through friendship and business connections are important as well.

The fabric of Kazakh society is maintained by observance of the basic rituals and ceremonies of life. One of the most vital and vibrant of these rituals is the wedding ceremony and the subsequent marriage. Marriage reinforces the importance of the family in Kazakh life and extends kinship ties. In traditional nomadic life, marriages were arranged by the parents of the bride and groom, sometimes well before either reached adolescence, although the actual wedding might not take place until years later. In general young people married early in life, and girls in particular might be married while still in their early teens. Today, the minimum legal age for marriage is eighteen, and arranged marriages are less common, but marriage still follows an ageold pattern. The prospective groom's father must meet with the father of the prospective bride and agree to a bride price, which is traditionally paid in livestock. If the young woman agrees to the marriage, the groom's father awards her jewelry and a cluster of owl feathers, a symbol that the union is approved by all parties. The wedding ceremony will take place in the following months and is likely to be a huge affair—all the relatives and friends of both families are expected to attend, and a gathering of several hundred guests is considered a modest wedding by Kazakh standards.

WOMEN'S STATUS IN SOCIETY

Kazakhstan is considered a Muslim country by many, but this label masks important cultural differences between Kazakh society and most of the Islamic world. In particular, the role and status of women differs between women in Kazakhstan and those from other Muslim countries, due to the relatively late historical conversion of the nomadic Kazakhs, the almost total absence of dogmatic traditions among them, and the strong influence of Russian cultural attitudes and practices. Wearing the veil was a convention never widely adopted among Kazakh women, and Soviet-era emphasis on equality for women in society further weakened traditional restrictions on women's role in society. It is commonplace for women of all ethnicities in Kazakhstan to work outside the home, pursue a higher education, own their own businesses, and be active in politics, although they are not represented proportionally in the government relative to their numbers in the population, nor are there many women in higher positions of authority.

One must be careful not to overgeneralize about the position of women in Kazakh society, however, because significant differences exist between women based on ethnicity, geographic location, and other characteristics. As is true in other developing countries, women in the cities tend to have many more opportunities for social enrichment and economic advancement than women living in the countryside, and they almost always enjoy a higher standard of living as well. This is especially the case for Russian women, who are much more urbanized than Kazakh women and who tend to pursue advanced educational opportunities at higher rates than Kazakh, Uzbek, or other traditionally "Muslim" women. There are few social restrictions on women of any group, how-

Woman worker operating a forklift, moving copper sheets at a factory in Ust-Kamengorsk. (Time Life Pictures/Getty Images)

ever, and women may venture forth without the restrictions on their mobility found in more conservative Muslim countries. The nontraditional status of women is highlighted by the somewhat ironic goal, articulated by the Kazakh regime in the 1990s, of encouraging women to stay at home and raise children in an effort to increase the country's birthrate.

The standing of women living in Kazakhstan's rural areas is much more difficult than that for urbanized women. First, employment opportunities are fewer in the countryside, and the jobs available tend to be low paying and require hard physical labor. Second, rates of unemployment are higher in the rural districts, and in the southern regions of the country women may make up close to 80 percent of the unemployed (International Women's Rights Watch 2000). The dire economic situation for some women has resulted in an increase in prostitution within the country (Nazpary 2002), and many young women have fallen victim to international traffickers who lure them abroad and force them into jobs as sex workers. Family responsibilities are typically greater for rural women as well, as average family size is considerably larger in the countryside, and health care is more difficult to obtain and of lower quality than in the cities. A serious and troublesome problem affecting women at all levels of society is domestic violence, an issue compounded by economic conditions and high rates of alcohol abuse among men. Some experts suggest that up to 60 percent of all women in Kazakhstan suffer at least one incident of domestic violence in their lifetimes (Shokamanov 2000). Alarmingly, suicide rates are high among women in Kazakhstan (Buckley 1997), another indication of the economic and social difficulties they face.

The differences in dress, mannerisms, and social behavior between women of varying ethnic groups is not as noticeable in Kazakhstan as in most other Central Asian countries because of the influence of Russian and European standards and mores. In the northern reaches of the country, where the Russian and German minorities are concentrated, the latest available (and affordable) fashions will be sported by women of all ages, whereas in the more conservative south and west, a more traditional lifestyle is the rule. Regardless of ethnic or religious affiliation, women in Kazakhstan must struggle to overcome the economic hardships that have plagued their country since independence—problems that have affected women disproportionately. These challenges must be met if Kazakhstan is to have a successful future.

RECREATION AND POPULAR CULTURE

Popular culture has fundamentally changed in Kazakhstan during the last twenty years. Until the late 1980s, most Western music, literature, film, and dress were all considered bad influences on Soviet youth, with only a few exceptions. Procuring these taboo items was difficult and expensive because their importation into the USSR was forbidden, and thus they could be had only via the black market or by trading with foreign visitors. For the most part, youth in the former Soviet Union experienced a kind of cultural blockade, isolating them to some degree from the remainder of the world.

In the last years of the USSR, these restrictions were eased somewhat, and with the complete demise of the Soviet system, a virtual flood of Western popular culture poured into the post-Soviet states. The Internet, videos, compact discs, DVDs, and other recent developments in media have assisted in the absorption of American and other foreign influences by young people in Kazakhstan. Dozens of street corner kiosks in Almaty alone offer foreign films and music, and Internet cafes allow access to the same via computer. Many people now own satellite dishes, which enable them to access television broadcasts from around the world, and foreign television serials, usually dubbed into Russian and broadcast via local airwaves, have become popular. At the same time, older forms of entertainment are also gaining popularity, especially among ethnic Kazakhs who view traditional music and sports as an important part of their heritage. The following section discusses some aspects of both traditional and modern recreation and entertainment in Kazakhstan.

Traditional Music

Music has been a central part of Kazakh life for thousands of years. Improvised songs, or *kui,* were performed by most Kazakhs at virtually any festival or rite, including funerals. The *akyn* was a traveling minstrel who had memorized hundreds of heroic songs, epic poems, and legendary tales and also improvised on these works. The *akyn* typically played at social gatherings and was highly respected. Another type of singer, the *jirshi,* used less improvisation and specialized in epics dealing with military prowess, serving as an oral historian for the Kazakh people in the centuries before they possessed a written language. Folk songs and epics played an integral part in the formation of a Kazakh identity in the nineteenth century, when a series of influential writers emerged among the Kazakhs, culminating in Abai, considered by most to be the founder of the Kazakh literary tradition. Abai's poems are known to all Kazakhs and are still sung at family gatherings and celebrations.

Dozens of traditional musical instruments were developed by the nomadic Kazakhs, another indication of the importance of musical expression in their culture. The trademark instrument of the Kazakh bards is the *dombra,* a two-stringed instrument that is both plucked and strummed. The dombra closely resembles the Kyrgyz *komuz,* and just as every Kyrgyz singer of epics is expected to master that instrument, so too is every Kazakh akyn expected to be proficient on the dombra. The *kobyz* is also an ancient instrument of the steppe that somewhat resembles a violin but typically has only two or three strings. A common wind instrument is the *choor,* a small flute. These instruments are often played solo but may be featured in an ensemble or small orchestra and accompanied by percussion instruments such as kettle drums. The jaw's harp is popular with children and young women, and is found across the region.

Modern Music and Music Video

Since Mikhail Gorbachev's policy of glasnost (openness) was implemented in the late 1980s, the barriers that once prevented the recordings of popular Western musicians from reaching the public in the former USSR have collapsed. Since the early 1990s, the latest songs produced by a wide spectrum of American, European, and Asian artists have been available in music kiosks on the street corners and in the bazaars of every major city in Kazakhstan. Virtually every genre is offered: rock, pop, hip-hop, easy listening, oldies, and so on. Only country music from North America seems to be absent from the vendors' stalls. In addition, a range of homegrown popular musicians has sprung up, most of them mimicking Western performers, but some developing an interesting blend of influences from both contemporary and traditional Kazakh music. Representatives of the latter style are Urker, a male trio that is popular with both youth and older people, and Tolkyn Zabirova, a female soloist, who also produces an eclectic mix of traditional and modern melodies and rhythms. Nurlan and Murat are a male duo who specialize in Kazakh hip-hop and rap music, and fans of heavy metal can rock to the music of bands such as Requiem, Holy Dragons, or Inkarna.

Most of the indigenous modern musicians in Kazakhstan are producing music videos because this is an excellent way to promote their recordings. Some of these productions are equivalent in quality to Western videos, although on occasion the production quality is lacking in sophistication compared with similar videos made in the U.S. and Europe. Kazakh music videos are far less suggestive and controversial than many of their counterparts in the West; female performers typically do not dress or dance in a provocative manner, although these standards are changing as the influence of Russian and Western performers increases. Lyrics typically are much more restrained; themes such as love for the homeland or dedication to the family are common. On the other hand, Western music videos have a large following as well and are viewed on "HitTV" (available across much of Kazakhstan), via satellite television, or downloaded off the Internet. A number of American performers are popular among young people in Kazakhstan, including Eminem, Britney Spears, 50 Cent, and Jennifer Lopez.

Television and Film

The Kazakh film industry received a major boost during World War II, when entire production studios from Moscow and Leningrad were relocated to Almaty, mostly with the aim of making wartime propaganda films. It was during this hiatus that the great Russian director Sergei Eisenstein filmed his epic masterpiece *Ivan the Terrible* in Kazakhstan. Since independence, several film studios have emerged, with Kazakhfilm being the most prominent. Local directors have teamed with European and U.S. partners to produce critically acclaimed films, but imported movies from the United States and Europe are more popular than those produced in Kazakhstan. Yet another sign of globalization, actors such as Sylvester Stallone, Tom Cruise, and Hugh Grant are likely to be more familiar to audiences in Kazakhstan than many of the country's own performers.

Television in Kazakhstan is much more interesting today than during the Soviet era, when there was little entertainment programming. Most programs are offered in Russian, especially in the north, but broadcasts in the Kazakh language are increasing. Reality and game shows broadcast from Russia, including a Russian version of *Survivor,* are watched with great interest throughout the country. Sporting events, national music and cultural festivals, and news broadcasts are regularly featured. Foreign programs were rarely aired by the Soviet authorities, but since the early 1990s many movies and serials from abroad have gained a following in Kazakhstan, with soap operas from Latin America being especially popular. A sizable percentage of the public has access to satellite television and therefore may watch a wide range of programming from around the world.

Sports

Like their cousins the Kyrgyz, the Kazakhs are great fans of sporting contests on horseback. These include the game of *kokpar,* wherein two teams of riders compete for the possession of a goat carcass that must be carried to the opposing goal. Variations on kokpar are found among several Central Asian peoples, and it appears to be quite an old sport in

A rider playing kokpar, *a traditional sport among Kazakhs. He holds a carcass across his saddle, with the aim of carrying it to the opposing team's goal. (Howell Paul/Corbis Sygma)*

the region. Other matches on horseback include wrestling with an opponent with the intent to throw him from the saddle; races of varying length, with some reaching 30 or 40 miles; and feats of skill where small objects are plucked from the ground while riding at full gallop, all requiring great strength and command of one's mount. In addition to these organized contests, hunting with eagles from horseback is a time-honored tradition among the Kazakhs. The hunter is called a *berkutchy* in Kazakh, and the birds used in the hunt are large mountain eagles, which require great skill in their handling and training. The berkutchy is a living icon among the Kazakhs, respected as a symbol of the essence of "Kazakhness," much in the same way that the cowboy is viewed in American culture.

Modern sports are also popular with the people of Kazakhstan. The country's long winters and mountains in the south provide ample chance for devotees of skiing (both downhill and cross-country), ice-skating, hockey, and other winter-time leisure activities. The short summers offer opportunities for hiking, trekking, and swimming, especially in the country's mountains and national parks. Boxing, wrestling, and weightlifting are popular with young men, and Kazakhstan has produced several Olympic champions in these sports as well as in numerous track and field events. As is the case across Central Asia, soccer is a popular national pastime, and after independence, a professional soccer league was established in Kazakhstan, with matches sometimes broadcast on local or national television channels. For those less physically inclined, chess is widely played by people of all ages, and strolling in the parks and visiting friends and family are popular diversions for virtually everyone.

KAZAKHSTAN AND THE WORLD

Sharing a border with Russia that stretches for almost 2,000 miles and a boundary with China that reaches almost 1,000 miles in length, Kazakhstan stands between giants. Geographic position alone would grant this land of endless steppe and snow-capped peaks great significance, but there are additional factors that give the country profound international significance.

Substantial deposits of petroleum and natural gas in western Kazakhstan may make the country a major supplier of energy to the world market in the twenty-first century, if the means to transport the oil to energy consumers can be constructed. Kazakhstan therefore is of importance not only to the economies of Europe and North America, but also to expanding Asian economies that are increasingly short of energy supplies.

President Nazarbayev has pursued a leadership role for Kazakhstan in Central Asia and in the broader CIS (Commonwealth of Independent States). In the mid-1990s,

Kazakhstan, along with Uzbekistan and Russia, committed troops to Tajikistan in an effort to quell that country's civil war, and Nazarbayev was a staunch supporter of the CIS in the early 1990s. In addition, the Kazakh president has brought forth his own initiatives for regional cooperation, including a proposal for a "Eurasian union" that would have superseded the floundering CIS. Although that suggestion did not gain traction in the region, Kazakhstan has been in the forefront on new regional cooperative organizations, including the Shanghai Cooperation Organization (SCO), consisting of Russia, China, Kazakhstan, Uzbekistan, Kyrgyzstan, and Tajikistan. The SCO began in 1996 as the Shanghai Five, consisting of the present member states except for Uzbekistan. In 2001, Uzbekistan joined, and the group evolved into the SCO, an organization committed to resolving security issues. Kazakhstan is a member of several regional economic organizations, including the Central Asian Economic Community; the Economic Cooperation Organization (ECO), a larger union that includes the five former Soviet states in Central Asia, as well as Afghanistan, Azerbaijan, Turkey, Iran, and Pakistan; and the Eurasian Economic Community (EEC), formed in 2001 and composed of Russia, Belarus, Kazakhstan, Tajikistan, and Kyrgyzstan (Zhalimbetova and Gleason 2001).

Almost immediately after gaining independence Kazakhstan developed a special relationship with the United States. As noted earlier, Kazakhstan was the only former Soviet republic in Central Asia to possess nuclear weapons when the USSR disintegrated, a situation that generated great concern in Washington due to Kazakhstan's proximity to the Middle East and the country's Muslim character. In addition, Kazakhstan's potentially large hydrocarbon reserves had attracted the attention of Western oil companies even before the country's independence, and a considerable number of dollars had already flowed into developing the deposits just east of the Caspian Sea. In 1994, U.S. experts gathered and removed a cache of radioactive material from Kazakhstan that could have been used in building atomic weapons, with the Kazakh government's acquiescence, and the United States also helped Kazakhstan destroy its nuclear arsenal. Additional military cooperation has come in the form of joint military exercises between U.S. and Kazakh forces and training of Kazakh soldiers by U.S. experts. The burgeoning relationship between Kazakhstan and the United States was met with concern and dismay by Kazakhstan's powerful neighbors, Russia and China. Kazakh-Russian relations have been rather rocky since 1991, due to a number of issues. The treatment and status of the large Russian minority in northern Kazakhstan has led to considerable friction between Moscow and Almaty (Kazakhstan's capital before 1998), and the Kazakh administration's pursuit of the United States as an ally and benefactor alarmed the Russian government, which still considers the Central Asian region to lie within its sphere of political and military influence. Kazakhstan has sought to allay these concerns by forming strategic partnerships with both Russia and China, a strategy most prominently displayed in the formation of the SCO (discussed earlier). Kazakhstan leases the Baikonur space center in the central part of the country to Russia, and Russian troops continue to staff some small military installations in Kazakhstan. In its turn, China has emerged as an important trading partner, and the Chinese have shown strong interest in Kazakhstan's energy resources, although the infrastructure to move oil across the steppe to western China remains undeveloped. The Nazarbayev regime has proven adroit at playing its three powerful friends—Russia, China, and the United States—against one another, a strategy that has worked well thus far and will ensure that Kazakhstan remains a major player on the world stage.

References

Buckley, Cynthia. 1997. "Suicide in Post-Soviet Kazakhstan: The Role of Stress, Age and Gender." *Central Asian Survey* 6(1), pp. 45–52.

George, Alexandra. 2001. *Journey into Kazakhstan: The True Face of the Nazarbayev Regime.* Lanham, MD: University Press of America, 2001.

International Women's Rights Action Watch 2000, January 26. "Status of Women in Kazakhstan under Specific CEDAW Articles." Available at: http://iwraw.igc.org/publications/countries/kazakhstan.htm .Accessed December 15, 2004.

Nazpary, Joma. 2002. *Post-Soviet Chaos: Violence and Dispossession in Kazakhstan.* Sterling, VA: Pluto Press, 2002.

Olcott, Martha Brill. *Kazakhstan: Unfulfilled Promise.* Washington, DC: Carnegie Endowment for International Peace, 2002.

Rowland, Richard. 2001. "Regional Population Change in Kazakhstan during the 1990s and the Impact of Nationality Population Patterns: Results from the Recent Census of Kazakhstan." *Post Soviet Geography and Economics* 42(8), pp. 571–614.

Shokamanov, Yuri. 2000. "The National Action Plan on Improving the Status of Women in the Republic of Kazakhstan and Improving of Gender Statistics." Working Paper No. 8, submitted to the Joint ECE/UNDP Workshop on Gender Statistics for Policy Monitoring and Benchmarking, Orvieto, Italy, October 9–10 2000. Available at www.unece.org/stats/documents/2000/10/gender.workshop/8.e.pdf# search='women%20in%20Kazakhstan'. Accessed January 4, 2005.

Zhalimbetova, Roza, and Gregory Gleason. 2001, June 20. "Eurasian Economic Community (EEC) Comes into Being," *Central Asia Caucasus Analyst.* Available at http://photius.com/eaec/creation_ 010531.html.

PART TWO
REFERENCE SECTION

Key Events in Kazakh History

1000–200 B.C.

The Scythians, sometimes called the Saka, settle the grasslands of north-central Eurasia. Fierce nomadic warriors who battle the Persian Empire to the west, they are also master goldsmiths, crafting exquisite and delicate jewelry from the precious metal. The loosely knit order of Scythian nomadic society will be emulated by many peoples who follow them in the steppe region.

160 B.C.

The Usuns, possibly a branch of the group the Chinese called the Hsing-nu, appear on the western slopes of the Tien Shan. Nomadic and likely speaking an early Turkic dialect, the Usun controlled the territory between the Fergana Valley in modern Kyrgyzstan northward to Lake Balkhash. They were overrun and absorbed by the Huns in the fourth century.

A.D. 751

By 715, Qutaiba ibn Muslim had brought much of the land between the Fergana Valley and the Amu Darya into the realm of Islam. In 751, Muslim forces encountered an army of the Tang dynasty and defeated it near the ancient city of Taraz, in southern Kazakhstan. This victory secured the region's place in the Muslim world.

1218

The governor of Otrar, a Silk Road settlement near the Syr Darya, executes the members of a Mongolian caravan. In retaliation, Genghis Khan invades the following year and lays waste to the entire region. Eventually, Mongol armies surge as far west as Hungry and Poland.

1385

Rise of Amir Timur (known as Tamerlane in the West). Timur constructs a vast empire that includes the entire Syr Darya basin and the Jeti-Su region. In honor of the Sufi adept Ahmed Yassavi, Timur builds a spectacular mausoleum over the holy man's tomb in the city of Turkestan. His descendants rule the heart of Central Asia for another century after his death.

1500–1600

Emergence of the Kazakh Khanate and the development of the three *juz,* or hordes. The collapse of Timurid rule to their south opened the way for the nomadic Turkic peoples, who roamed the rolling steppe lands of north of the Amu Darya and Syr Darya rivers, to coalesce gradually into a loose confederation divided into three tribes: the Lesser, Middle, and Greater Juz.

1723

The Great Catastrophe: Buddhist Kalmyks, sometimes called Jungars, invade the Talas River valley. Within a few years, the Kalmyks drive the Kazakh population far to the west, seizing all of the Jeti-su. Thousands of Kazakhs lose their herds and grazing lands, and many die in the ensuing chaos.

1694–1731

Primarily as a result of the Kalmyk threat, the head of the Lesser Juz, Abdul Khayr, seeks assistance from the Russian Empire. By accepting Russian protection, the Lesser Juz become vassals of the Russian Empire, initiating the Russian colonization of the Kazakh steppe. The Russians soon begin building forts in the lands of the Middle Juz.

1837

Large-scale revolt against the Russians, led by Kenesary Khan. A khan of the Middle Juz, Kenesary challenged the absorption of Kazakh lands and the establishment of Tsarist authority. A highly capable military strategist, the uprising is not subdued until 1844.

1854

Founding of Fort Verny, later to become Almaty.

1895–1916

Massive migration of settlers from Russia and Ukraine to the northern steppe, and later to the southern reaches of the country. This influx of Slavic settlement meant the confiscation of millions of acres of Kazakh grazing lands. In approximately twenty years, almost 1.5 million colonists settle in Kazakhstan.

1916

Uprising by Kazakhs and other Central Asian peoples. Russian policies of land confiscation and higher taxes had already incensed many Kazakhs, when in 1916 the Russian government ordered the conscription of thousands of Central Asians to fight the Germans and their allies. The result was a widespread insurrection that cost thousands of lives and severely damaged the countryside.

1917

In February, Tsar Nicholas II abdicates, and the following October the Bolsheviks seize power in several cities in the Russian Empire, including many in Kazakhstan. In November, the Alash Orda, a political party composed of Kazakh intellectuals, advocates an autonomous state for the Kazakhs and attempts to form a government but loses control to the Bolsheviks.

1928

Stalin's regime implements the collectivization of agriculture in Kazakhstan. This policy is met with fierce resistance by the Kazakhs, who slaughter their livestock rather than surrender the animals to state control. Famine strikes the steppe, with nearly 2 million people, or 40 percent of the Kazakh population, perishing over the next decade.

1936

Formation of the Kazakh Soviet Socialist Republic (SSR).

1937

Mass arrests and executions of Kazakh Communist Party members. Most of those eliminated are accused of nationalist tendencies and betraying the revolution. One of the most prominent to be tried and liquidated is Turar Ryskulov, one of the earliest leaders of the Bolshevik movement in Kazakhstan.

1940

Written Kazakh is shifted from the Latin to the Cyrillic script.

1941–1945

During World War II much of the USSR's industrial plant is relocated to Kazakhstan, increasing the Kazakh SSR's role in Soviet industry. Stalin agrees to the establishment of "spiritual boards" to administer to the country's Muslim population. The board governing Central Asia is located in Tashkent.

1958

Nikita Khrushchev initiates the so-called Virgin Lands Program, designed to bring millions of additional acres of land into production in Kazakhstan. To cultivate the new lands, hundreds of thousands of Russian and Ukrainian "volunteers" are brought to the northern Kazakh SSR, increasing the proportion of Slavs in Kazakhstan's population.

1979

The Tengiz oil deposit in western Kazakh SSR is discovered by Soviet geologists.

1986

In December, riots rock the capital of Alma Ata, when the longtime first party secretary, Dinmukhamed Kunaev, is replaced by an ethnic Russian, Gennady Kolbin. Estimates of the number of protestors killed range from a dozen to several hundred.

1989

Writer Olzhas Suleimenov forms the Nevada-Semipalatinsk Antinuclear Movement, to protest Soviet nuclear testing in the Kazakh SSR. The Soviet regime agrees to close the testing zone later the same year.

1991

In August, a coup against Mikhail Gorbachev fails, signaling the end of the USSR. On December 1, Nursultan Nazarbayev is elected to the new office of president, and fifteen days later, Kazakhstan declares its independence.

1993

Introduction of the national currency, the *tenge*, and adoption of a national constitution, creating a powerful presidency and making Kazakh the state language. In December, Nazarbayev dissolves the parliament and begins ruling by decree.

1995

On August 30, voters approve a new constitution creating a bicameral legislature and granting President Nazarbayev extensive powers.

1997

Discovery of Kashagan oil field under the north Caspian Sea, lying within Kazakhstan's territorial waters.

1999

In January, Nazarbayev is reelected to the presidency for another seven-year term, in an election widely criticized for irregularities.

2003

Agreement reached on allowing Kazakh petroleum to reach international markets via a pipeline running from Baku, Azerbaijan, to Ceyhan, Turkey.

2005

The first section of the Baku-Tblisi-Ceyhan pipeline opens. The pipeline is expected to carry the majority of Kazakstan's oil wealth from the Caspian Basin to world markets.

Significant People, Places, and Events

Abylai Khan (?–1781)   Abylai Khan is considered one of the greatest *batyrs,* or warriors, of the Kazakh nation. A khan of the Middle Juz, he was a shrewd and sophisticated negotiator who resisted the complete absorption of his people into the Russian Empire. Abylai, although nominally bound to the Russians by treaty and pledge, skillfully used his relationship with the Manchu court and the Kalmyks to maintain as much independence for the Kazakhs, caught between these aggressive, expansionist powers, as was possible and is considered by some historians to be a key figure in reuniting the Kazakhs after the disasters of the Great Catastrophe.

al-Farabi (870–950)   One of the greatest thinkers in history, al-Farabi was not ethnically Kazakh but was born in what is today southern Kazakhstan. He received his early training there, before migrating to the intellectual and political hubs of Baghdad and Damascus, where he spent the remainder of his life. Al-Farabi wrote influential tracts on political theory and metaphysics and had a profound impact on musical theory, being one of the first scholars to analyze that subject in detail. His influence in the Muslim world has been compared with that of Aristotle on Western philosophy.

Alma Ata Events   On December 16, 1986, Mikhail Gorbachev, who had been leader of the Soviet Union for less than two years, removed the long-serving first party secretary of the Kazakh Communist Party, Dinmukhamed Kunaev, from his post. By the next morning, large crowds of demonstrators had gathered in the main square of Alma Ata to protest the action. Many of those present were angry that an ethnic Russian from outside Kazakhstan, Gennady Kolbin, had been appointed as Kunaev's replacement. The actual size of the crowd is somewhat unclear, but some reports suggest that there may have been several thousand people on the square. When security forces attempted to disperse the group, violence broke out, and a number of demonstrators died, although the exact figure is unknown.

Altynsaryn, Ibrahim (1841–1889) After receiving an education in the Russian schools in Kazakhstan, Altynsaryn emerged as the greatest educational reformer of his day. A Russophile, he held that the "civilizing" influence of Russian rule on the nomadic Kazakhs would assist in modernizing Kazakh society, and he advocated the abandonment of traditional lifestyles for sedentary farming, a practice many Kazakhs disdained. Altynsaryn produced a textbook on the Kazakh language and wrote the first Russian-Kazakh dictionary, helping to advance literacy among the Kazakhs.

Aral Sea A body of salt water located in western Kazakhstan that is split by the border with Uzbekistan. In 1960, the Aral was the world's fourth-largest lake, but overuse of the two streams supplying it with recharge water, the Amu Darya and Syr Darya, resulted in a collapse of the sea and surrounding ecosystem. The sea has shrunk so drastically over the past forty years that the Kazakh city of Aralsk, once a port on the Aral, is now located almost thirty miles from the shoreline. Through the construction of a dam the Kazakh government appears to have stabilized a portion of the Aral and has reintroduced a salt-tolerant species of flounder in some areas.

Astana City named the capital of Kazakhstan in 1998 in a highly controversial move. Formerly known as Akmola in the early 1990s, and Tselinograd during the Soviet era, Astana is a rail hub and industrial city that also served as the focal point of the Virgin Lands Program of the late 1950s. Russians are the largest ethnic group in the city, but the Kazakh population has been increasing in recent years. Since the late 1990s, a significant amount of investment has flowed into the city, as the Kazakh government attempts to make this provincial capital into a showpiece for the entire country.

Auezov, Mukhtar (1897–1961)   Generally considered the most influential Kazakh writer of the Soviet era, Auezov is often referred to as Mukhtar the Great. He was a playwright, novelist, biographer, and scholar. Auezov wrote a lengthy biography of Abai Kunanbayev, *The Way of Abai,* helping to establish Abai as the founding father of modern Kazakh literature and a national hero for the Kazakhs. Auezov gained early fame with the publication of a play based on the Kazakh folktale of Enlik and Kebek, two lovers whose clans are in conflict and who defy the wishes of their parents. A number of Auezov's works were adapted into screenplays and made into films.

Baikonur Cosmodrome   Located along the Syr Darya river, approximately 150 miles directly east of the Aral Sea, this space launch facility was constructed during the Soviet era, and every rocket sent into space by the USSR originated from this location. The first man in space, Yuri Gagarin, blasted off from Baikonur. After the collapse of the Soviet Union, the status of Baikonur was somewhat unclear. Eventually Kazakhstan agreed to lease the facility to Russia for more than $100 million a year for seventy years. Unfortunately, unlike Cape Canaveral in the United States, spectators are not allowed to view launches, and the entire area around the facility is closed to visitors.

Brezhnev, Leonid (1906–1982)   Brezhnev served as the first party secretary of the Kazakh Communist Party for less than one year, but his impact on the Kazakh SSR was substantial. Brezhnev was appointed the head of the Kazakh Communist Party by Nikita Khrushchev in 1955 in response to opposition among many in the Kazakh leadership to Khrushchev's plan to bring the "virgin lands" of the republic into production. In only nine months, Brezhnev brought the dissidents to heel, and the Virgin Lands Program was well under way by early 1956. Brezhnev was subsequently awarded with a position in Moscow, and in less than ten years, he would become the leader of the entire USSR.

Bukeikhanov, Ali Khan (1869–1932) At the turn of the twentieth century, an anti-tsarist movement emerged among a portion of the Kazakh intelligentsia. The foremost figure in this group was Bukeikhanov, who was a professor and publisher and descended from Kazakh nobility. Bukeikhanov published scathing critiques of Russian policy in the steppe and held that the ultimate goal of the tsarist administration was the annihilation of Kazakh identity and culture. Bukeikhanov was a central figure in the formation of the Alash Orda party, which formed an independent government in Kazakhstan for a short time after the Bolshevik Revolution.

Chimbulak A major ski resort just outside of Almaty and one of the most popular recreation spots in Central Asia, Chimbulak is located at an elevation of almost 7,000 feet. The resort is also a starting point for trekkers who wish to cross the Ala Tau range and hike to Lake Issyk Kul in Kyrgyzstan, a journey of about four or five days.

Dulatov, Mir Yakup (1885–1935) Dulatov was a key figure in the Alash Orda movement and served as one of the editors of the newspaper *Kazak,* the official paper of the Alash party. He wrote extensively on politics in Kazakhstan before and during the Bolshevik Revolution and was perhaps the most outspoken opponent of cooperation with the Bolsheviks, whom he greatly distrusted. Condemned for his nationalist tendencies by most Soviet historians, Dulatov's reputation was reevaluated during the glasnost period of the late 1980s.

Goloshchekin, Filipp (1876–1941)   The period from the early 1920s to the late 1930s represents the darkest epoch in the history of the Kazakh people, and Filipp Goloshchekin, first secretary of the Kazakh Regional Committee of the Communist Party, presided over this calamitous era. From Goloshchekin's arrival in the region in 1923 to his execution in 1941 (some sources give the date as 1938), approximately 2 million Kazakhs died resisting Soviet policies. Goloshchekin ruthlessly implemented Stalin's orders to collectivize agriculture in 1928 and also began the construction of an extensive system of prison camps—the "Gulag," as it was first called by Alexander Solzhenitsyn, one of its many residents.

Jeti-Su (Russian: Semireche)   Meaning "seven rivers," the Jeti-su has been a key region of Central Asia for at least a millennium. The boundaries of the Jeti-su roughly follow the Tien Shan in the south to Lake Balkhash in the north and run from the Chinese border in the east to the Muyunkum Desert in the west. Because of the area's well-watered and productive soils, the Jeti-su historically has served as the heartland of several civilizations since the Muslim conquest. The Russians built Fort Verny (Almaty) to secure control of the Jeti-su during the era of the Great Game, and the region served as a base for Russian conquest of Tashkent and the Fergana Valley.

Kazhegeldin, Akezhan (1952–)   An outspoken critic of the Nazarbayev regime, Kazhegeldin served as prime minister from 1994 to 1997. He resigned his post in October 1997, presumably forced out by Nazarbayev, who feared that Kazhegeldin was becoming increasingly popular and was on the verge of challenging Nazarbayev's control of the government. In 1999, Kazhegeldin organized the Republican People's Party of Kazakhstan (RNPK) and attempted to challenge

Nazarbayev for the presidency but was prevented from running for the office by court order. He has lived in exile since 1999 and was sentenced to a ten-year prison term in 2001 by a Kazakh court.

Kunaev, Dinmukhamed (1912–1993) Kunaev served for a total of 25 years as the first secretary of the Kazakh Communist Party and thus was the most powerful figure in the Kazakh SSR during that period. Kunaev was first appointed to the post of first secretary in 1959 by Nikita Khrushchev but was demoted in 1962. Khrushchev's successor, Leonid Brezhnev, reappointed Kunaev to head the Kazakh party in 1964. Kunaev's removal in December 1986 and replacement by an ethnic Russian sparked rioting by young Kazakhs in the capital city of Alma-Ata, resulting in dozens, and possibly hundreds, of deaths.

Kunanbayev, Abai (1845–1904) Abai is generally considered the founder of modern Kazakh literature and is widely revered as Kazakhstan's greatest man of letters. Abai infused his work with many themes and motifs from Islam, especially Sufism, but he was also a proponent of the adoption of Russian culture by Kazakhs. Abai's father, in fact, served as an administrator for the tsarist government; Abai himself held several positions in the Russian colonial administration and even wrote some legal statutes. Nevertheless, Abai is viewed in Kazakhstan today as a national hero who masterfully blended literary and philosophical elements from both Islamic and Western culture.

Lake Balkhash An enormous crescent-shaped lake in eastern Kazakhstan, Lake Balkhash is located about 250 miles north of Almaty, the capital city. Balkhash is a highly unusual body of water in that the western portion of the lake is fresh water, while the eastern section is salty. The primary river feeding the lake is the Ili River, which originates in the Tien Shan in China and flows northward to the lake. Recent diversion of much of the flow of the Ili and other streams draining into Balkhash has led to concern that the lake is shrinking, and some reports indicate that the surface may have been already reduced by as much as 770 square miles. Because demand for water is expected to increase in both western China and eastern Kazakhstan in the future, the ecology of the lake may suffer.

Medeo The world's largest outdoor ice-skating facility, Medeo is located only a short distance from Almaty. It is actually a stadium that lies at approximately 5,000 feet in elevation, just below the Chimbulak ski resort. The skating rink itself is nearly 400 yards long, and numerous Soviet and now Kazakh speed and figure skaters have trained there. Many international competitions have been held at Medeo, and dozens of speed-skating records have been set at the facility, partially due, perhaps, to the rink's elevation. On weekends, the general public may use the ice, and it is a favorite place for recreation.

Nazarbayev, Nursultan (1940–) Nazarbayev is the president of Kazakhstan and has held that position since the country's independence in 1991. Nazarbayev's rise to prominence is a Kazakh rags-to-riches story. Born on a collective farm in southern Kazakhstan, Nazarbayev became a steel worker in the city of Temirtau, in central Kazakhstan, in 1959. He joined the Communist Party and over the next two decades rose rapidly through the ranks. In 1990, after the dismissal of Gennady Kolbin as first party secretary, Nazarbayev was given the position and quickly proved himself to be a charismatic leader. In the aftermath of Soviet collapse he was elected Kazakhstan's first president but became more authoritarian in the 1990s.

Novi Uzen   The site of ethnic rioting between Kazakhs and various groups from the Caucasus in the spring of 1990, Novi Uzen is located on the Mangyshlak Peninsula in far western Kazakhstan. The town's economy is dependent on the processing of natural gas and in 1990 unemployment had risen dramatically in the area. Tensions boiled over between local Kazakhs and imported workers from the Caucasus region, and the violence lasted for several days, with a number of people killed and seriously injured. These events probably hastened the dismissal of the first party secretary at the time, Gennady Kolbin, and led to the appointment of Nursultan Nazarbayev.

Otrar   The site of an ancient ruined city, Otrar is of great historical importance in Central Asia, for at least three reasons. First, Otrar was near the birthplace of one of the Islamic world's greatest minds, the philosopher al-Farabi, who probably received his early education in one of Otrar's *medressehs* before he moved to the Middle East. Second, three centuries after the time of al-Farabi, the governor of Otrar put to death the members of an entourage from Mongolia, obviously one of history's greatest blunders, for it brought the wrath of Genghis Khan upon Central Asia, and ultimately Russia and Europe. Finally, Otrar was the city in which Amir Timur (Tamerlane) died while on his way to conquer China.

Oralmandar   The oralmandar are Kazakhs who have returned from abroad since the country's independence. As of the late 1990s, they numbered several hundred thousand. The Kazakh government has encouraged their return, and most have immigrated to Kazakhstan from Mongolia, Turkey, Afghanistan, China, and Iran, as well as from the other former Soviet republics. Some of the oralmandar, particularly those who do not speak Russian, have had difficulty adjusting to life in Kazakhstan.

Polygon   The Polygon is the infamous Soviet-era nuclear testing zone in eastern Kazakhstan. Nearly 20,000 square miles in area, it is located only about 70 miles to the west of Semey (formerly Semipalatinsk), a city of several hundred thousand inhabitants. To make matters worse, the prevailing winds blow toward the east, meaning that large doses of radioactivity blew over the city and surrounding villages for more than forty years, as the Soviets tested almost 500 atomic weapons in the region during that period. Statistics indicate that the incidence of many cancers is several times the average in this part of Kazakhstan, and other health problems also occur at catastrophic rates.

Ryskulov, Turar (1894–1938) Ryskulov was a radical Kazakh who opposed the tsarist administration in Kazakhstan, and became the leading Communist figure in the region in the years immediately after the Bolshevik Revolution. He participated in the uprising of 1916 and later became the head of the Kazakh Communist Party in 1920, although he quickly fell from power. He later published a history of the revolution in Kazakhstan. He was arrested and executed in 1938 during the Stalinist purges.

Semipalatinsk (Semey) Semipalatinsk was founded as a Cossack fort in the early 1700s, along the Irtysh River in the northeastern corner of Kazakhstan. Most of the inhabitants are Russian, and the city still has many buildings and homes made from wood, taken from the forests nearby. One of the city's more famous residents was Fyodor Dostoyevsky, who spent several years in exile in the city in the mid-nineteenth century and met his wife there. In the late twentieth century, Semipalatinsk became famous for another reason—the damage done to the city's inhabitants by decades of Soviet nuclear testing. Although the testing has stopped for more than a decade, rates of cancer and birth defects in the area continue to exceed the national average in Kazakhstan.

Shaiakhmetov, Zhumabai (1902–1966)   Shaiakhmetov was the first ethnic Kazakh to be appointed first party secretary of the Kazakh Communist Party. Significantly, he did not assume this post until 1946, more than 25 years after the Bolshevik Revolution. He broke with Nikita Khrushchev over the latter's plans to develop the "virgin lands" in Kazakhstan and was dismissed in 1959.

Speransky, Mikhail (1772–1839)   One of the most influential politicians of his day, Speransky had significant impact on the administration of the Middle Juz when he was governor general of Siberia in the 1820s. Speransky's reforms were limited to the Middle Juz because that group was under the control of the Siberian regional governor. Speransky imposed an administrative framework and legal code on the Kazakhs of the Middle Juz that was designed to encourage them to abandon nomadism and to adopt farming, in an early attempt to "settle" the Kazakhs. Many Kazakhs resented the limitations imposed by Russia, and numerous revolts over the next two decades were the result.

Suleimenov, Olzhas (1936–)   A politician, writer, and activist, Suleimenov is well known in Kazakhstan and across Central Asia. His masterpiece is *Az i Ya,* an examination of the linguistic and cultural connections between the Kazakhs and Turkic culture in Central Asia, based on a reading of the Russian epic *The Lay of Igor.* In 1989, Suleimenov formed the Nevada-Semipalatinsk Antinuclear Movement, linking activists in the United States and Soviet Union. Nevada-Semipalatinsk gathered the signatures of more than a million people in Kazakhstan on petitions against nuclear testing and played a key role in the closing of the nuclear testing zone in eastern Kazakhstan. Suleimenov has held several posts in the government since independence.

Taraz   Known as Aulie-Ata in the nineteenth century and as

Zhambyl during the Soviet era, the city of Taraz dates from at least 100 B.C. It was an important stopping point on the caravan routes of the Silk Road and was a major city in the empire of the Karakhanid Turks. It lies near the border with Uzbekistan in southern Kazakhstan. Taraz contains an interesting museum and several ancient mausoleums. Once heavily polluted by fertilizer plants, the city is now a much healthier place, as the largest plants have closed in recent years.

Tauke Khan (?–1715)   During the late 1600s the Kalmyks (Jungars) began an expansion into Kazakh lands in the Jeti-su and Syr Darya valley. Tauke Khan, the last leader of a truly unified Kazakh Khanate, attempted to rally the Kazakh forces against the invading Kalmyks but was defeated in 1698. Afterward, the Kazakhs were forced to fight a defensive war and retreat further into the depths of the steppe, until the disastrous defeat of 1723, resulting in the Great Catastrophe.

Turkestan   An ancient city along the Syr Darya, Turkestan is located about 100 miles north of the Kazakhstan-Uzbekistan border. The city was founded possibly as early as A.D. 400 and by the Middle Ages had become an important center of Sufism, especially after the Sufi sheik Ahmed Yassavi took up residence in the town. After Yassavi's death, his modest tomb became a site of pilgrimage, but in the late 1300s Amir Timur built a much larger mausoleum over the original tomb. The structure is marked by an enormous turquoise dome and is one of the finest examples of Islamic architecture in Central Asia.

Valikhanov, Cholkan (1835–1865)   Valikhanov was a scholar, spy, explorer, and artist and possessed one of the most gifted minds of the early nineteenth century. After receiving a military education in Russia, he went to work for the tsarist government, collecting information on the peoples, cultures, and natural history of the more remote parts of the

Fergana Valley and Tien Shan. He was later sent across the Tien Shan to the city of Kashgar to gather intelligence for Russia. Valikhanov befriended the Russian writer Fyodor Dostoyevsky when the latter was exiled to eastern Kazakhstan for several years and was frequently critical of Russia's militaristic policies in Central Asia. He died young, at the age of thirty.

Yassavi, Ahmed (1103–1166) Yassavi was a Sufi adept and poet, who founded a new *tariqa,* a Sufi order, that bears his name. He lived in the city of Turkestan and was buried in a simple tomb there until the 1390s, when Amir Timur, evidently an admirer, built a magnificent mausoleum over his crypt.

Zhabayev, Zhambyl (1846–1945) An *akyn,* or musical bard, Zhambyl's life straddled the Bolshevik Revolution and the transition from Russian imperialism to Soviet totalitarianism. Like others of the akyn tradition, Zhambyl accompanied himself on the *dombra*, a traditional stringed instrument. In the 1930s, Zhambyl became famous for his tributes to the Soviet system and to Stalin personally, and upon the creation of the Kazakh SSR, the city of Taraz was renamed in his honor. After Kazakhstan's independence, Zhambyl's reputation declined and Taraz reverted to its old name, partially because of the embarrassing, fawning character of Zhambyl's odes to a leader and a political system that destroyed millions of his countrymen.

Language, Food, and Etiquette in Kazakhstan

LANGUAGE

Kazakhstan has an official language, Kazakh, and a language of "interethnic communication," Russian. Although a slight majority of the population is ethnically Kazakh, a significant portion of this group is not conversant in their own tongue and speaks Russian as a first language. Moreover, few non-Kazakhs have a working knowledge of Kazakh, and Russian continues to function as the main language for interethnic communication. The Kazakh government has tirelessly promoted the Kazakh language since independence, making Kazakh a major language of education and offering free Kazakh language lessons on state television, among other efforts. These may be gradually bearing fruit, but by and large the use of Russian remains widespread, especially in the cities of northern Kazakhstan. Although a language law passed in the 1990s requires all Kazakh citizens to learn Kazakh by 2006, this will certainly not be the case.

Kazakh is a Turkic language with strong influences from Mongolian and from other Turkic tongues. It shares many commonalities in grammar and vocabulary with other Turkic languages in Central Asia and like them has borrowed much of its technical lexicon from Russian. Kazakh was written in the Arabic script until the late 1920s when the Soviet government shifted the language to the use of the Latin alphabet, following the lead of Turkey and Soviet Azerbaijan. In 1940, yet another shift in the writing system occurred, when almost all the languages of Central Asia were switched to the Cyrillic alphabet.

For Kazakh, this required the addition of several letters beyond the standard thirty-three-letter script used for Russian. Spoken Kazakh has three dialects based mostly on the three *juz* (hordes), but the distinctions between these variants are slight, and all are mutually intelligible.

Structurally, Kazakh is an agglutinative language, adding suffixes and particles to words that modify meaning. These may negate the noun or verb, change its grammatical case, change the tense of a verb, or serve some other function. This means that a single word may contain much more information than the typical word in English, and in fact, a single word in Kazakh may require an entire sentence when rendered into English. Because of this efficiency, Kazakh, like other Turkic tongues, may be spoken quite rapidly, and considerable information may be conveyed in only a few words or phrases.

The following are several useful and common phrases in both Russian and Kazakh:

Useful and common phrases in Kazakh:

Qayirly tan	Good morning
Kosh keldinizder	Welcome
Rakmet	Thank you
Tusinbeymin	I do not understand
Ya	Yes
Zhok	No
Kansha?	How much?
Zhaksi	Good
Zhaman	Bad
Kaida?	Where is . . .?
Agylshynsa bilesizbe?	Do you speak English?

Useful and common phrases in Russian:

Dobroya ootra	Good morning
Das vedaniya	Good-bye

Kak dela?	How are you?
Da	Yes
Nyet	No
Kak vas zavut?	What is your name?
Menya zavut . . .	My name is . . .
Horosho	Good
Ploha	Bad

FOOD AND BEVERAGES

Taking a meal in traditional Kazakh society is not simply a process of obtaining nourishment. Meals are important social events, especially if a guest is present, and given the tradition of hospitality in Central Asia, visitors frequently share one's food and company. In Kazakhstan, the invitation to share the host's *dastarkhan,* or tablecloth, represents the essence of Kazakh hospitality and tradition. The dastarkhan is usually spread on the floor and sumptuously laden with fruits, nuts, and other snacks—but this is only the beginning of the meal, and many more dishes will arrive before the feast is over. Once the meal has begun, it will be a rare guest indeed who is able to resist either his own appetite or the constant entreaties of his hosts to consume ever more food.

Although Kazakhs are "less Islamic" than many other Muslims in Central Asia, some traditions and prohibitions must be observed when taking a meal. One should never touch or pass food with the left hand, and one's feet must be kept away from the dastarkhan. The latter is usually accomplished by sitting cross-legged, with the feet folded under the thighs. Bread is often torn into chunks and placed at various locations around the table, and one should be careful not to place a piece of bread upside down, nor should bread ever be thrown away in Central Asian society. Stale bread is broken up and placed outside for birds or other animals to eat.

Common Kazakh Dishes

Meat Dishes. There are three common types of meat served in Kazakhstan—mutton, beef, and horse meat. The latter, much to U.S. visitors' revulsion, is considered a delicacy, and the heads of both sheep and horses may be served as part of a feast. It often falls to the guest of honor to carve the head and serve various pieces to others at the gathering—each portion carries a symbolic meaning. Chicken and fish are also frequently eaten but more commonly as appetizers or in soup.

Mutton Dishes. Mutton is the main meat in many dishes found in Kazakh cuisine. The national dish of the Kazakhs might be considered *beshbarmak,* a mutton stew made with noodles. *Basturma* is grilled mutton that has been marinated with vinegar and onions and is traditionally served with cucumbers, tomatoes, and bread. *Shashlik* consists of pieces of mutton or beef skewed and grilled over an open flame; stands selling this dish are found on many streets throughout Kazakhstan. Shashlik, if made from mutton, will typically include chunks of fat from the sheep's tail alternated with the meat. This is considered a delicacy, and regardless of the type of meat, shashlik is often served with onions and *non,* or traditional flatbread. *Plov* is a rice dish that is usually topped with pieces of mutton or beef, and *sorpa,* a meat and vegetable stew is frequently served at the beginning of a meal. *Kespe* is a meaty noodle soup that is often served at the beginning of a meal.

Horse-Meat Dishes. The flesh of the horse is considered a special treat among Kazakhs, and numerous dishes are made with it. Perhaps the most common is *kazy,* a spicy horse-meat sausage that is frequently served as an appetizer. *Zhal* is a fatty smoked meat that is also popular, and *shuzhuk* is a smoked sausage made from horse meat. As mentioned earlier, the head of a slaughtered horse is sometimes presented as the center piece of a feast, which is then carved and distributed among the diners.

Breads and Related Foods. Various types of bread are essential to the Kazakh diet. Non is an unleavened bread that is baked in a round clay oven, called a *tandir.* Russian speakers call this bread *lepyoshka,* and it is the most common form of bread in Kazakhstan. Non is served with virtually every meal and is torn into pieces at the table, usually by the host or eldest person, and distributed to all those present. *Baursak* is fried bread that is dipped in sugar or eaten with sour cream, often for breakfast or a snack. *Blini* are thin pancakes that are usually served with sour cream or sugar and may be served at any time of the day. Kasha is a porridge usually prepared for breakfast and may be made from buckwheat, oats, millet, or rice. A popular and quick meal can be made of *lagman,* a dish of thick, boiled noodles. *Gutap* are delicious fritters that are mixed with spices and onions and deep-fried, and served with sour cream.

Milk Products. As a nomadic culture, the Kazakh people obtained much of their sustenance from the animals they maintained, and many dairy foods are a common element of Kazakh meals. Butter, cream, cheese, and yogurt are frequently eaten by themselves or with other foods. *Airan* is a tart yogurt made from goat's or mare's milk, and *irimshik* is a common snack made from the dried curd of cow's or goat's milk. A variety of cheeses are made from cow's milk, and often from goat's milk as well. Milk itself is typically sold fresh on the street or in the bazaar and must be boiled before it is drunk.

Common Kazakh Beverages

Tea. Tea is served with every meal and social gathering. Black tea is most common and may be taken with sugar, and on occasion Kazakhs and other Central Asians may drink tea with milk or cream. Tea must always be served and drunk hot, even in the searing summers of Kazakhstan; many people believe that cool tea is unhealthy. Black tea is widely popular, but green tea is also drunk, especially for its supposed health benefits.

Alcoholic Beverages. Despite the Muslim prohibition against consumption of alcoholic beverages, Kazakhs have for much of their history produced and consumed such products. Kazakh nomads made at least two types of fermented drinks. Fermented mare's milk, or *kumiss,* is widely drunk today in Kazakhstan, and *shubat,* or fermented camel's milk, is also available, although not as popular as kumiss. Kazakhs believe these drinks have curative properties, and they are considered special treats and thus frequently offered to guests. Just as popular are vodka, cognac, wine, and beer, all of which will flow freely at almost any party or celebration in Kazakhstan.

Soft Drinks. Soft drinks are increasingly popular in Kazakh society. Relatively speaking, soft drinks are much more expensive for people in Central Asia than in the United States and are not drunk as frequently. U.S. visitors will find it odd that these beverages are frequently served at room temperature, without ice. Among the Slavic population and some Kazakhs, *kvass,* a drink made from bread, is popular and often sold on the street in cities in northern Kazakhstan.

ETIQUETTE

Society in Kazakhstan is multifaceted, with the result that traditions and standards of conduct vary according to ethnic group and geographic location. For example, European groups in Kazakhstan (Slavs and Germans) have traditions and values that may differ markedly from those of the Muslim groups (Kazakhs, Uzbeks, and others). Furthermore, there are additional distinctions between urbanized and rural people, especially among the Muslim groups. What follows is a general outline of expected behaviors within the more traditional communities of the country, because these represent the most unfamiliar cultural territory to a Western visitor. Although not necessarily universal, these standards of behavior are widely observed in many parts of Kazakhstan.

Taking Off Shoes. As is typical across Central Asia, one is expected to remove shoes when entering a home or mosque. House shoes may be provided by the host, if visiting a private residence. Streets in Kazakhstan are dirty and dusty, and one's shoes will quickly become covered with dirt after just a short stroll. Removing shoes helps to keep the home clean, and this custom is observed in much of Asia and the Middle East.

Use of Hands and Feet. In general, one should use the left hand sparingly in social situations, and especially avoid passing food with it. Do not shake hands with someone across a threshold of a door or entrance to a home—many people believe this brings bad luck. When sitting on the floor, one should avoid touching one's feet, and should not point the sole of one's foot toward someone else. The best way to avoid this is to fold the feet under or behind the legs. By no means should one's feet come near the table or any food, and one should never prop his or her feet up on a table or desk.

Social Hierarchy and Respect. Showing deference to those who are older, even if they are strangers, is an expected part of social behavior in Kazakh culture. This is part of what Kazakhs call *sybaga,* or "old traditions." At mealtime the eldest person present is accorded the honor of leading the conversation, and others present are expected to defer to his or her judgment. The eldest person will also be served first, unless there is a guest present, in which case the guest is usually provided for first. Refusing an offering of food may be seen as disrespectful, and one is expected to at least try the dish being offered. A person who is disrespectful to elders or superiors is considered uncultured and ignorant.

Public Display of Affection between Opposite Sexes. The appropriateness of physical contact between the sexes in public varies according to the ethnic group and setting. Among Slavs and urbanized Kazakhs, holding hands and kissing in public is generally acceptable, if done discreetly. More traditional Kazakhs and Uzbeks in the southern, rural regions of the country do not kiss or show affection publicly, and such behavior is frowned on by more conservative Muslims. This prohibition applies even to married couples and especially to single females.

Sitting. Although meals may be served at a table, it is traditional in Kazakh society to take one's meals while sitting on the floor. As mentioned earlier, under such circumstances it is important to sit with one's feet away from both the food and from others who are dining.

Nose Blowing. It is generally best to avoid blowing one's nose in public, particularly at mealtime. If possible, it is appropriate to leave the table or gathering and use a handkerchief in private. Public nose blowing is more acceptable in northern Kazakhstan than in the southern region.

Bargaining. In the traditional bazaars of Kazakhstan, all prices are negotiable, and one is expected to bargain for the final sum. As is typical under such circumstances, the seller always begins with a price substantially higher than what he or she eventually expects to receive. Bargaining the price is an art in which Central Asians take pride, and one who fails to deal for the cost of an item, even one that is of relatively low cost, will be seen as gullible.

Business Cards. It is fashionable for professionals to carry and exchange business cards in Kazakhstan. It is considered good manners and a sign of seriousness to offer one's own card and to ask for one in return.

Clothes. Styles of dress in Kazakhstan are not as conservative as those encountered in neighboring Uzbekistan, except in the rural areas of the south. In general, clothing styles for women are similar to those found in Russia, particularly among Slavic women. Kazakh women may dress slightly more conservatively but never go veiled, and in the larger cities where there is a significant Slavic population, women often mimic the standards of their Russian counterparts. Mature women may wear a scarf, but this is done as a matter of convention and has nothing to do with religious requirements, unless the woman in question intends to visit a mosque or church. Men typically dress conservatively and seldom wear shorts, even in the hot summer months. If invited as a guest to someone's home, it is expected that one will appear "dressed up," and professional men nearly always wear a tie and coat when working.

Kazakhstan-Related Organizations

BUSINESS AND ECONOMIC

The following is a brief listing of various groups and organizations focused on commerce and business development in Kazakhstan. A search of the Internet will reveal many more because the business environment is dynamic, and new groups are constantly appearing. When calling locations in Kazakhstan from outside the country, one must dial the country code (7) and the respective city code. The city code for Almaty is (327).

American Chamber of Commerce in Kazakhstan
Telephone: (3272) 58-79-38
Fax: (3272) 58-79-42
E-mail: info@amcham.kz
Web site: http://www.amcham.kz
    The American Chamber of Commerce in Kazakhstan has almost 160 members, who range from multinational corporations to local businesses. The chamber's mission is to serve as a forum for the exchange of ideas and information on doing business in Kazakhstan and assist in business development.

Kazakhstan Foreign Investors Council
Suite 216, 67 Aiteke Bi Street
Almaty, Kazakhstan 480091
Telephone: (3272) 72-08-27
Fax: (3272) 50-61-05
E-mail: director@fic.kz; assistant@fic.kz
Web site: http://www.fic.kz
    The Kazakhstan Foreign Investors Council was created to

facilitate dialogue between investors and the government of
Kazakhstan and provide opportunities for discussion of
investment issues.

Kazakhstan Stock Exchange
Box 140
Almaty, Kazakhstan 050000
Telephone: (3272) 72-98-98
Fax: (3272) 72-09-25
E-mail: kase@kase.kz; info@kase.kz
Web site: http://www.kase.kz

U.S.-Kazakhstan Business Association
1200 G Street, NW
Suite 827
Washington, DC 20005
Telephone: (202) 434-8791
Fax: (202) 638-3040
E-mail: ExDir@uskba.net
Web site: http://www.uskba.net
    The U.S.-Kazakhstan Business Association provides infor-
mation on business opportunities in Kazakhstan, serves as a
forum for the exchange of ideas and views between business
people from both countries, and promotes communication
between government and business officials.

U. S.-Kazakhstan Chamber of Commerce
Telephone: (212) 752-5566
E-mail: info@uskazakhstanchamberofcommerce
    .8k.comddress.com
Web site:http://www.uskazakhstanchamberofcommerce.8k
    .com
    This organization assists in business development in Ka-
zakhstan by encouraging dialogue between American and
Kazakh businesspeople, organizing events to showcase busi-

ness opportunities in Kazakhstan, and developing programs to increase awareness of business in Kazakhstan.

CULTURE, EDUCATION, AND EXCHANGE

Fulbright Association of Kazakhstan
92 Taugul-1, Apt. 62
Almaty, Kazakhstan 480042
Telephone: (3272) 20-94-64
E-mail: z2001a@freenet.kz

The Fulbright Association provides opportunities for educators, professionals and students to participate in exchange programs for several months, up to a year. The overall goal of the Fulbright Program is to foster mutual understanding and cooperation between peoples of different nations via the mechanism of education and collaboration.

Green Women Ecological News Agency
Apt. 73, h.2, distr. Koktem-2
Almaty, Kazakhstan 480090
Telephone: (3272) 75-49-96
Fax: (3272) 75-49-96
E-mail: greenwomen@nursat.kz
http://www.greenwomen.freenet.kz

The Green Women Ecological News Agency seeks to increase awareness and knowledge of environmental issues in Central Asia through the publication of magazines, bulletins, and reports and to increase public participation in resolving environmental issues.

International Business School
8-a Abai Avenue
Almaty, Kazakhstan 480100
E-mail: bsuzhiko@ibs.kz

Kazakh Institute of Management, Economics and Strategic Research (KIMEP)
4 Abay Avenue
Almaty, Kazakhstan 050010
Telephone: (3272) 70-42-13
Fax: (3272) 70-42-11
E-mail: admis@kimep.kz
Web site: http://www.kimep.kz

KIMEP is one of Kazakhstan's premier universities, offering courses in business, economics, and social sciences. Most classes are taught in English.

Kazakhstan Women's Information Network (KWIN)
c/o Alfia Abikenova
Almaty Women Information Center
Telephone: (3272) 65-25-00
Fax: (3272) 67-84-26
E-mail: a_alfia@yahoo.com

This is a nongovernmental organization (NGO) that serves as an umbrella organization for other NGOs in Kazakhstan that focus on women's needs. The goal of KWIN is to pool resources and information between those groups working to improve the condition of women in Kazakhstan.

Youth Information Services of Kazakhstan
E-mail: almaty-ynet@netel.kz
Web site: http://www.youth.kz

This organization seeks to foster communication among young people in Kazakhstan and provide information and training toward the development of civil society. The organization has branches in fifteen cities in Kazakhstan and offers seminars and other educational programs.

GOVERNMENT

Embassy of Kazakhstan
1401 16th Street, NW
Washington, DC 20036
Telephone: (202) 232-5488
Fax: (202) 232-5845
E-mail: Kazakh.embusa@verizon.net
Consular section: Kazakh.consul@verizon.net
Web site: http://www.kazakhembus.com
    The Kazakhstan Embassy Web site is extremely useful and contains dozens of links and other information.

New York Consular Section
866 United Nations Plaza, Suite 586-A
New York, NY 10017
Telephone: (212) 888-3024
Fax: (212) 888-3025
E-mail: kzconsulny@un.int
Web site: http://www.kazconsulny.org

TOURISM

Kazakhstan offers many opportunities for outdoor enthusiasts and those interested in culture and history. Although distant from North America, Japan, and Australia, the country is safe, and the people are warm and receptive to guests. There are spectacular landscapes to enjoy and magnificent cultural monuments almost a thousand years old. Like the other countries in the region, Kazakhstan is a bargain for the traveler, because food and accommodations can be had for relatively little cost, if one is traveling on a tight budget. There are more than seventy tourist agencies in Kazakhstan offering a wide range of tours and services—most are listed on the Kazakh Embassy Web site. A few follow, and many others may be found by searching the Internet.

Silk Road Kazakhstan
98 Zheltoksan Street
Almaty, Kazakhstan 480091
Telephone: (3272) 33-35-12
Fax: (3272) 62-91-06
E-mail: ncsilkroad@hotmail.com
Web site: http://www.zzk.tourkz.com

Hotel Complex Otrar
73 Gogol Street
Almaty, Kazakhstan
Telephone: (3272) 33-80-34
Fax: (3272) 33-20-13
E-mail: s-otrar@mail.group.kz

Silk Road Business Services
LTD88 Sharipova Street
Almaty, Kazakhstan
Telephone: (3272) 92-40-42
Fax: (3272) 67-63-19
E-mail: spadventurs@nursat.kz

Annotated Bibliography of Recommended Works on Kazakhstan

The following books, articles and Web sites provide additional information for those who wish to learn more about Kazakhstan. This list is by no means comprehensive, but these works represent additional sources of information on the general topics presented in the narrative section. Some of the resources provided here might fall under several headings and have been grouped according to the narrative outline.

GEOGRAPHY AND HISTORY OF KAZAKHSTAN

Becker, Seymour. 1994. "The Russian Conquest of Central Asia and Kazakhstan: Motives, Methods, Consequences." In *Central Asia: Its Strategic Importance and Future Prospects,* edited by Hafeez Malik. New York: St. Martin's Press.

One of the best summaries of Russian policy and practice in the steppe lands of Central Asia available to the general reader. Becker's treatment is impartial yet critical, and he methodically assesses the Russian strategy in the context of larger geopolitical issues of the nineteenth century in Central Asia. The "civilizing" mission of Russian policy resulted in outcomes both negative and positive for the Kazakh nation, and Becker offers insight into each of these.

Beisenova, Aliya. 1998. "Environmental Problems in Kazakhstan." In *Sustainable Development in Central Asia,* edited by Shirin Akiner, Sander Tideman, and Jon Hay. New York: St. Martin's Press.

This is a general overview of environmental degradation in Kazakhstan. The impact of industrialization on a number of urban areas is discussed, as is the ecological threat to Kazakhstan's water supplies. The latter is a matter of some concern, as demand for water in the region continues to rise. The last section of the chapter addresses the environmental conditions specifically in the city of Almaty, Kazakhstan's largest urban area.

Conquest, Robert. 1986. *The Harvest of Sorrow.* New York: Oxford University Press.

Conquest's chapter titled "Central Asia and the Kazakh Tragedy" is required reading for any who wish to develop an understanding of the impact of Soviet rule on the Kazakh nation. The horrors and devastation of collectivization in the steppe remain largely untold and unexamined by Western scholars, but Conquest's work goes a long way toward redressing this oversight.

Kazakhstan Home Page. Available at: http://www.kazakhstan .com

Contains articles and analysis on current events in Kazakhstan, plus numerous links to topics on economics, business, and history. A quick and reliable source of information on many subjects connected to Kazakhstan.

Olcott, Martha. 1995. *The Kazakhs.* 2d ed. Stanford, CA: Hoover Institution Press.

Olcott's book is the most comprehensive treatment of the history and politics of the Kazakh people available in English. The focus of her work is on the Soviet and post-Soviet periods, and she offers a detailed discussion of the impact of Soviet actions and policies on the current situation in the country. The discussion of independent Kazakhstan is of course somewhat dated now but still offers a clear description and analysis of Kazakh politics in the formative years of the new country.

Rottier, Peter. 2003. "The Kazakness of Sedentarization: Promoting Progress as Tradition in Response to the Land Problem." *Central Asian Survey* 22(1), pp. 67–81.
   A study of the impact of Russian colonization on nomadic life among the Kazakhs. Rottier examines several aspects of Kazakh identity in this context, including the role of the *akyns*, or bards, in preserving Kazakh tradition, as well as the approach of the small group of Kazakh intellectuals to the "land question," that is, the problem of maintaining territorial control of the traditional grazing regions while under pressure from the Russian administration to abandon nomadism.

Rowland, Richard. 2001. "Regional Population Change in Kazakhstan during the 1990s and the Impact of Nationality Population Patterns: Results from the Recent Census of Kazakhstan." *Post Soviet Geography and Economics* 42(8), pp. 571–614.
   Rowland analyzes the qualities and trends in the population geography of Kazakhstan, using both an ethnic framework and an urban-rural approach. Numerous insights are offered based on the differential growth rates and varying patterns of migration among Kazakhstan's ethnic groups.

Rumer, Boris. 1989. *Soviet Central Asia: A Tragic Experiment.* Boston: Unwin Hyman.
   A devastating critique of Soviet agricultural and economic policies and their impact on Central Asia. Romer's work is one of the most detailed studies produced in English on the destructive character of the "cotton monoculture" in Central Asia, a problem that has not disappeared with the fall of the Soviet empire.

THE ECONOMY OF KAZAKHSTAN

Eicher, Sharon. 2001. "When Does a Transition Economy Become a Market Economy? The Example of Kazakhstan." *Journal of Central Asian Studies* VI(1), pp. 2–18.

A recent assessment of the economic transition in Kazakhstan and a critique of the methods utilized to label various economies as "transitional" or "market-oriented." Contains a number of useful tables.

Esentugelov, Arystan. 1996. "Kazakhstan: Problems and Prospects of Reform and Development." In *Central Asia in Transition: Dilemmas of Political and Economic Development,* edited by Boris Rumer. Armonk, NY: M.E. Sharpe.

This is a balanced and thoughtful analysis of Kazakhstan's economic situation in the mid-1990s. Although some of the commentary is obviously out of date, much of the information presented continues to have relevance. For example, the final section, "Prospects," contains policy recommendations that remain pertinent for economic development in Kazakhstan, and the author cautions against the country relying too heavily on Western markets, particularly the petroleum market, for future growth.

Peck, Anne. 1999. "Foreign Investments in Kazakhstan's Mineral Industries." *Post-Soviet Geography and Economics* 40(7), pp. 471–518.

A geographic perspective on the spatial investment patterns associated with Kazakhstan's significant and diverse mineral resources.

Rasizade, Alec. 2002. "The Mythology of Munificent Caspian Bonanza and Its Concomitant Pipeline Geopolitics." *Central Asian Survey* 21(1), pp. 37–54.

A critical assessment of U.S. policy and strategy in the development and exploitation of Caspian Sea hydrocarbon resources. There is considerable emphasis on Kazakhstan's part in the geopolitical dynamics that surround the issues of moving the energy wealth of the Caspian basin to the global market. Rasizade argues that instability in the region must be addressed along with transport issues if the region is to become a reliable source of energy.

UNDP Kazakhstan. 2004. *Poverty in Kazakhstan: Causes and Cures.* No. UNDPKAZ 08. Available at www.undp.kz/library_of_publications/center_view.html?id=2617. Accessed January 27, 2005.

This lengthy report provides a wealth of data regarding the growth of poverty in Kazakhstan in the post-Soviet period. Special emphasis is placed on articulating the causes of poverty and describing the conditions of those most affected: women, the elderly, children, and residents of rural areas. The most comprehensive study of poverty done on the country in recent years.

KAZAKH INSTITUTIONS

Altoma, Reef. 1994. "The Influence of Islam in Post-Soviet Kazakhstan." In *Central Asia in Historical Perspective,* edited by Beatrice F. Manz. Boulder, CO: Westview Press.

An interesting assessment of the role Islam plays in emerging Kazakh society. Altoma considers Islam in the context of foreign policy, its impact on the political dynamics of Kazakhstan, and the interaction between state institutions and law and Islam. Her conclusions show that although Islam plays a part in Kazakh identity, the history of the faith among the Kazakhs weakens any tendency to politicize Islam, despite the fact that Islam plays a more visible role in Kazakh society in the post-Soviet period.

Gleason, Gregory. 1997. *The Central Asian States: Discovering Independence.* Boulder, CO: Westview Press.

A useful description of the major players and issues in Kazakh politics in the early 1990s.

George, Alexandra. 2001. *Journey into Kazakhstan: The True Face of the Nazarbayev Regime.* Lanham, MD: University Press of America.

As the title suggests, this is an exposé of the political situation in post-Soviet Kazakhstan. The author builds a convincing case that the Nazarbayev regime has drifted toward dictatorship rather than building democracy in the 1990s, through interviews with many political actors in the country. A wide range of issues is examined, including freedom of the media, economic policy, and environmental damage.

Katsiev, Oleg. 1999. "Prospects for Development of an Independent Media in Kazakhstan." In *Civil Society in Central Asia,* edited by M. Holt Ruffin and Daniel Waugh. Seattle: University of Washington Press.

A review of media development in Kazakhstan since independence. Katsiev traces the origins of independent media in the country and describes the efforts by the Nazarbayev regime to control and silence those outlets that are critical of government policy. The chapter addresses the conditions of both print and broadcast media and contains two tables on tender fees for radio and television stations.

Nowicki, Marvin. "Local Government Reform in Kazakhstan." *Journal of Central Asian Studies* 1(2), pp. 21–34.

An informed summary of the restructuring of the local administrative network after Kazakhstan's independence. Provides useful diagrams and tables.

Olcott, Martha Brill. 2002. *Kazakhstan: Unfulfilled Promise.* Washington, DC: Carnegie Endowment for International Peace.

An updated companion volume to Olcott's *The Kazakhs,*

this book transcends the earlier work in several ways because of Olcott's broader approach to her subject and its less cumbersome, detail-laden style. Here she addresses the failures of an independent Kazakhstan to progress substantially toward the country's enormous potential, along with the causes and consequences of this failure. Required reading for anyone who wishes to comprehend the challenges facing this huge and fascinating country.

Surucu, Cengiz. 2002. "Modernity, Nationalism, Resistance: Identity Politics in Post-Soviet Kazakhstan." *Central Asia Survey* 21(4), pp. 385–402.

Surucu skillfully articulates the dynamics between those he terms "cosmopolitan" and the movement he identifies as "Kazakh nationalism." The struggle between these perspectives is rooted in Soviet modernization efforts, which were designed to eliminate the various allegiances and levels of identity that had historically existed in Kazakh society. In the aftermath of Soviet disintegration, these competing schools of identity construction are shaping the concept of an emergent Kazakh identity.

KAZAKH SOCIETY AND CONTEMPORARY ISSUES

Buckley, Cynthia. 1997. "Suicide in Post-Soviet Kazakhstan: The Role of Stress, Age and Gender." *Central Asian Survey* 6(1), pp. 45–52.

Suicide rates rose significantly in the early 1990s in Kazakhstan, and Buckley describes the various causes and patterns associated with this increase. Her findings show that men are more likely to commit suicide than women in the post-Soviet era, and that the older a man gets, the higher the likelihood of suicide. Somewhat surprisingly, among women the rate is higher in younger women. A rare and revealing look at this phenomenon in Kazakhstan.

Expat.nursat.kz. Available at: http://expat.nursat.kz. Accessed February 16, 2005.

An excellent source of information on culture, history, and living in Kazakhstan. A user-friendly Web site with many links.

Janabel, Jiger. 1996. "When National Ambition Conflicts with Reality: Studies on Kazakhstan's Ethnic Relations." *Central Asian Survey* 15(1), pp. 5–21.

An examination and discussion of the ethnic politics in Kazakhstan in the mid-1990s, with particular focus on the views of Kazakhs toward the Russians. Much of the discussion is centered on the declining economic situation and how this may affect the political landscape. The study is somewhat dated and occasionally presents some dubious assertions but overall offers insight into the dynamics of ethnically based politics in Kazakhstan.

Nazpary, Joma. 2002. *Post-Soviet Chaos: Violence and Dispossession in Kazakhstan.* Sterling, VA: Pluto Press.

This is the only sociological analysis of its kind available in English. Nazpary has conducted extensive research on the impact of the economic transition on Kazakh society, particularly on women. His study of the dispossessed is disturbing because it reveals the darker aspects of life in post-Soviet Kazakhstan. His research identifies and examines the ways in which people cope with their declining quality of life.

Sarsembayev, Azamat. 1999. "Imagine Communities: Kazak Nationalism and Kazakification in the 1990s." *Central Asian Survey* 18(3), pp. 319–346.

This article tackles the controversial process of "Kazakification" undertaken by the Nazarbayev regime in the 1990s. Kazakification is the process whereby the previously dominant Russian culture is replaced by characteristics that are uniquely Kazakh, especially concerning the use of language.

The Kazakh regime has viewed this shift as vital to building a Kazakh national identity, but its effect on the Russian community has been to increase emigration.

Schatz, Edward. 2000. "The Politics of Multiple Identities: Lineage and Ethnicity in Kazakhstan." *Europe-Asia Studies* 52(3), pp. 489–506.
An in-depth look at the complex issue of identity among Kazakhs in the post-Soviet era. The various expressions of identity among Kazakhs are affected by what Schatz terms "directionality," and he argues that efforts to form a unitary Kazakh nationality have actually reinforced clan and tribal identities among Kazakhs, and he views this as a major political issue in the emerging society in Kazakhstan.

KYRGYZSTAN

PART ONE
NARRATIVE SECTION

The Geography and History of Kyrgyzstan

A Kyrgyz folktale relates how Ashik, a poor orphan boy, befriends an injured frog who rewards him with a magic pebble. Gifted with this power, Ashik is able to defeat the Black Khan, an evil ruler who himself has supernatural abilities and who is determined to destroy Ashik and his village. The story of Ashik is in some ways an appropriate metaphor for modern Kyrgyzstan, a country "orphaned" by the collapse of the Soviet Union. The Black Khan is represented by the multitude of problems that beset this beautiful and remote country, but what of the magic pebble? Surely the vital "magic" of Kyrgyzstan today is the resolve of its people to revive their ancient culture and traditions and at the same time move rapidly to integrate into the world community.

Kyrgyzstan is fundamentally different from its larger neighbors Uzbekistan and Kazakhstan. It is much smaller, consists mostly of highlands with only limited agricultural land, and with the exception of a significant gold deposit lacks the generous endowment of resources, especially oil and gas, which those Central Asian states enjoy. On the other hand, because of the relative lack of resources and industrialization, Kyrgyzstan suffered less ecological damage while under Soviet rule, and its mountain fastness gives one resource that is in increasingly short supply in the rest of the region—water. Add to these advantages spectacular alpine scenery, one of the most scenic mountain lakes in the world, Issyk Kul, and a relatively successful record of attracting foreign investment and assistance in the post-Soviet era, and Kyrgyzstan shows considerable potential to become the "Switzerland of the East," a label the country's promotional literature already unabashedly employs when attempting to lure visitors and investors.

To meet this potential, the country must overcome an isolated geography, a stunted and outdated transportation and communications infrastructure, a recent history of small but recurrent acts of terrorist violence, and conflict between the majority Kyrgyz and the largest minority group, the Uzbeks. The latter issue led to one of the deadliest episodes of ethnic violence to rock the USSR in its last years, when Kyrgyz and Uzbeks attacked one another near the southern city of Osh in 1990, resulting in possibly 300 deaths. Although the country has avoided a repetition of this tragedy, tensions remain between the two groups, who are separated not only by culture and language, but also geographically, with most of the Uzbek population concentrated in the Fergana Valley in the south. Lacking a "magic pebble," the residents of Kyrgyzstan must face these difficulties and rely on themselves to secure the future stability and growth of their rugged yet beautiful nation.

PHYSICAL AND HUMAN GEOGRAPHY

The dominant feature of the Kyrgyz landscape is elevation. Even if one is located in one of the country's several large valleys, the mountains always loom on the horizon, a constant reminder of their dominance. The average elevation of the landscape in Kyrgyzstan is approximately 8,200 feet, and the second-highest peak in former Soviet Central Asia, Jonish Chokosu (Peak Victory), stands at 24,400 feet at the eastern margin of the country. It is here in southeastern Kyrgyzstan that the majestic Tien Shan reach their highest elevation, forming a wall of rock and ice between Central Asia and western China. Running just north and parallel to the main chain of the Tien Shan is the Terskey Ala Too, a subrange of the main body of the Tien Shan, and separated from them by the valley of the Naryn River. The Naryn neatly bisects the coun-

Lake Issyk Kul, in north-central Kyrgyzstan. The lake is a major vacation destination for many in Central Asia. (Photo courtesy of Reuel Hanks)

try, flowing westward into the Fergana Valley and eventually reaching Uzbekistan. The city of Naryn sits at the eastern end of the river's lowland in central Kyrgyzstan, astride the road leading to China via the Torugart Pass, a break in the Tien Shan lying above 11,000 feet.

In the northeast, Lake Issyk Kul sits in a deep depression between the Terskey Ala Too and yet another parallel range stretching along the northern border, the Kungay Ala Too. Issyk Kul means "hot lake" in Kyrgyz, and this name is due to the interesting fact that the lake fails to freeze during the winter months. It is somewhat unclear why the lake does not freeze, although the reason is probably due to warmth retained in the water from the summer months as well as the lake's salinity (Sinnott 1992). Issyk Kul extends for about 90 miles and is about 30 miles across its widest point. Although the water is remarkably clear, the lake is deep, reaching a maximum depth of close to 2,000 feet. One of the largest alpine lakes in the world, Issyk Kul has no outlet and is fed by numerous small streams that flow down the slopes of the mountains that bracket it to the north and south. Several fish species live in its waters, and small-scale commercial fishing helps to support the local economy.

Near the western end of Issyk Kul another of the country's rivers originates, flowing almost to the lake and then bending northward and forming part of the border between Kyrgyzstan and Kazakhstan; this is the Chui River. The valley of the Chui in the north-central region of the country is an important lowland, containing Kyrgyzstan's capital and largest city, Bishkek. Lying to the west, and separated from the Chui valley by yet another modest range of mountains, the Kyrgyz Ala Too, is the valley of the Talas River. The Talas, like the Chui, flows northwestward into Kazakhstan, but before reaching the border provides much needed irrigation water for this corner of Kyrgyzstan.

Southward of the Talas region, across a rugged terrain split by the valley of the Naryn River, lies the third vital lowland of the country—Kyrgyzstan's share of the Fergana Valley. Although Kyrgyzstan was awarded only a meager portion of this rich agricultural region by Soviet cartographers in the 1920s, nevertheless three significant cities are clustered in the valley on the Kyrgyz side: Jalalabad, Uzgen, and Osh, progressing from north to south. The latter two are ancient Silk Road cities, and both were established over a thousand years ago. The Fergana Valley is Kyrgyzstan's most densely populated region and also holds most of the Uzbek minority. This fertile, productive corner of the country witnessed savage ethnic rioting between Kyrgyz and Uzbeks in 1990 near the city of Osh, and due to continuing instability, isolation, and distance from Bishkek, it remains a source of concern for the government. During the winter months, the highway connecting Osh to Bishkek is often blocked at higher elevations by heavy snowfalls, further dividing the north from the south. The economic potential of this region may soon increase, as it contains one of the few passes through the mountainous frontier into China, the Irkeshtam Pass. Recently opened, this opening to China may allow for increased trade between western China and Kyrgyzstan.

Southwest of the Fergana Valley an elongated southern arm of Kyrgyzstan stretches between Uzbekistan and Tajikistan, a remote and sparsely populated land of isolated villages situated among jagged mountain peaks. This is Batken oblast (province), the least developed of Kyrgystan's regions, and also the poorest. A region of stunning beauty, there is little opportunity for agriculture or industry, and the main activities are herding and some limited mining. Batken does show some potential as a tourist destination, at least for mountain climbers, hikers, and other outdoor enthusiasts because the landscape is stunning in its wild beauty, and much of it remains completely unspoiled and undeveloped. For this potential to be met, shortcomings in transportation and tourist infrastructure must be addressed. Unfortunately, little of the available investment capital in Kyrgyzstan has been directed to Batken, as other more populated and accessible parts of the country have taken priority.

A final and essential point that must be made concerning Kyrgyzstan's geography again relates to elevation. The country's expansive mountainous terrain contains an abundance of an increasingly scarce and precious resource in Central Asia—water. The mountains of Kyrgyzstan hold several thousand glaciers, some of them massive, like the famous South Inylchek Glacier of the Tien Shan, which extends for nearly thirty miles. In addition, the country boasts almost two thousand lakes, most of them containing fresh water. Along with the Naryn, Talas, and other streams, these sources of water represent not only a vital resource for the future of the entire region, but also future political leverage and influence for Kyrgyzstan with its larger, more powerful neighbors, in particular, Uzbekistan and Kazakhstan. It seems certain that as demand for water inevitably increases in Central Asia, Kyrgyzstan's standing will also grow, because the lakes and glaciers of this isolated, beautiful country represent virtually the only location where additional water may be found. Ironically, the difficult terrain of Kyrgyzstan in the future may deliver its most valuable commodity.

Climate and Ecology

Kyrgyzstan's location at the center of the Eurasian landmass ensures that the country experiences a continental climate, with the typical temperature extremes that characterize locations at the heart of continents. Temperature variation depends not only on latitude, but in such a mountainous country, elevation, too, plays an important role in determining the local range of temperature. In the northern valleys of the Talas and Chui rivers, temperatures in winter may drop to well below freezing, although milder readings of 10 to 15 degrees (Fahrenheit) above the freezing mark are common as well. In the southern stretches of the country, particularly in the Fergana Valley, winters are warmer and may be rather comfortable compared with much of the remainder of Kyrgyzstan. Nearly 90 percent of the landscape is mountainous, and at the higher elevations winters can be extremely cold and inhospitable, with temperatures remaining well below freezing during the winter months. On the other hand, summer temperatures are relatively mild, with temperatures above 90 degrees Fahrenheit common only in the Fergana Valley, where occasionally high temperatures may exceed 100 degrees Fahrenheit.

The patterns for precipitation across the country also show considerable variation for such a small nation. In the north and east, drier conditions prevail because the air masses that reach this part of the country have had much of the moisture they contain wrung from them by the mountainous peaks over which they are carried. The south and southwest are wetter, however, because of the higher elevation of these regions, which brings on more abundant cloud formation and

Radioactive waste from a Soviet uranium processing plant spreads along the banks of the Maili Suu River, near the Fergana Valley in southwest Kyrgyzstan. The Soviets dumped some 2 million cubic meters of uranium waste along the river between 1948 and 1968. (Staton R. Winter/Getty Images)

results in greater precipitation, especially in the form of snow. The precipitation at higher altitudes across Kyrgyzstan provides a steady source of water during the growing season for the entire country, and indeed for much of the entire region of Central Asia.

Kyrgyzstan did not suffer the environmental catastrophes of the Soviet era that struck its neighbors Uzbekistan and Kazakhstan, partially as a result of its topography and remoteness. Nevertheless, the country did not entirely escape the ecological mismanagement that characterized Soviet administration either, and significant challenges loom in protecting and preserving the quality of Kyrgyzstan's environment. Among the most important are the numerous abandoned uranium mines that dot the landscape, a residue of the Soviet period when the Kyrgyz SSR was a major supplier of uranium to the Soviet government. Runoff and seepage from these facilities is a constant threat to water quality in the communities located near them, and further contamination of water supplies is a potential problem. In addition, several incidents of accidental spillage of toxins into major water bodies in the post-Soviet period have resulted in loss of life and serious damage, as was the case when an overturned truck dumped cyanide into a stream feeding Issyk Kul in 1998.

Deforestation and rising global temperatures are additional environmental concerns in Kyrgyzstan. By some estimates, the country has lost half of its forested acreage since World War II, and since independence, economic decline, rising poverty rates, and increases in population growth in some areas have led to more losses. In some rural districts, wood has become a major source of fuel, and uncontrolled cutting for local use has resulted in a significant loss of trees in many parts of Kyrgyzstan. This in turn gives rise to greater erosion of the hillsides and loss of topsoil, reductions in local water quality in streams and lakes, and problems with siltation in some lakes. Warmer temperatures in recent decades have contributed to the retreat of many of Kyrgyzstan's glaciers, a worrisome development in a country with increasing demands on its water supplies and that provides water to much of the rest of Central Asia.

Political Geography

When the borders of Soviet Socialist Republics (SSRs) began to take shape in Central Asia in the aftermath of the Bolshevik Revolution, Soviet ethnographers encountered difficulty in distinguishing some nomadic peoples, particularly the Kazakhs from the Kyrgyz. Initially, this confusion arose due to some scholars and officials labeling the Kazakhs "Kyrgyz," and employing the name "Kara Kyrgyz," or "Black Kyrgyz" for those groups who would later be collectively identified as the Kyrgyz nationality. Some of this confusion was due to the weak self-identity of the groups themselves, whose tribal and clan loyalties at the time far outweighed any sense of a larger national identity. By the mid-1920s, both the Kazakhs and the Kyrgyz had been more accurately defined as Soviet "nationalities" and were assigned specific territories that were, at least in theory, historically connected to their recently identified ethnic identity. The Kara Kyrgyz Autonomous Oblast was formed in 1924 and the next year was elevated to the Kyrgyz Autonomous Soviet Socialist Republic (Kyrgyz ASSR), a unit lying within the administration of the Russian Federated Soviet Socialist Republic (RFSSR), which the next year was divided into seven oblasts. Granting the Kyrgyz people a delineated territory as their homeland clearly assisted in solidifying the concept of *Kyrgyzchylyk,* or "Kyrgyzness."

The borders of the new territorial units in Central Asia did not exactly conform to the location of the various ethnic groups, however, and in the case of Kyrgyzstan, significant numbers of Uzbeks living in the eastern end of the Fergana Valley were enclosed within the Kyrgyz ASSR, and, as was true elsewhere in the region, many of the urban areas held large numbers of Slavs, particularly the capital city of Pishpek, the name of which was changed to Frunze in 1926 (and later Bishkek in 1991). The inclusion of these minority groups would set the stage for later ethnic tensions and clashes, and the lack of precision in setting the boundaries of the Kyrgyz ASSR, as was the case with other political territories in Central Asia, would contribute to border disputes between independent Kyrgyzstan and its neighbors in the 1990s.

In 1936, the Kyrgyz ASSR was promoted to full Soviet Socialist Republic status, officially becoming the Kyrgyz SSR and adopting a new constitution patterned after those of existing republics. This change in status helped to further the notion of a Kyrgyz nation, because it placed the Kyrgyz on par with other peoples who long had possessed an indisputable identity, such as the Russians, Georgians, and Armenians. Soviet policy from the 1940s to the 1990s tended to reinforce the notion of Kyrgyzchylyk, and the collapse of the USSR in

1991 resulted in the appearance of an independent Kyrgyz state for the first time in history. Decisions of Soviet administrators continue to haunt the young nation, however, which must find answers to ethnic friction, boundary irregularities, and other difficulties brought about by that bygone era.

Population Characteristics

Ethnic and Religious Geography

From its inception, the territory assigned to the Kyrgyz by the Soviet government held numerous ethnic groups, and Soviet policy, especially in the 1930s and 1940s, further complicated the ethnic landscape of this small Central Asian Soviet republic by relocating various peoples there. As recently as 1979, the Kyrgyz did not represent a majority of the population in the Kyrgyz SSR, and Slavs (mostly ethnic Russians) accounted for nearly 30 percent of Kyrgyzstan's people. The large Slavic component of the population was the result of massive immigration to the region both before and after the Bolshevik Revolution, while others were "relocated" to Kyrgyzstan, such as many Tatars, Germans, and Koreans, when Josef Stalin questioned their loyalties to the Soviet regime. The years since the early 1980s have witnessed profound changes in the ethnic makeup of Kyrgyzstan, a process discussed in detail later in the section on "Distribution and Growth."

The origins of the Kyrgyz are somewhat obscure, although it is clear that they are related to several of the ethnic groups that reside in Central Asia. They are closely connected to the Kazakhs and Karakalpaks, and more generally to other Turkic peoples of the region. It seems reasonably certain that ancestors of the modern Kyrgyz migrated to Central Asia from Siberia, probably from a homeland near the Yenisey River. Exactly when this process began is unknown, but by A.D. 1000, it is likely that numerous Kyrgyz were living in the Tien Shan along what is today the border region between Kyrgyzs-

A Kyrgyz yurt from the early 20th century. (Library of Congress)

tan and China. There they practiced transhumance, the nomadic process of moving herds of animals to pastures at lower elevations during colder months and returning to higher grazing lands during the summer. The Kyrgyz call the winter grazing land the *kyshtoo,* and the summer pasture in the mountains is the *jailoo.*

Until the 1800s, the Kyrgyz were loosely connected, a more or less confederated collection of tribes and clans with no overarching central authority. The *ail,* a village of an extended family, served as the basic unit of social organization, and the *yurt,* a structure composed of a wooden frame covered by felt textiles, was the basic dwelling. The *sanjira,* or tribes, of the Kyrgyz remain an essential element of the identity of every Kyrgyz. Originally there may have been forty sanjira because some scholars believe that the origin of the name "Kyrgyz" may be from a Turkic root meaning "forty." The tribes are broadly divided on a geographic basis, with the Ong Kanat, or "right wing," living in the north and the Sol Kanat, or "left wing," traditionally residing in the southern part of the country. In general, because of a longer interaction with and exposure to Russian culture, the tribes of the Ong Kanat have acquired more Russian cultural traits than their cousins in the south.

The second-largest group in Kyrgyzstan is the Uzbeks, who make up about 14 percent of the population. The Uzbeks are overwhelmingly concentrated in the Fergana Valley in the southwestern corner of Kyrgyzstan, and although they share some cultural commonalities with the Kyrgyz, they are ethnically distinct. These distinctions include a stronger attachment to Islam among the Uzbeks; differing clothing styles, especially the headgear worn by men; and, of course, differences in language. The *doppa,* or skullcap, that is characteristic of Uzbek men differs markedly from the peaked, felt *kalpak* worn by Kyrgyz men, and this attribute alone is often enough to identify instantaneously a man's ethnicity.

Until recently, the Russians were the largest minority in the country, but the Russian population has experienced an astonishing decline. In the late 1970s, Russians represented almost 30 percent of Kyrgyzstan's population, but by 2002, that figure had dropped to only about 11 percent. This dramatic shift is due to several factors, the most significant of which is the large-scale emigration of Russians from the country beginning in the 1970s, a movement that gained momentum after independence. The mass exodus of Russians, combined with higher birthrates among the Kyrgyz and Uzbeks, has resulted in the steady erosion of the Russian percentage in the population. Those Russians who have remained are mostly urban, concentrated in Bishkek, Talas, and other cities in the northern valleys of the country. Ironically, the Russian language retains its role as a common language among the country's various groups. As is the case in other Central Asian states, the exit of the Russian population has not been healthy for Kyrgyzstan's economy and development because many who have left are highly skilled and educated professionals.

Two other peoples, who once accounted for significant percentages of the population, have also left Kyrgyzstan in huge numbers in recent decades. Ukrainians represented 2.5 percent of the population in 1989, but like their fellow Slavs the Russians, they have left Kyrgyzstan in large numbers since the late 1970s, and since Kyrgyzstan's independence in 1991, more than 50 percent of the Ukrainian population has emigrated. After the Russian conquest of Central Asia and during the first decades of Communist control, thousands of Germans migrated from European Russia (mostly the Volga basin) to Kyrgyzstan, where they generally engaged in farming. Following the pattern of the Slavs, Germans began leaving Central Asia in significant numbers in the late 1970s, but after independence, this flow turned into a flood. In the 1990s, the German population in Kyrgyzstan declined by nearly 80 percent, and the rate of emigration remains high, as the German population returns to either Russia or Germany or migrates to other countries located outside of Central Asia.

Unlike these non-Muslim minorities, the traditionally Islamic minority groups in Kyrgyzstan have not emigrated in nearly the same proportions as the Slavs and Germans, although many Crimean Tatars have left in the 1990s. In total, the Kazakhs, Tatars (those originally from the lower Volga basin), Uighurs, Tajiks, and Dungans (ethnic Chinese who converted to Islam) represent around 5 percent of the population. Most of the ancestors of the Dungan community arrived as refugees from western China in the 1800s, when the Chinese government began persecuting Muslims in its western provinces. In addition, there are communities of Koreans and Armenians in most of the larger cities, the former arriving in the region as a result of being deported from eastern Siberia by Stalin, who doubted their loyalties to the Soviet state. Although small in number, some minority peoples play valuable roles in Kyrgyz society. For example, the Koreans and Dungans, despite their "alien" origins, are frequently leaders in business, commerce, and science, and both communities generally enjoy a higher standard of living than the majority of the population.

The majority of the Kyrgyz were converted to Islam rather late in Central Asian history because of their nomadic lifestyle and their relative isolation from the oasis cities along the Silk Road. The Kyrgyz tribes were exposed to Islamic tenets and practice around the time of their migration from Siberia, probably initially by Sufi adepts, and the Kyrgyz became overwhelmingly Sunni Muslims over the course of several centuries (Imart 1986). Today they are still regarded by many scholars as having some of the weakest links of any Central Asian people to the faith, especially when compared with the Uzbeks and the Tajiks. As Islam gradually took root among the Kyrgyz, it did not entirely displace existing systems of belief, often labeled "shamanism," "totemism," or "folk religion" by scholars of the region. This form of worship emphasized elemental forces of nature, often represented by the power of a specific animal or the sky, moon, sun, or other symbols of the natural world. Another common example of totemism in modern Kyrgyzstan is the placing of votive offerings, often strips of cloth or paper, at holy sites, in the hope of bringing about good fortune for the worshipper.

In Kyrgyzstan today there is a clear geographic division of Islamic religiosity, based mostly on ethnicity. Islamic belief is stronger in the southern portion of the country, where a large Uzbek population is concentrated in the Fergana Valley, while in the northern reaches of the country where the Kyrgyz dominate, strict devotion to Islamic strictures and ritual among the Kyrgyz is rare. The Islamic heritage of the Kyrgyz is evident in post-Soviet Kyrgyzstan, however, in the form of numerous new, albeit rather small, mosques that have appeared all over the country, often constructed with foreign funds. Since 1999, the country has experienced periodic incidents of terrorist violence, most allegedly the work of Muslim extremists, although the frequency of such events has diminished since the removal of the Taliban government in Afghanistan in 2001. These developments have alarmed the already uneasy non-Muslim minorities, and former president Askar Akayev took pains while he was in office to assure both non-Muslims and moderate Muslims alike that the postindependence emphasis on the country's Islamic heritage does not augur a move toward an Islamic government.

The Kyrgyz language belongs to the Uralic-Altaic language family and is related to the other Turkic languages of Central Asia, especially Kazakh. Kyrgyz lacked a written form until the twentieth century, when a system of writing the language based on Arabic script was developed early in the Soviet period. This was later modified to a Latin alphabet in 1928, but that in turn was replaced by a modified Cyrillic alphabet in 1940. The lack of a written language did not prevent the Kyrgyz from cultivating a literary heritage, as the tradition of oral epics, including the most famous of these, *Manas,* has developed to the level of high art among the Kyrgyz. Unlike their cousins the Kazakhs, the Kyrgyz maintained their language in the face of Russification during Soviet administration, and most Kyrgyz today are conversant in their native language and have a good working knowledge of Russian. In the years just after independence there were efforts to make Kyrgyz the exclusive language of public discourse and law, but public outcry by Russians and other minorities resulted in this policy being withdrawn, and in 1996 Russian was actually made an "official" language alongside Kyrgyz.

Distribution and Growth

Kyrgyzstan has a total population of nearly 5 million, and the population density in the country is rather high for such a mountainous nation—about sixty people per square mile. The distribution of the population is uneven, however, with approximately half of Kyrgyzstan's people living in the Fergana Valley oblasts of Osh and Jalalabad, and nearly a third in Osh oblast alone. In the north, the valleys of the Talas and Chiu rivers and the area around Lake Issyk Kul have the greatest concentrations of population. On the other hand, some areas in the northeast of the country are virtually uninhabited because of the elevation and difficult mountain environment.

Population growth rates differ greatly among Kyrgyzstan's various ethnic groups, with Muslim peoples generally having higher rates, and several non-Muslim minorities showing a steep decline of their numbers in recent years. According to the Soviet census conducted in 1979, Kyrgyz made up less than 50 percent of the Kyrgyz SSR's population but today account for two-thirds of the total population, and this share is expected to increase further in coming years. This dramatic increase is due to two factors. First, the Kyrgyz have a relatively high rate of natural increase compared with many other groups in the country; second, the mass emigration of Slavs and Germans from Kyrgyzstan over the last several decades, and especially during the 1990s, has helped to increase the proportion of Kyrgyz in the country. The average age among the Slavs and Germans who remain in Kyrgyzstan is much higher than among the other ethnic groups, and their rate of natural increase is low, factors that ensure their representation in the country's population will continue to decrease. The Uzbeks, who have a fairly high rate of natural increase, have displaced the Russians as the second-largest ethnic group, and their numbers are expected to continue expanding for the foreseeable future.

Migration and Urbanization

The demographic balance between Kyrgyzstan's various peoples has undergone a seismic shift in the last two decades, as several groups have left the country in large numbers. The most significant of these in terms of sheer quantity is the out-migration of Russians and Ukrainians, who began leaving in significant volume as early as the 1970s. Statistics indicate that this mass departure reached near epic proportions after independence in 1991, as the Russian population dropped by 34 percent between 1989 and 1999, and the Ukrainians declined by 53 percent, although the absolute number of Ukrainians was much lower because their population was significantly smaller than that of their Slavic cousins, the Russians. As is true in the other Central Asian states, the economic and social consequences for Kyrgyzstan of losing the Slavic population, representing many professionals, technicians, and businesspeople, have inhibited the country's efforts at economic advancement.

Another group whose numbers belie their economic importance are the Germans, whose exit, like Germans in Kazakhstan, has picked up steam since the collapse of the USSR. The Germans represented only 2.4 percent of the population of the Kyrgyz SSR in 1989, or about 100,000 people, but in the decade between 1989 and 1999 more than 60,000 left Kyrgyzstan, a trend that has slowed, but not halted. This is yet another group that historically has produced prosperous and industrious farmers, entrepreneurs, and scholars, and their loss has not been helpful to Kyrgyzstan's fledgling economy. The European exodus of Slavs and Germans from Kyrgyzstan has been fueled by resentment over official language policy, particularly in the early 1990s before Russian was elevated to official status with Kyrgyz; fears of Islamic "fundamentalism" and violence; economic uncertainty and decline in Kyrgyzstan after independence; and general displeasure with the loss of status many Slavs enjoyed before the decline of Soviet power. Most of these emigrants have left the Central Asian region entirely, returning to their ethnic homelands or to countries outside the former Soviet bloc.

The population of Kyrgyzstan has lived primarily in rural areas for most of history, and even in the twentieth century no more than about 38 percent of the people in the Kyrgyz SSR were urbanized. In fact, the proportion of those who were urbanized in Kyrgyzstan has been declining over the last several decades, dropping from 38.3 percent in 1979, to 38.1 percent in 1989, to only 34.8 percent in 1999 (Abazov 2004). The decline in urbanization has been fed by two trends. First, the flight of much of the Russian population, which historically was heavily urbanized in Kyrgyzstan, contributed significantly to the overall drop in urbanization over the last twenty years. In addition, higher rates of natural increase among both Kyrgyz and Uzbeks, who tend to reside in rural locations, also added to the general losses in urbanization during the same period. The largest city by far is Bishkek (formerly Frunze), which is officially listed as holding a population of about 700,000, and the next largest city is Osh, with a population slightly greater than 250,000. No other city in the country reaches even 100,000 residents.

HISTORY
Early History

The territory of modern Kyrgyzstan is dotted with evidence of inhabitation from as early as 3000 B.C., and it is likely that nomadic tribes occupied the area well before that time. Much of the evidence appears in the form of petroglyphs, and two sites in particular indicate not only early human settlement, but also a climate that must have been somewhat warmer than today. The rock carvings at Saimaly Tash, an isolated location in southern Kyrgyzstan, range in age from 3000 B.C. to as recent as A.D. 1000, indicating that Saimaly Tash has held great religious and cultural significance for numerous peoples who occupied this part of Kyrgyzstan over the course of many centuries. Many of the drawings represent animals, and some show what appear to be religious rituals as well as agricultural practices, hinting that some of the earliest peoples of the region may not have been entirely nomadic. Similar artwork at Cholpan Ata, near Lake Issyk Kul, although not as old as some of the depictions at Saimaly Tash, nevertheless provides invaluable insight into the lives of the ancient residents of Kyrgyzstan.

Some of those who left their mark at Saimaly Tash were Scythians, a nomadic and warlike people who gained control of the steppes and mountain valleys of central and eastern Central Asia in the eighth century B.C. The Scythians or Saka, as they were sometimes called, were skilled workers of gold and masters of mounted warfare. These nomadic peoples built no great cities but instead followed a transitory way of life for centuries. Yet the Scythians developed enough communication and organization among their far-flung clusters of horses and wagons that they may be called the first "civilization" of the steppes. The Scythians waged war against the Persians to their west, at one point frustrating the great Persian ruler Darius, who was forced to abandon his campaign against them. By the second century B.C., the eastern tribes of Scythians, who lived in the river valleys and around Lake Issyk Kul in what is today northern Kyrgyzstan, had been absorbed by a group Chinese chroniclers call the Wusun (in some sources, Usun). This fierce people built their capital on the shores of Issyk Kul but were likely displaced by the Hunnic invasions of Central Asia that began in the first century B.C.

In the second century B.C., the Chinese Empire established trading relations with city states in the Fergana Valley, at the time under the control of the Sogdians. The Chinese were especially interested in trading for horses and soon discovered that silk, which at the time only they could produce, was in great demand there and further west, all the way to the Roman Empire. Thus silk (and many other commodities) began to flow westward, and goods and money moved in the opposite direction, giving rise to the famous Silk Road. One branch of this ancient trade route passed through Kyrgyzstan, and the cities of Osh, Uzgen, and Jul, an ancient city located

An ancient caravansary in Kyrgyzstan, along the old Silk Road. (Janet Wishnetsky/Corbis)

near the site of modern Bishkek, all functioned as important Silk Road commerce centers.

The Huns held much of eastern Central Asia for five centuries, until they were dispersed by another army of nomadic invaders, the Turks, in A.D. 565. These Turkish warriors were part of a larger empire that came to exist in two parts, an Eastern Khanate centered on Mongolia and southern Siberia, and the Western Turkish Khanate, with its capital at least part of the year near Issyk Kul. Powerful for a time, the Turks weakened themselves by frequent intrigue and conflict between the two portions of the empire and ultimately were defeated by the Chinese, who cleverly played one khanate off against the other. The collapse of Turkish authority in Central Asia allowed the Chinese to expand their border in the region greatly to the west—by A.D. 744, the Tang dynasty had added the Talas basin and the Issyk Kul region to their empire, as well as other territory west of the Tien Shan. Chinese influence likely would have been extended even further to the west had not the arrival of a new force of invaders, inspired by a new faith, prevented them from pushing deeper into the heart of Central Asia.

Muslim armies under the great general Qutaiba had subjugated the Silk Road cities of Bukhara and Samarkand between A.D. 709 and 712 and pushed into the Fergana region by 715. Although forced to repress frequent rebellions in Bukhara and Samarkand, the Muslim army, which was composed mostly of Arabs but contained soldiers from many ethnic groups, eventually consolidated its hold over the Silk Road cities and by 750 had advanced to the very doorstep of Chinese territory in northern Kyrgyzstan. In 751 the two armies clashed near the Talas River, a battle of huge significance for the history of Central Asia and for world history. The Chinese were badly defeated and forced to withdraw to the eastern slopes of the Tien Shan. At the same time, the Muslims took many prisoners, including some who taught their Islamic captors the process of making paper, a technology later passed to Europe. The Battle of Talas River secured Central Asia as part of the Dar ul Islam, or "realm of Islam," for it would be a 1,000 years before the Chinese pushed again to the western side of the Tien Shan, and then only for a short time.

There is general agreement that the ancestors of the modern Kyrgyz migrated into the western Tien Shan and associated basins from Siberia. The exact location of their original homeland in that region is debated, although probably a majority of Kyrgyz scholars believe that it was likely located near the Yenisey River. There is also general accord among scholars that this migration was more or less complete by A.D. 1100. By that date, the territory of modern Kyrgyzstan was at the heart of the Karakhanid Empire, founded by another Turkic but decidedly Muslim people, who established capitals at both Uzgen and Burana, near Tokmak in northern Kyrgyzstan. The five centuries from A.D. 1100 to 1600 in Central Asia represent a period of almost constant warfare and invasion, for the Karakhanids in turn would be followed by the

Seljuks, the Khitans, the Mongols under Genghis Khan, Amir Timur (Tamerlane), and finally the Shaybanids (see the discussion on early history in the section on Uzbekistan).

Perhaps the most destructive invaders the Kyrgyz faced were the Kalmyks (referred to as the Oirats or Jungars in some sources), a Buddhist Mongol people who penetrated Central Asia in the 1600s and competed with indigenous nomadic peoples for pasture and water, especially the Kazakhs and Kyrgyz. The Kalmyk invasion was a time of great difficulty but may have contributed to Kyrgyz unity because the isolated and disparate tribes were forced to collaborate in their resistance to this new adversary. After a century and a half internal conflict finally weakened the Kalmyks, to the extent that the majority attempted to return to western China, where they were resettled under the watchful eyes of Chinese officials. Ironically, the departure of the Kalmyks merely paved the way for yet another emergent power to encroach on the valleys and mountain redoubts of the Kyrgyz, this time from the Fergana Valley city of Kokand.

An Uzbek tribe, the Ming (not connected to the Chinese dynasty of the same name) had constructed a palace at Kokand, in the western part of the Fergana Valley, in the early 1700s. From this rather modest base the Khans of Kokand, as the rulers came to call themselves, progressively expanded their reach to include much of southern Kazakhstan, eastern Uzbekistan, and most of Kyrgyzstan and Tajikistan. The Kyrgyz vigorously resisted incorporation into the khanate and, once brought under the yoke of Kokand, frequently rebelled but lacked the organization and weaponry to break free. After a century of resisting the domination and cruelty of the Kokand regime, many Kyrgyz acquired assistance and protection from a most unexpected source—the Russians. After two centuries of gradually penetrating the steppe lands of Central Asia, by the middle of the 1800s the Russians had arrived at the foothills of the Tien Shan, an event that would completely reshape Central Asia's culture, history, and geography.

The Imperial Russian Period

The advent of the Russians into Central Asia was accomplished primarily through military conquest, although in some instances the tsar's authority was welcomed with little resistance. Among the Kyrgyz, some of whom had sought the Russian Empire's protection as far back as the early 1800s, Russian intervention in the region was seen as a useful counterweight to the aggressive regime in Kokand. When the Russian government established protectorates over several northern Kyrgyz tribes in the middle of the nineteenth century, the stage was set for an eventual showdown between the tsar's forces and those of the Khan of Kokand. Russian generals began peeling away portions of the Khanate's territory, capturing Tashkent in 1865 and in 1875 taking three crucial cities in the Fergana Valley: Kokand, Osh, and Andijan. The following year the Russians simply absorbed what remained of the chaotic khanate into its new province of Turkistan, thereby placing all of the Kyrgyz tribes west of the Tien Shan under Russian rule. Some Kyrgyz tribes, including those led by Kurmanjan Datkha, whom the Russians considered a Kyrgyz "queen," joined the Russians in ousting the Kokand government.

Tsarist administration brought many changes to traditional life among the Kyrgyz. The lifestyle of transhumance was weakened by the arrival of commercial agriculture and a market economy. Expansion of the transportation and urban structures disrupted the traditional nomadic system, and expanded trade both with Russia and other locations in Central Asia, resulting in many Kyrgyz abandoning the herding and hunting activities of their forefathers and becoming tradesmen, merchants, or farmers. A number of forts built by the Khanate of Kokand were converted into larger urban sites by Russian military officials, and the economic and social opportunities these and other cities offered under the new regime drew many Kyrgyz to them. Land ownership, always a somewhat vague and indefinite concept among Kyrgyz nomads, became concretely defined under Russian law, undermining the ability of the Kyrgyz to follow their herds. Thus the social fabric of traditional Kyrgyz life was slowly but inevitably unraveled.

Absorption into the Russian Empire brought not only social and economic changes for the Kyrgyz, but also changes in the cultural and ethnic landscape, as thousands of settlers from other corners of the empire arrived in Kyrgyzstan, at the invitation of the region's new rulers. Groups of Russian settlers had established small communities in Kyrgyzstan as early as the 1860s, and by the 1890s, numerous Slavic and German farming settlements dotted the "unclaimed" lands in the region, most of which had been seasonal pasturage that the tsarist administrators appropriated for the new colonists. At the turn of the century, some 30,000 Slavs and Germans from European Russia were tilling the valleys of Kyrgyzstan. A second and larger migration of Slavs into Kyrgyzstan took place in the first decade of the twentieth century, when as many as 70,000 immigrants may have arrived. Not only did the immigrants turn lands that had previously been pasture into cropland, they also helped accelerate the cultural changes that were already under way.

Ironically, while the influx of both Russian control and Russian settlers sapped the foundations of traditional Kyrgyz culture, these new elements in Kyrgyz life also had the effect of crystallizing Kyrgyz identity. By the early part of the twentieth century, an indigenous elite had developed among the Kyrgyz, most of whom were products of the Russian educational system but who frequently came to identify themselves not by tribal or clan criteria, but more universally as "Kyrgyz." Advances in literacy, including instruction in Kyrgyz as well as Russian, allowed a Kyrgyz literature to appear for the first time, at least in print. The great epic poem *Manas,* a paean to a legendary *batyr,* or Kyrgyz warrior, had been passed through generations of Kyrgyz orally, but rising literacy among the Kyrgyz made the story more accessible. *Manas* and other epic tales were indisputably a central element of Kyrgyz identity and served to unify the Kyrgyz at a time when many of their traditions were threatened by the encroachment of Russian civilization.

Under such conditions of rapid social and cultural change, conflict between the Kyrgyz and the newcomers was probably unavoidable. Tensions arising from religious differences were especially acute, and one of the most serious uprisings was indeed led by a Muslim leader in 1898. The Andijan Uprising began with the call to arms by a Sufi adept in the Fergana Valley city of the same name, who declared a jihad (holy war) against the Russian government and settlers. Muslim rebels first attacked the Russian troops stationed at Andijan, and subsequent attacks followed in other cities in the Fergana region, including Osh. The majority of those carrying the fight to the Russians may have been ethnically Uzbek, but it is clear that significant numbers of Kyrgyz joined the rebellion before it was forcefully suppressed by superior Russian firepower. Local Russian officials were surprised by the level of disaffection among their Central Asian subjects and in the aftermath of the uprising instituted changes designed to placate local grievances.

The violence of 1898 would not be the last episode of open rebellion by the tsar's restive Central Asian subjects. In the first decades of the new century, cultural tensions remained high between the Muslims and their Russian overlords, and combined with deteriorating economic conditions in the early years of World War I, led to an even larger and more serious insurrection. The main spark that ignited this conflagration was a military order in 1916 calling for Central Asians to be drafted into the Russian army. Central Asians reacted ferociously in an armed rebellion that involved most of the region. The government responded with a scorched earth policy, taking a terrible toll among the local population. In Kyrgyzstan, thousands of Kyrgyz attempted to flee the fighting by escaping across the Tien Shan to China, but the passes were snowed in, and huge numbers perished from exposure and starvation. Well over 100,000 Kyrgyz died as a result of the violence, and the stage was set for a political upheaval that would sweep the imperial government from power.

The Soviet Period

The February Revolution in 1917 and the tsar's abdication the following month had little immediate impact on life in Kyrgyzstan. Among the Slavic population a few workers' "soviets" (committees) had formed in the spring after Tsar Nicholas II relinquished power, but enthusiasm for political change was confined mostly to the Russian immigrant population, as few Kyrgyz had been allowed to take part in the existing political system and had little experience in such matters. When the Bolsheviks seized power in St. Petersburg later in the year, Kyrgyzstan and the entire Central Asian region were experiencing rapid economic decline, and support for the new Communist regime remained tempered. The political situation swiftly became chaotic, as various committees and groups competed for control, with the Bolsheviks (Reds) and the Anti-Bolsheviks (Whites) becoming the primary players by 1919. That same year Mikhail Frunze, a Russian native of Pishpek (Bishkek), was assigned by the Bolsheviks to drive the White Army from eastern Central Asia, a task he accomplished decisively within the next year and a half.

Some Kyrgyz fought for either the Red or White forces during the revolutionary years, but the majority remained on the sidelines or formed their own resistance to the Bolsheviks. Among the latter were the so-called Basmachi, a Turkic term applied by their adversaries meaning "bandits." Certainly the Basmachi contained some criminal elements, but the majority were motivated by religious opposition to the Bolsheviks or were generally against continued Slavic domination of Kyrgyzstan and had taken part in the 1916 revolt. Some groups of Basmachi allied themselves with the White forces in the Fergana Valley and for a time captured and held a number of the major cities in that region, including Osh and Jalalabad. Frunze was able to uproot them, however, and with the consolidation of Bolshevik power, the Basmachi were reduced to following isolated, guerrilla warfare tactics, which harassed the Bolshevik authorities but had little possibility of ousting them. Although dispersed and disorganized, some Basmachi continued their struggle into the 1930s.

After 1920, the Bolshevik hold on Central Asia was secure, although scattered resistance persisted for some time thereafter. Following Vladimir Lenin's prescriptions regarding nationalities policy in the Soviet Union, a political union formally established in 1922, the land of the old tsarist territorial unit of Turkistan was subdivided on the basis of "national" (ethnic) groupings. Thus the Uzbeks and Turkmen were awarded Soviet Socialist Republics in 1924, while the Kyrgyz were assigned the Kara-Kyrgyz Autonomous Oblast, later to become the Kyrgyz Autonomous Soviet Socialist Republic, and finally elevated to the Kyrgyz Soviet Socialist Republic in 1936 (Soucek 2000, 224). The creation of the Kyrgyz SSR was vital to strengthening Kyrgyz national identity in that for the first time in history a specific territory was identified as the homeland of the Kyrgyz nation, a shared space that held the genesis of the Kyrgyz people. Whether this was historically accurate was less important than the fact that many Kyrgyz came to view the Kyrgyz SSR, or simply "Kyrgyzya," as their indisputable homeland.

Soviet rule brought some positive changes for the Kyrgyz people. Literacy rates, although they had grown modestly under the Russian imperial regime, skyrocketed under Soviet administration, and women became more politically and economically active. Yet the excesses of the Soviet system far outweighed the benefits it brought, particularly after Josef Stalin assumed complete control of the Soviet state in 1928. In the 1920s and early 1930s, many Kyrgyz joined the Communist Party, and the first party leader in Soviet Kyrgyzstan was Abdulkadyr Urazbekov, an ethnic Kyrgyz. This process resulted in a local Communist elite, although Slavs tended to be represented in Communist Party bodies in a higher proportion than in the general population. Between 1936 and 1938, Stalin purged local communists across the USSR, and in the Kyrgyz SSR nearly the entire government leadership, almost 150 people, was shot in secret near the town of Chong Tash, with their bodies disposed of in a mass grave.

The most devastating policy of the Stalinist years was the collectivization of agriculture. The traditional nomadic way of life for the Kyrgyz was nearly destroyed by Stalin's program to collectivize all agricultural land in the USSR. The effort to collectivize was enforced between 1928 and 1932, and during those years wholesale changes swept Central Asia. Rather than turn their livestock over to the state, thousands of Kyrgyz followed the lead of their Kazakh cousins and slaughtered their animals by the millions, often leaving their carcasses in the fields to rot. Hundreds of thousands of Kyrgyz died in the drive to create the *kolkhozi,* or collective farms. Many thousands of others fled the region into China to escape Soviet tyranny. The wealthiest members of Kyrgyz society, the *manaps,* who frequently owned large herds of animals and were traditionally the leaders in Kyrgyz society, had their property confiscated and were imprisoned or exiled to Siberian camps. Some of the social linkages among the various Kyrgyz clans was maintained by entire tribes or extended clans forming a kolkhoz where such relationships might be preserved, but overall collectivization had devastating consequences for many Kyrgyz.

Demographic and economic changes accompanied the social changes implemented by Stalin and other Soviet leaders. Soviet policy designed to increase economic development in Kyrgyzstan led to a greater level of industrialization, but this in turn led to a shortage of trained labor. Many Kyrgyz were either unwilling to work in factories or lacked the education and training to perform such work. In response, many thousands of Slavic immigrants were brought to Kyrgyzstan to staff the growing number of enterprises. Soviet census data indicate that, between 1926 and 1939, both the Russian and Ukrainian populations in the Kyrgyz SSR more than doubled, mostly due to the influx of laborers from other parts of the USSR. During World War II, entire factories, along with their workforces, were relocated to Kyrgyzstan, resulting in yet another boost to the Russian population, a trend that continued after the war. Other ethnic groups were forcibly removed to Kyrgyzstan from far-flung corners of the Soviet Empire, the outcome of Stalin's doubts concerning their loyalties to the Soviet state.

In the 1980s, many of the inherent contradictions and imbalances in the Soviet economy and in Soviet society had become obvious to all but the most committed Communist ideologues. Mikhail Gorbachev became leader of the USSR in early 1985, and from the outset, he gave notice that he would be a new breed of Soviet leader. His policies of glasnost (openness) and perestroika (restructuring), slowly accepted and implemented initially, gradually led to a societywide evaluation of the Soviet experiment. For the first time in the history of the USSR, public criticism of not only the Soviet system but the ideology that generated it were allowed to flourish. Both reformist policies were slow to take root in Kyrgyzstan, but eventually Kyrgyz writers, artists, and other intellectuals began to call for greater use of the Kyrgyz language and for reversing the decline of Kyrgyz culture suffered under the Soviet system. Finally, a mass movement emerged to make Kyrgyz a "state" language of equal status with Russian, a clear signal that the Kyrgyz would no longer be content with the status quo in their homeland. Kyrgyz was promoted to official standing in 1989.

Near the end of the Soviet era tensions that had remained submerged under the veneer of "socialist brotherhood" violently broke to the surface, revealing a serious rift between the Kyrgyz SSR's largest Muslim groups. The conflict was centered in Osh oblast in the Fergana Valley, where long-simmering antagonisms between the local Uzbek population and the Kyrgyz in the region suddenly erupted in a bloodbath that raged for two weeks and claimed hundreds of lives. The fighting had several causes. First, many Uzbeks felt that their interests had been ignored when Soviet authorities failed to make Uzbek a third "state language" alongside Kyrgyz. In addition, in Osh oblast many Kyrgyz believed that Uzbeks unfairly dominated the economy and controlled a larger proportion of the land than they were due. When local authorities appropriated a section of an Uzbek kolkhoz and assigned it to Kyrgyz farmers, some young Uzbeks began agitating for the incorporation of Osh and other "Uzbek" territories into Uzbekistan. Mobs of Kyrgyz and Uzbek youths attacked members of the opposite ethnic group, and Soviet army units were required to end the rioting (Anderson 1999). The façade of peace and tranquility among Kyrgyzstan's peoples had been shattered, with few realizing at the time that, within a year and a half, the Soviet system would collapse.

Independent Kyrgyzstan

Askar Akayev was elected to the post of president of the Kyrgyz SSR in October 1990. Akayev was a physicist and had little connection to the Communist Party, a fact that increased his popularity among many in Kyrgyzstan. The Kyrgyz SSR formerly declared independence on August 31, 1991, in the midst of the abortive coup against Mikhail Gorbachev. Unlike most other Central Asian leaders in the USSR, Akayev immediately condemned those who were attempting to overthrow Gorbachev and in fact ordered local forces into the streets of Bishkek to protect his own position. Akayev benefited greatly from his personal popularity and could claim to be the only leader in Central Asia who was not under the control of the Communist Party. By the end of the year, Akayev had won the presidential election for independent Kyrgyzstan, running unopposed.

Akayev moved swiftly to create a new political culture in his country, and Kyrgyzstan quickly outpaced other former Soviet republics in the region in terms of democratic reform. Akayev frequently emphasized the need for "civil society" to evolve, and within a short period the new country was sporting an independent press, political parties of varying persuasion, and nongovernmental organizations (NGOs). By the middle of the decade, however, the political atmosphere in Kyrgyzstan began a swing toward authoritarianism. Akayev, who himself was accused of corruption by some newspapers, intimidated and harassed those who openly questioned his behavior and motives. In the 2000 presidential election, Akayev's strongest opponent, former vice president Felix Kulov, was barred from the election on the basis of his poor knowledge of Kyrgyz and was later arrested on questionable charges, along with other opponents of Akayev. Widespread voting irregularities, pressure by the government against its critics, and Akayev's apparent reluctance to relinquish power all undermined the country's effort to build a civil society. In March 2005, the Akayev regime collapsed after demonstrators forced the president to flee the country. Felix Kulov was freed from prison, and many of Akayev's opponents took up posts in a provisional government, with new presidential elections to be held in June 2005.

From the earliest days of independence, Kyrgyzstan followed a "shock therapy" strategy, designed to overhaul the country's economic structures as quickly as possible. Kyrgyzstan was the first former Soviet republic in Central Asia to introduce a national currency (the *som*) and vigorously pursued a program of privatization of enterprises, foreign investment, and economic reform. For most of the 1990s, the Kyrgyz economy was plagued by high levels of inflation (in the early 1990s exceeding 1,000 percent), unemployment, lower than expected rates of foreign direct investment, and declines in the gross domestic product. By 2001, however, there were signs that the economy was not only stabilizing but expanding. This process was boosted by the influx of military aid and soldiers during and after the autumn 2001, when the United States, and later Russia, established military bases near Bishkek, in response to the U.S. campaign in Afghanistan.

The demise of the Soviet system allowed the Kyrgyz openly to rediscover and celebrate their cultural heritage. At the core of the Kyrgyz heritage is the epic *Manas,* the reexamination of which was encouraged by the Akaev government. In 1995, the 1,000-year anniversary of the poem was observed with huge fanfare in Bishkek, and several schools for budding *manaschi,* or traditional reciters of the epic, have been opened. In addition, the country's Islamic past, reviled under Soviet authority, has been resurrected and restored to a place of honor, especially in the southern part of Kyrgyzstan, where the Uzbeks, more devout than many Kyrgyz, dominate. Yet even in the northern oblasts, new mosques have appeared in recent years, often funded by foreign organizations or governments. These fundamental elements of identity are seen as crucial to the construction of national identity, although many in the remaining Slavic population see such emphasis as alien, isolating, and even hostile.

After the terrorist attacks on September 11, 2001, in the United States, Kyrgyzstan, literally overnight, acquired an increased geopolitical significance. Early in the Bush administration's War on Terror, the Akaev government offered its support to Americans, and within a few weeks U.S. aircraft were stationed in the country. When military action was initiated against the Taliban in the fall of 2001, many combat flights were launched from Kyrgyz territory—Kyrgyzstan, a former Soviet republic, had become a vital ally of the United States. This new relationship brought certain benefits, especially in the form of military and economic aid, but was viewed with trepidation by some in Kyrgyzstan, who feared that openly siding with the Americans would invite retaliation by Islamic extremists. Russia also eyed the U.S. presence in its "backyard" with some alarm, and Kyrgyzstan allowed the Russian government to construct its own military facility in the country, not far from the U.S. base. Nearly overnight, Kyrgyzstan had become a strategic partner of both powers.

FINDING THE PAST, FACING THE FUTURE

The citizens of Kyrgyzstan have discovered over the last decade and a half that independence brings both freedom and responsibility, and building a new society based on democratic principles and a free market is fraught with peril. The initial euphoria has passed, and much hard work toward shaping a state and society that will be successful in a globalized world remains undone. The Akayev regime's backsliding into authoritarianism had many in Kyrgyzstan, as well as many potential foreign investors and partners, waiting for the government's next step. Akayev's abrupt departure from the country's political scene left a sense of both euphoria and uncertainty among many. But the "magic pebble" may yet be within reach—the desire of the Kyrgyz people to succeed and to take their rightful place among the community of nations. The spirit of *Manas* has been reawakened, and like their great hero, the Kyrgyz stand ready to meet all challenges.

References

Abazov, Rafis. 2004. *Historical Dictionary of Kyrgyzstan*. Lanham, MD: Scarecrow Press.

Anderson, John. 1999. *Kyrgyzstan: Central Asia's Island of Democracy?* Amsterdam: Harwood Academic.

Imart, Guy. 1986. "The Islamic Impact on Traditional Kirghiz Ethnicity." *Nationalities Papers* 14(1–2), pp. 65–88.

Sinnott, Peter. 1992. "The Physical Geography of Soviet Central Asia and the Aral Sea Problem." In *Geographic Perspectives on Soviet Central Asia,* edited by Robert Lewis. New York: Routledge.

Soucek, Svat. 2000. *A History of Inner Asia*. New York: Cambridge University Press.

The Economy of Kyrgyzstan

In the years just after independence, many inside Kyrgyzstan and without held considerable hope that the country would serve as a beacon of reform for Central Asia, providing an example of successful transition from a command economy to a globalized, free-market system. Perhaps the foremost reason for this optimism and great expectation was the person of President Askar Akayev himself, who as the only leader in the region who had not been tempered in the cauldron of the Communist Party, represented a clear departure from the past. Indeed, in Kyrgyzstan's first years as a sovereign nation, the rate of reform was bold and impressive, especially when compared with some of the country's neighbors. Yet the "shock therapy" strategy that Kyrgyzstan's leadership followed did not yield results to the degree expected. The country's relatively low level of development inherited from the Soviet era, as well as its geographic isolation, were greater obstacles to advancement than many had anticipated.

Kyrgyzstan's economy was completely transformed under the Soviet system. What had been a traditional, nomadic society with little industrial activity and rather limited agricultural production was within a few decades restructured into a semi-industrialized economy with sedentary agriculture as its most important component. Kyrgyzstan's main economic role within the Soviet Union, however, was providing rare and strategic natural resources, especially strategic metals such as antinomy, gold, lead, zinc, and mercury. Having emerged from the USSR, Kyrgyzstan has struggled to overcome this role and redress the economic structural imbalances of its recent past.

The economic transition has been difficult, despite the ambitious program pursued by the Akayev government. Following the advice of specialists from the International Monetary Fund (IMF), Kyrgyz authorities initiated wholesale privatization in all sectors of the economy, released price controls, and introduced a convertible national currency, the *som,* in 1993. Kyrgyzstan was therefore the first of the Central Asian states to leave the so-called ruble zone and the first to integrate its currency with the global economy. This broad restructuring of the Kyrgyz economy was rewarded in 1998, when Kyrgyzstan, one of the poorest countries to emerge from the former USSR, became the first former Soviet republic to join the World Trade Organization (WTO). Despite the rapidity and depth of the transition, however, the economic situation in Kyrgyzstan worsened in the first five years of independence. After 1995, the economy appeared to turn the corner, and economic growth has been modest, but generally consistent, since 1996.

AGRICULTURE

In 2001, agriculture accounted for the largest share of the Kyrgyz economy and was easily the most important component of the economy. According to the IMF, the agricultural sector represented slightly more than 35 percent of the country's gross domestic product (GDP) in 2001, a modest increase from the last year of Soviet administration, when agriculture contributed just over 34 percent of the Kyrgyz SSR's economic production. Among former Soviet republics, Kyrgyzstan's economy was more dependent on the agricultural sector than any other, and only agriculture in Uzbekistan approached the figure found in Kyrgyzstan. In addition, well over half of all employment in Kyrgyzstan was in agriculture, highlighting the essential role of this portion of the Kyrgyz economy.

Since the mid-1990s, the production of most agricultural commodities has increased, in some cases dramatically. Besides ores and other raw materials, agricultural products

A Kyrgyz shepherd tends his sheep from horseback, near the Tien Shan. (Janet Wishnetsky/Corbis)

represent the country's biggest exports and remain vital to Kyrgyzstan's future.

Cropping Pattern

Kyrgyzstan's mountainous terrain severely limits agricultural potential. Slightly more than half of the country can be utilized for agricultural production, but the great bulk of this land is useful only for grazing. Only 7 percent of Kyrgyzstan is considered arable, or capable of growing crops, yet despite this limitation, the output of some crops is sizable. Crop production is concentrated along the main river valleys, with the most important region being the Fergana Valley. Here the combination of an extensive irrigation system and fertile soils, with a slightly longer growing season than in the north, results in a diverse agricultural landscape, with cash crops, such as cotton and tobacco, numerous orchards, vineyards, potato and beet fields, and various grains all occupying portions of the available farmland. In the north, the valleys of the Chu and Talas rivers, along with the lowlands around Lake Issyk Kul, complement the abundance of the Fergana region.

In addition to the impressive increases in total volume of agricultural commodities that Kyrgyz farmers achieved in the latter part of the 1990s, there was a dramatic rise in the yield of many crops. For example, average yields of grain between 1995 and 2001 increased by 56 percent, and for the same time period average yields of melons went up by 149 percent. These remarkable gains in yields may be attributed to several factors, including better farming techniques and the privatization of farmland. The first years of turning over the collective farms (*kolkhozi*) to private production were chaotic, but by the mid-1990s much of the disruption of this process had been overcome, resulting in substantial improvements in yields and productivity.

Most of the country's agricultural land is useful only for grazing, and animal husbandry was the traditional way of life for the Kyrgyz people. Animal products, particularly wool and meat, remain a substantial part of the country's agricultural exports, although production of both remained stagnant during the late 1990s. Kyrgyz herders have practiced a seasonal migration of their flocks for centuries between pastures at differing elevations, a practice known as transhumance. Although severely curtailed after the collectivization of agriculture in the 1930s, some Kyrgyz still observe this seasonal cycle. The summer pastures, located at higher elevations, are referred to as the *jailoo.* During this time the entire extended family will typically occupy a *yurt,* a large tent composed of a wooden frame covered by animal skins. During the long winter months, the herders and their flocks move back to lower elevations, usually to valleys protected from harsh winds, which are called the *kyshtoo.*

The production of food crops has seen a significant boost

since the mid-1990s. In 2001, Kyrgyz farmers produced almost 2 million tons of grain, including wheat, barley, corn, and rice, with wheat representing more than half the total. That figure represented almost exactly twice the production in 1995, an increase that was common to almost all agricultural commodities. For example, the volume of potatoes harvested in Kyrgyzstan in 2001 was more than twice the amount produced in 1995, and similar gains were achieved in the production of fruits and berries, vegetables, and melons. Only wool production remained stagnant, failing to rise significantly from levels in the mid-1990s. Most of the fruit, vegetables, and melons grown in Kyrgyzstan are for local consumption, because these treats are served with nearly every meal. As is true elsewhere in Central Asia, in the late summer many street corners in Bishkek, Osh, and other large cities are occupied by enormous piles of watermelons or the yellow sweet melon known simply as *dinya* in Russian, and both are frequently served as the final course at dinner or at social gatherings.

Land Ownership and Reform

Before the arrival of the Russian administration in the nineteenth century, land tenure in Kyrgyzstan was a rather loose system, with certain clans, led by *manaps,* or local tribal leaders, controlling most of the grazing lands and pastures. The arrival of immigrant farmers from Russia and Ukraine and the subsequent appropriation of "empty" lands meant that some system of land ownership was required, and under the Russian imperial administration, formalized procedures were set in place to recognize legal ownership of land. The great majority of Kyrgyz remained nomadic, however, and therefore most of the propertied farmers were the recent immigrants, who continued to pour into the region, drawn by the allure of "free" land.

After the establishment of Soviet authority, major changes

to land ownership and control were implemented, and some redistribution of land was undertaken in the first years of Soviet administration. This early policy would change, however, particularly with the campaign to collectivize agriculture in the 1920s and early 1930s. The Soviet regime became determined to "settle" the nomadic peoples of Central Asia, primarily the Kazakhs and the Kyrgyz. To that end, the Kyrgyz were forcibly located onto collective farms, or kolkhozi, and less frequently onto *sovkhozi,* or state farms, the latter generally being somewhat larger. The lands of the kolkhozi and sovkhozi were owned by the state, as were the machinery, buildings, and livestock (Abazov 2004). The Kyrgyz reaction to the confiscation of their pastures and livestock was both tragic and immediate: millions of animals were slaughtered by their owners, rather than turning them over to the Soviet authorities, and many Kyrgyz simply fled to western China. For nearly all the Kyrgyz, collectivization spelled the end of a way of life their ancestors had followed for centuries.

The decline of the USSR in 1991 also meant the collapse of Soviet ideology, and with it, collectivized agriculture in Kyrgyzstan. The Kyrgyz government moved swiftly to return land to private ownership over the opposition of some entrenched bureaucrats and politicians, breaking up the kolkhozi into agricultural cooperatives, and initially leasing the land to farmers for a period of 99 years. Farmers had the option of establishing individual enterprises or banding together into cooperatives. Considerable confusion and uncertainty plagued the process of privatization in the first years of independence, however, and the result was a serious drop in agricultural production, as many farmers simply produced enough for their own immediate needs. Numbers of livestock also went into a steep decline as many animals were slaughtered for food.

The initial period of disruption surrounding privatization was followed by a recovery in agricultural production in the late 1990s, as Kyrgyz farmers adjusted to new market conditions. Productivity was also boosted by aid and assistance from international donor agencies such as the IMF and the World Bank, which made loans available and offered educational programs designed to help inexperienced producers with technical and financial issues.

By some estimates, more than half the agricultural land in Kyrgyzstan had been returned to private ownership by the late 1990s, a process that has continued unabated into the new century. Kyrgyzstan's experience with privatization may serve as a model for other Central Asian states, which have lagged somewhat behind in shifting agricultural lands to the private sector. Kyrgyzstan appears poised to resume its role as a major exporter of agricultural products and to expand its markets to a broader regional, and perhaps eventually, global scale.

INDUSTRY

Virtually no industry existed in Kyrgyzstan before the Bolshevik Revolution. The Kyrgyz were overwhelmingly agrarian and nomadic until the 1920s, when a limited number of enterprises were built in the Kyrgyz SSR, along with attempts to exploit valuable deposits of mineral resources. The level of industrial activity was increased dramatically during the World War II, when entire factories were shifted to the Kyrgyz republic to make them less vulnerable to German attack, and at the same time, Kyrgyzstan became an important source for coal and metallic ores. In general, however, the Kyrgyz SSR received a much lower share of industrial investment under the Soviet administration than did other Soviet Socialist Republics, even most of those in Central Asia. The region was utilized by Soviet planners and officials as a storehouse of raw materials and resources, which were extracted, and then processed and refined in other parts of the Soviet Union, and subsequently returned to Kyrgyzstan in the form of higher-value finished goods.

By 1991, when Kyrgyzstan suddenly became independent, the modest industrial base that had been constructed was antiquated and inefficient. Machinery and technology were badly out-of-date, and the country's enterprises were completely lacking any knowledge or experience with the management, marketing, and accounting strategies that would allow Kyrgyz producers to compete in the global marketplace. The country desperately needed capital investment, but little local capital was available, because the concept of purchasing stock was alien to most people, and few had much disposable income to invest at any rate. As was the case in Uzbekistan, foreign investment fell short of expectations, and the overseas capital that did arrive was concentrated in mining and other rather short-term investments that generated fewer jobs.

The Kyrgyz government pursued a vigorous program in the early 1990s to privatize both industrial property and agricultural holdings, at the same time introducing the national currency, the som. Coupled with the disruption of previous markets and suppliers, these events sent Kyrgyz industrial production into a tailspin, and output witnessed a disastrous decline during the first half of the 1990s. Entire factories simply shut down, with thousands of workers losing their jobs. Added to these problems was the exodus of a large portion of the skilled, highly educated workforce, mostly Russians, who left seeking better economic conditions in Russia or for other reasons. By 1996, the signs of an economic recovery were clear, and except for a brief dip in 1999, industrial production has grown steadily since that year. Some industrial goods, however, once mainstays of Kyrgyzstan's industrial base, have virtually disappeared in the transition, including electric engines, trucks, washing machines, and other durable goods. According to Kyrgyz government statistics, in 2000, industry accounted for less than 10 percent of Kyrgyzstan's GDP, whereas at the beginning of the 1990s, it represented nearly 30 percent.

Although industrial production of machinery and con-

Metallurgist smelting copper and drawing copper cable in a factory located in the Fergana Valley of Kyrgyzstan. (Shepard Sherbell/Corbis Saba)

sumer goods has severely declined in independent Kyrgyzstan, some remaining sectors have shown promise, especially mining and energy. Although coal production has plummeted, a large gold mine at Kumtor was established with the aid of Canadian investors in the late 1990s, and in 2001 contributed 9 percent of Kyrgyzstan's GDP, a huge share for a single enterprise. In 2002, the Kumtor mine produced in excess of twenty tons of gold, and it is expected that other potential gold deposits in Kyrgyzstan will soon be worked, if world gold prices remain stable and relatively high.

Kyrgyzstan's mountainous terrain and numerous swiftly flowing streams provide great potential for electrical generation, and after many delays, a large hydroelectric dam was inaugurated at Tash Kumyr in 2001. Increased investment in the country's hydroelectrical potential could allow Kyrgyzstan to develop into a major exporter of electricity to Uzbekistan, Kazakhstan, and even possibly western China and parts of southern Siberia. Food processing is another industrial activity that the country appears poised to enter, as this sector of industry is clearly underdeveloped, and both the local and nearby export markets show considerable potential for expansion. Standing in the way of industrial and business growth are the systemic obstacles of corruption and bureaucracy. Kyrgyz entrepreneurs face daunting levels of paperwork just to establish and maintain a business, and often bribery is the only means of getting things accomplished. Such barriers only serve to inhibit economic advancement and preserve low standards of living, thereby adding to general frustration and disappointment.

SERVICES

Because of the state monopoly under communism, the service sector in Kyrgyzstan and other parts of the USSR was badly underdeveloped during the Soviet period. The collapse of the command economy brought with it an immediate demand for services that had previously been essentially nonexistent under the former regime, such as financial services, private insurance, consulting, information management services, and others. By 2004, the service sector accounted for 38 percent of the total GDP in Kyrgyzstan, almost the same as agriculture, and the service sector provided jobs to 30 percent of the workforce. With the decline of industrial production in the 1990s, the expanding service sector in Kyrgyzstan has taken on additional significance.

Many of the current services available in Kyrgyzstan have been created since 1991. For example, under the Soviet administration, no securities markets existed in the country, but after independence, the Kyrgyz government established the legal framework for a stock market, which began operations in 1995. By 1999, more than 10 million stocks were traded on the Kyrgyz exchange—a paltry number compared with major markets in Europe, Japan, and the United States, but a significant increase over previous years. Banking services were privatized, and by 2003 a number of independent banks were offering basic services to the Kyrgyz public. The government has also taken steps to stimulate the development of a domestic insurance industry, with modest results.

The expansion of the service sector in the Kyrgyz economy has offset the contraction of industrial activity that hampered the country through most of the 1990s. The importance of growth in services is magnified by the recent shrinkage in the agricultural sector, once far and away the largest part of the economy. Only services have shown sustained growth in Kyrgyzstan since independence, and this sector appears to have the greatest potential for continued expansion, particularly if larger numbers of tourists are successfully enticed to visit the country in the near future. The Kyrgyz economy is still struggling with the transition to free-market capitalism, however, and more time and effort will be required before the full array of services, found in Western economies, takes root.

POVERTY

The concept of poverty in Kyrgyzstan must be approached with caution, particularly when making comparisons with other countries or regions. Generally, social scientists approach the concept of poverty using a relative standard that varies according to the society and region in question. A recent report by the IMF utilizes three methods to assess poverty in Kyrgyzstan, reinforcing that there is no uniform definition of poverty even within the same country, nor is the term always used in the same way. When considering poverty in Kyrgyzstan, therefore, the Western reader must keep in mind that many of those listed as "living in poverty" in North America or Europe would belong to the middle or possibly upper class in Kyrgyzstan, where overall living standards are much lower.

While a part of the USSR, the Kyrgyz SSR was one of the

poorest and least developed Soviet republics. The economic disruption brought on by the sudden and unexpected dissolution of the USSR in turn generated quite difficult times for most Kyrgyz. The first five years of independence in particular witnessed an extreme decline in quality of life for many. By 1996, government sources were reporting that approximately 60 percent of the population lived in poverty, and many Kyrgyz families were altering their traditional lifestyles, including limiting the number of visits to relatives, a fundamental activity in Central Asian culture (Howell 1996). Ironically, the assistance of family and friends appears to have been a key factor in helping many people cope with the economic crisis, as these sources provided food and small personal loans to those most in need.

As is true across Central Asia, in Kyrgyzstan during the crisis of early independence, and still today, the rural regions hold a higher percentage of poor than do urban areas. In 1993 in Jalalabad Oblast, the percentage of households considered to be poor in rural districts was more than twice the percentage of poor households in the cities (Howell 1996). This disparity led to increased migration to the country's urban areas, particularly by young males seeking employment opportunities. In 1997, the Yntymak movement assisted hundreds of unemployed young men from eastern Kyrgyzstan in reaching the capital of Bishkek, a shift that increased social and political tensions there (Anderson 1999). In addition, a broader geographic division may be observed in the country regarding levels of income and standards of living. The northern reaches of Kyrgyzstan, particularly Chui Oblast, have higher average incomes and are somewhat better off than the southern regions, with Batken Oblast representing the poorest region in the country, and one of the most poverty-stricken areas in Central Asia. In regions where average family size was larger and birthrates were higher, such as Naryn and Osh oblasts, some children could not attend school because they lacked winter clothing (Anderson 1999).

By the late 1990s, the Kyrgyz economy appeared to be improving, as many vital economic indicators began to move upward. Unemployment rates began to decline, and even the crippled industrial sector showed some signs of regeneration, as productivity increased. Between 1999 and 2002, a significant drop in poverty was achieved. In 1999, 60 percent of the rural population was under the official poverty line, but by 2002 that figure had decreased to 47 percent—still a shockingly high percentage, but clearly conditions for those living in the countryside were improving (IMF 2004). Improvement was also registered for poverty levels in the cities, although the decline in poverty there was more modest. In 1999, slightly more than 42 percent of the urban population lived in poverty, whereas by 2002 the rate had fallen to just over 39 percent. The IMF estimated in a recent report that poverty rates will continue to diminish through the next decade in Kyrgyzstan and that the worst period of economic transition from Communism to capitalism appears to have passed (IMF 2004).

TRANSPORTATION AND COMMUNICATION

Geography alone inhibits Kyrgyzstan's linkages to the rest of the world, as well as the internal network of transportation and communication. Landlocked at the heart of the Eurasian landmass, Kyrgyzstan is a long way from the world's sea-lanes, a considerable disadvantage to international trade. The rugged nature of most of the country's landscape makes expanding the roadways and rail connections expensive and time-consuming, and the extreme elevation in some sections of the country results in some roads being blocked by heavy snowfalls during the winter. The existing networks for transport and communication are insufficient and antiquated, and considerable investment for this sector of the economy must be found if Kyrgyzstan is to overcome the disadvantages of its

Young Kyrgyz woman using old telephone, Bishkek. (Keren Su/Corbis)

location and domestic topography. A key challenge for the future will be finding such investment, which will almost certainly have to come from international donor agencies, such as the World Bank and IMF.

Improving the transportation infrastructure is essential if the country hopes to attract increasing numbers of tourists, a goal seen as crucial to expanding the Kyrgyz economy in the long term. Since independence, the main airport at Manas, near the capital of Bishkek, has been renovated with assistance from Japan but is still considerably smaller and serviced by fewer international carriers than neighboring airports in Tashkent or Almaty. The country's national airline, Kyrgyzstan Aba Joldoru, experienced a severe drop in business in the mid-1990s, although by 2002 the company was planning to expand service to several major cities in Asia and the Middle East. Most of the airline's fleet dates from the Soviet period however, and if the new connections result in increased traffic, Aba Joldoru will need to acquire newer, more modern aircraft. Within Kyrgyzstan, most major cities are serviced by Aba Joldoru, in most cases with daily flights.

The road, rail, and telecommunications systems in the country are all badly in need of repair and upgrading. The main north-south artery is the Bishkek-Osh highway, which was improved in the late 1990s with assistance from several international lending agencies. Many of the roadways in the southern and eastern sections of the country remain in poor condition, however, and additional improvement and expansion is needed. After independence, the country's railways were privatized, but Kyrgyzstan has only slightly over 200 miles of track, and much of the eastern half of the country has almost no rail connections at all. The government has suggested the possibility of building a rail link to China, but thus far no work has begun because of financial difficulties and political instability. Kyrgyzstan inherited an underdeveloped communications system from the Soviet era, a system plagued by poor quality of performance and equipment. The telecommunications system was held in monopoly by KYR-GYZTELECOM after independence, and some improvements were implemented in the 1990s, again with the financial help of international partners. Fiber optic cable was installed in several oblasts, and improved facilities for cellular connections were also constructed.

TOURISM: A POTENTIAL ENGINE OF GROWTH?

Like Uzbekistan and Kazakhstan, Kyrgyzstan faces sizable obstacles in its effort to attract tourists. Kyrgyzstan is even more remote than its two neighbors, and its main airport at Manas, near Bishkek, is smaller and less developed than the facilities offered by both Tashkent and Almaty. The sheer distance from some of the world's major source regions of tourists, that is, Japan and the United States, is a major barrier itself, as travelers must endure an extended flight of at

Kyrgyz on horseback near the shore of Issyk Kul. (Nevada Wier/Corbis)

least ten hours, and perhaps twenty hours if flying from North America. Flights to Kyrgyzstan are less frequent, and fewer airlines service the country than is the case with Uzbekistan and Kazakhstan. Tourist infrastructure inside the country is underdeveloped as well, although recent years have seen some improvements, particularly in Bishkek and around Issyk Kul, Kyrgyzstan's number-one tourist attraction. These shortcomings clearly inhibit expansion of this sector of the economy. Currently, only a tiny percentage of tourists visiting Kyrgyzstan come from outside Central Asia.

If sufficient investment were found to expand and modernize facilities and infrastructure, tourism has great potential in Kyrgyzstan. Spectacular mountain scenery and abundant opportunities for hiking, trekking, climbing, and skiing could make Kyrgyzstan a winter playground for tourists seeking outdoor alpine adventure, and the beauty and beaches of Issyk Kul could easily draw thousands of visitors from all over the world during the summer period. The government has attempted to stimulate tourism through official promotions, such as designating 2001 the "Year of Tourism," but these have seen modest results.

Some initiatives toward ecotourism and low-impact cultural tourism have born fruit. One organization, Community Based Tourism, offers opportunities for homestays, "dude ranch" experiences working with Kyrgyz herders and farmers, and related activities that require little expansion of existing infrastructure or an increased level of services and amenities. Although this type of tourism may be well suited to the requirements of some visitors and has a limited impact both on local lifestyles and the environment, it is likely to attract only a modest number of foreign guests. If tourism is to be the boon to the economy that some in Kyrgyzstan hope for, the country must find a successful formula for drawing both investment dollars and increased numbers of travelers.

ECONOMIC PERFORMANCE AND BARRIERS TO GROWTH

Askar Akayev's willingness to take his country through a difficult yet necessary process of structural reforms placed Kyrgyzstan in a more favorable position to attract investors and tourists than some of its neighbors, and it is likely that his successor as president will continue this strategy. Recent years have brought a spate of positive economic data and trends, the sort of success that builds confidence in the Kyrgyz economy both at home and abroad. But not all of the economy's problems have been solved, or even adequately addressed. Graft and corruption still are common features of the business environment in Kyrgyzstan, poverty rates and unemployment remain alarmingly high, and the Akayev administration's back pedaling on democratic reform and harassment of opposition figures tarnished the country's reputation as the most "democratic" of the Central Asian states in the last years of his administration, slowing the rate of foreign investment.

To ensure continued expansion of the economy, create additional jobs and improve the transportation system, the Kyrgyz regime must maintain a delicate balancing act with its larger neighbors, chiefly Uzbekistan and Kazakhstan. Both serve as gateways to Kyrgyzstan for the world outside Central Asia, and they are the country's most important economic partners as well. In some respects, Kyrgyzstan's fate is tied to that of both of its larger partners, for it is difficult to envision a stable and prosperous Kyrgyzstan without the same conditions emerging in its neighbors to the north and west. Kyrgyzstan's leverage in the region is bound to increase in the future, however, for the country controls a good deal of what will soon be the region's most vital and precious resource—water. Ultimately, it may be Kyrgyzstan's command of this commodity that enlarges its economic and political status in the region.

CONCLUSION

There is reason to be cautiously optimistic about the future of the Kyrgyz economy. Kyrgyzstan's government pursued aggressive policies directed at restructuring the economy in the early 1990s, and after a painful period of adjustment, these actions appear to finally be bearing fruit. Kyrgyzstan was in the forefront among former Soviet Central Asian states in adopting a convertible currency and remains the only country among that group to be admitted to the World Trade Organization. In recent years, poverty rates have declined, inflation rates are down, and productivity and output in most sectors of the economy are increasing. Serious obstacles to growth remain, however, especially in the long term. Kyrgyzstan remains dependent on donor agencies for investment capital, and the transportation and communications networks in the country are badly underdeveloped. Tourism holds great potential as an engine for economic expansion and job creation, but the country's geographic isolation must be overcome. Yet despite these daunting challenges, the Kyrgyz people appear determined to guide their beautiful, remote land into the twenty-first century, while nurturing and strengthening their unique cultural heritage.

References

Abazov, Rafis. 2004. *Historical Dictionary of Kyrgyzstan.* Lanham, MD: Scarecrow Press.

Anderson, John. 1999. *Kyrgyzstan: Central Asia's Island of Democracy?* Amsterdam: Harwood Academic.

Howell, Jude. 1996. "Coping with Transition: Insights from Kyrgyzstan," *Third World Quarterly* 17(1), pp. 53–68.

International Monetary Fund. 2004. "Kyrgyz Republic: Poverty Reduction Strategy Paper Progress Report." IMF Country Report No. 04/200. Washington, DC: Author. Available at: http://www.imf.org. Accessed January 30, 2005.

Kyrgyz Institutions

Upon reaching independence in 1991, Kyrgyzstan differed fundamentally from the other newly independent states in Central Asia: it was the only country of the five where the head of the country was not a former Communist Party boss. It was certainly true that Askar Akayev, the country's new president, had been a member of the Communist Party, but he was seen as an outsider who sought reform and progress for the country. Kyrgyzstan's political situation was also unusual in that Absamat Masaliyev, the last first party secretary to hold office, was voted out of power and replaced by Akayev *before* the collapse of the USSR. In the atmosphere of euphoria and hope after independence, many commentators inside and outside of Kyrgyzstan labeled the country an "island of democracy," a label that seemed appropriate when the political environment of Kyrgyzstan was compared with that of its neighbors. The country had an active, independent media that frequently criticized the actions of the government, true opposition parties were allowed to form and function, and the commitment of the Kyrgyz administration to rapid and profound economic restructuring was apparent.

In the mid-1990s, the island began to sink into a sea of rising authoritarianism, as Akayev maneuvered to secure ever more political power for himself and to undermine the process of democratization. Political opponents, many of them former colleagues and supporters, were intimidated and sometimes imprisoned on charges of "corruption," a charge leveled at a virtual host of Akayev critics and challengers. Although Kyrgyzstan's political environment remained open and democratic compared with Turkmenistan or Uzbekistan, the backsliding toward dictatorship troubled some of the country's international donors and supporters. In 2002, the Kyrgyz government promoted a national program titled "Kyrgyzstan Is a Home of Human Rights," but sloganeering was not enough to convince the regime's critics. Violent demonstations in Bishkek in March 2005 forced Akayev to flee the country, opening a new era in Kyrgyz politics, marked by both hope and uncertainty about the country's future.

GOVERNMENT AND POLITICS

Kyrgyzstan's present political situation cannot be understood without reference to the Soviet period, when the notion of a Kyrgyz identity and specific territory associated with that identity were forged. The following section presents an overview of the Soviet period from the early 1960s through independence, the period when the political convictions and views of Kyrgyzstan's contemporary political players were forged.

Turdakun Usubaliyev:
Party Boss and Patron (1961–1985)

Turdakun Usubaliyev ran the Kyrgyz Communist Party as the first secretary for nearly a quarter of a century and in many ways became a modern-day Central Asian potentate. Through an extensive system of patronage and kinship ties, Usubaliyev changed the ethnic makeup of the Kyrgyz Communist Party, turning the organization from one dominated by ethnic Slavs into a party that was predominantly Kyrgyz. By placing his loyalists in positions of influence throughout the Kyrgyz Soviet Socialist Republic, Usubaliyev was able to control the party apparatus essentially unchallenged for decades. Firmly committed to the Soviet system, Usubaliyev sought to modernize what some propagandists in Moscow believed was one of the most backward and feudal corners of the USSR, and the effects of his long tenure at the helm of the Kyrgyz Communist Party continue to shape Kyrgyzstan today, particularly in terms of social and economic issues.

Under Usubaliyev's leadership, comparatively large amounts of investment flowed into the republic, especially into the industrial sector, a poorly funded part of the Kyrgyz economy before the 1960s. By the 1970s, however, the central Soviet administration was devoting millions of rubles to developing industry and power generation in Kyrgyzstan. Much of this funding was expended on the construction of large hydroelectric dams, which not only produced electricity for the Kyrgyz SSR but could supply some of the surrounding republics with electric power as well. Other investment went toward extracting and processing the considerable mineral wealth Kyrgyzstan possessed, as well as to industries related to the agricultural sector, such as food processing and the manufacture of farm machinery. The 1960s and 1970s witnessed steady increases in industrial output, a trend that would begin to falter by the 1980s.

The central reason the Kyrgyz first secretary was successful in bringing large sums of investment to his republic was his loyalty and commitment to Moscow's policies regarding the creation of a Soviet identity. This notion came at the expense of national (ethnic) differences in the Kyrgyz SSR and other republics. Kyrgyz was replaced by Russian as the language of governance and higher education, following a general trend of Russification of the minority ethnic groups in the Soviet Union. Few among the Kyrgyz elite expressed concern about the loss of identity in the 1960s and 1970s, but by the 1980s a number of intellectuals were issuing muted, indirect critiques of Usubaliyev's promotion of Soviet policies designed to erode Kyrgyzchylyk, or "Kyrgyzness" (Bohr 1996, 389). By far the most famous and influential of these critics was Chingiz Aitmatov, a famous Kyrgyz writer whose father had been executed by Stalin's secret police and whose novel *The Day Lasts More Than a Hundred Years* called into question the validity of Soviet policy toward the heritage of Central Asians.

Despite the economic development that had transpired during his watch, by the 1980s weaknesses in both society and the economy in the Kyrgyz SSR were becoming apparent. The Kyrgyz SSR remained one of the poorest regions in the USSR, and Usubaliyev's entrenched rule had engendered a republican government that was deeply corrupted. In the early 1980s, the central government in Moscow began to harshly criticize some aspects of society in Kyrgyzstan, particularly what were frequently characterized in the press as "religious vestiges" or "nationalist traditions." These were code terms for the persistence of Islamic beliefs and practices that the Soviet regime had spent decades attempting to eliminate and that were experiencing something of a revival in the Kyrgyz SSR, especially in the southern part of the republic. When Mikhail Gorbachev became the leader of the USSR in early 1985, Usubaliyev was removed amid charges of corruption and incompetence.

Absamat Masaliyev's Tenure (1985–1991)

The rise of Mikhail Gorbachev to the head of the Communist Party of the Soviet Union also raised the star of Absamat Masaliyev, a staunch Kyrgyz Communist who had risen through the ranks of the party for twenty years. Gorbachev was instrumental in Masaliyev's election to the position of Kyrgyz first secretary in 1985. Ironically, although Gorbachev was hailed as a reformer early on, Masaliyev was resistant to the implementation of Gorbachev's social liberalization policy, glasnost. Masaliyev also found himself saddled with increasingly intractable problems in his small republic, including a declining economic situation and the exodus of many of Kyrgyzstan's Slavic residents, a trend that had begun in the 1970s (Anderson 1999). By the mid-1980s, the entire USSR was faced with an impending economic crisis, and the impressive levels of investment that the center had bestowed on the Kyrgyz SSR were no longer forthcoming. Despite the deteriorating socioeconomic conditions in his republic, Masaliyev held to rigid, conservative policies on both the economic and social fronts.

In 1989, the first visible challenge to Masaliyev and Communist rule surfaced. Several thousand unemployed young men from eastern Kyrgyzstan traveled to the capital city, Frunze (now Bishkek), and formed Ashar, an organization designed to convince the authorities to grant land to the group. Within a few months, the members of Ashar had simply occupied several tracts of land around the city and built crude houses there, while the Communist authorities reacted cautiously (Huskey 1993, 405). The success of Ashar emboldened others, and within a year numerous "informal" groups had formed in Kyrgyzstan, including the Democratic Movement of Kyrgyzstan, a coalition that claimed to have several hundred thousand members and quickly emerged as a central player in the changing political situation in the republic. A key issue that motivated many of the newly formed organizations was the status of the Kyrgyz language. In an effort to placate the rising number of activists who decried the widespread use of Russian as opposed to Kyrgyz, the authorities made Kyrgyz the "official language" of the Kyrgyz SSR in late 1989.

The façade of "socialist brotherhood" completely collapsed in Kyrgyzstan in the summer of 1990, when ethnic riots broke out near the city of Osh, in the southern part of the republic. Brutal fighting between mobs of Uzbeks and Kyrgyz continued for several days, with several hundred people killed and thousands injured. Masaliyev's tentative and bungling response to the crisis damaged his reputation as a leader further, and his support, even within the Communist Party itself, began to collapse. In 1990, a new post of president was established in the republic, and to nearly everyone's surprise, the Supreme Soviet, a body composed of Kyrgyz Communist Party members, did not elect Masaliyev to the position. Instead the members chose a relatively unknown and politically inexperienced figure, Askar Akayev, to be the Kyrgyz president. Akayev showed immediately that he was sympathetic to the cause of the reformers, meeting with a wide variety of opposition groups. In April 1991, Absamat Masaliyev resigned as first party secretary, effectively ending the control of the Communist Party in Kyrgyzstan. During the attempted coup against Mikhail Gorbachev four months later, President Akayev immediately denounced those involved and banned the Communist Party in Kyrgyzstan, courageous steps that greatly enhanced his status as a leader in the eyes of many citizens in Kyrgyzstan.

Kyrgyz Independence (1991–)

The Kyrgyz SSR declared its independence from the USSR within days of the abortive putsch against Gorbachev in August 1991. Two months later, Askar Akayev ran unopposed in a general election for the presidency of the new country and won a large majority of the vote. In December 1991, Akayev, along with most of the new leaders of other post-Soviet countries, signed the charter in Alma-Ata, Kazakhstan, that created the Commonwealth of Independent States (CIS). In 1992, Akayev chose Felix Kulov to serve as the country's first vice president, and work began on a new constitution for Kyrgyzstan. Political freedom flourished in the country, as independent newspapers and new political parties sprang up virtually overnight. Economic reforms moved more quickly than in any other part of the former Soviet Central Asia, and in response the country joined the International Monetary Fund (IMF) and World Bank, making it eligible for badly needed economic assistance. Kyrgyzstan also joined the United Nations and established diplomatic relations with a host of countries, including the United States, which quickly came to view Kyrgyzstan as the most democratic of the new states in Central Asia.

The second year of Kyrgyzstan's independence represented

a benchmark in the country's history, as Akayev moved quickly forward on both the economic and political fronts. Kyrgyzstan sent shock waves throughout the Central Asian region when the government introduced a national currency, the *som*, later that year. This created friction with some of Kyrgyzstan's neighbors, especially Uzbekistan, which retained the ruble as its currency for the time being. In the spring of 1993, the Kyrgyz parliament, the Jogorku Kenesh, approved the country's new constitution, clearing the way for a national referendum on the document the next year. Because of Akayev's growing reputation as a reformer and advocate of free-market economics and political pluralism, foreign assistance began pouring into the country, both from international donor agencies and from a wide range of private investors from abroad. Frequent scandals involving financial improprieties plagued the government, however, and several high-ranking officials in Akayev's administration were forced to resign. Akayev was not implicated in any of the scandals, but the image of his administration was becoming tarnished both within the country and with his many supporters in the international community.

By the mid-1990s, several signs indicated that the Akayev administration was drifting toward authoritarianism. Akayev's decision to dismiss the Jogorku Kenesh in 1994 led to a political crisis in the country. Akayev demanded changes to the constitution that would replace the former unicameral Jogorku Kenesh with a body composed of two houses and that would reduce the number of representatives holding seats from more than 300 to just 105. These changes were eventually approved, and a new parliament was seated the next year. In 1995, Akayev requested a national referendum that would allow him to remain in office for five more years without being reelected by popular mandate, a request the Jogorku Kenesh denied, as such a referendum would violate the provisions of the constitution. Akayev won the presidential election that year nevertheless, but his government continued to be dogged

Kyrgyz president Askar Akayev casts his ballot during the presidential election in Bishkek, October 29, 2000. Akayev was forced from office in March 2005 by demonstrators demanding democratic reforms. (Reuters/Corbis)

by charges of corruption and bribery. In the meantime, the economic situation in Kyrgyzstan steadily worsened, as poverty rates skyrocketed and productivity plummeted.

By the late 1990s, economic conditions in Kyrgyzstan, although still dire in many parts of the countryside, were improving overall. This was a fortuitous development for President Akayev, who was up for reelection in 2000 and was facing a rising chorus of criticism from his political opponents. In 1999, the Ar-Namys Party was formed by Akayev's former vice president, Felix Kulov, who also had headed the country's security service for a time. Kulov represented Akayev's most serious potential challenger, but Kulov decided not to run for office because he lacked a good command of the Kyrgyz language and therefore could not meet the language requirement. Akayev won the election handily, but once again both opposition parties and international observers criticized the process as failing to meet acceptable standards. Shortly after the election, Felix Kulov was arrested and later convicted on charges of corruption, and sentenced to seven years in prison, effectively removing him form the political scene in Kyrgyzstan.

The increasingly authoritarian bent of the Akayev administration concerned many observers of the Kyrgyz political scene. Media outlets critical of the president and his policies continued to be harassed and closed down, and opponents or potential opponents were intimidated or charged with crimes, damaging their reputations and preventing them from seeking office. The increasing frustration felt by many in the country reached critical mass in late March 2005, after two rounds of parliamentary elections that some believed were rigged to favor candidates who supported Akayev. On March 24, a demonstration in Bishkek swept Akayev from power, as an angry crowd stormed government buildings and freed Felix Kulov, a popular opposition leader, from prison. A provisional government led by Kurmanbek Bakiev, another prominent opposition figure, is in control of the country until a new president is elected, an event scheduled for the summer of 2005.

RELIGION AND SOCIETY

The two most numerous ethnic groups in Kyrgyzstan, the Kyrgyz and the Uzbeks, are both Muslim, but the history and influence of Islam differs significantly between these two peoples. For the Uzbeks living in the Fergana Valley, Islam has been a way of life for centuries, as their urbanized ancestors were converted to the faith almost a millennium and a half ago. In contrast, many of the Kyrgyz were brought into the Islamic realm only in the last two hundred years, and like their cousins the Kazakhs, the Kyrgyz retained a fair portion of their previous belief system, resulting in "folk Islam." There are Christian believers in Kyrgyzstan as well (mostly Russian Orthodox), but the focus of this section is on the Muslim population of the country because it represents the largest body of religious believers, as well as what has emerged as the dominant cultural group since Kyrgyzstan's independence. The discussion begins with a short description of the basic attributes of Islam, followed by a description of Islam's status under the Soviet government and in Kyrgyzstan today.

The genesis of Islam begins with the birth of one man, the Prophet Muhammad, in A.D. 570. Muslims believe that Muhammed was different from any other human being who has ever lived, or will ever live, in that he was chosen by God (Allah, in Arabic) to reveal the true and complete message of God to humanity. This message was transmitted to Muhammed over the course of some twenty-two years and was eventually compiled into the holy book of Islam, the Koran. After Muhammed's death in A.D. 632, Islam developed many sects and movements, but certain rituals and beliefs are common to all Muslims. The most important of these are the

Five Pillars of Islam, consisting of five activities every devout Muslim must observe.

The first pillar is the profession of faith, a simple declarative sentence that must be said with sincerity and passion: "There is but one God, Allah, and Muhammed is his prophet." Thus stated, the speaker has joined the Islamic community but is expected to adhere to the remaining pillars as well. The second pillar is daily prayer, and Muslims are required to pray five times each day while facing in the direction of the holy city of Mecca. Third, Muslims must be generous to the poor when they are able and therefore are expected to pay alms for distribution to those less fortunate at least once a year. Ramadan is the fourth pillar and is the month when Muslims may not eat, drink any liquid, or have sexual relations during the daylight hours. Only pregnant women and those who are gravely ill are excused from observing Ramadan, but they are expected to observe the fast later on their own. The last pillar is the *hajj,* the pilgrimage to the holy city of Mecca, which every Muslim must make at least once in his or her lifetime, unless the individual is too poor or too sick to make the journey to Saudi Arabia.

Islamic warriors entered Central Asia in the eighth century, moving mostly along the pathways linking the region's urban settlements and reaching as far eastward as the Fergana Valley. In these areas they encountered a wide variety of religions, including Zoroastrianism, Manichaeism, Christianity, and others. Over the next two centuries, most of the sedentary population living in the oasis centers along the old Silk Road was converted from these faiths to Islam, but those nomadic peoples living in the steppes to the north or secluded in mountain valleys to the east were not readily converted and had only occasional contact with Muslim culture and ideas. Over time, the gradual blending of Islamic strictures with older shamanism and animistic beliefs among these groups resulted in a hybrid, folk Islam. Regardless of whether they were nomads or city dwellers, almost all the Muslims of Central Asia came to follow the Sunni sect of the faith, as Shiism, the other major sect, never made serious inroads into Central Asian Islamic culture.

By around 1200, one would have encountered two distinct Islamic zones on the territory of modern Kyrgyzstan. Southern cities such as Osh, Jalalabad, and Uzgen were solidly part of the Islamic world, following traditions similar to those found in Damascus, Baghdad, and Cairo. In the river valleys and mountains of the north, however, the nomadic ancestors of the modern Kyrgyz were nominally Muslim, but by some measures were only marginally attached to the standards and behaviors of the wider Islamic world. A clear example would be provided by the appearance of women in public. In the southern cities, women would wear the veil, or *paranja,* when outside the home, but the wives and daughters of the northern herdsmen never adopted this custom, and in fact were more socially and politically active than their counterparts in the south. Much of what the nomadic Kyrgyz knew of Islam they learned from Sufi missionaries, who carried their tolerant, devotional style of Islam to those outside the urban areas (for a more detailed account of Sufism, see the section on Uzbekistan institutions). Some Kyrgyz were not converted to Islam until the eighteenth and nineteenth centuries.

Authorities of the Russian Empire had to contend with Islamic uprisings periodically in Central Asia, but by and large the tsar's representatives did not interfere with the local religious environment and certainly did not attempt any campaign to eradicate Islam in favor of Christianity among the indigenous Central Asians. The advent of Soviet power in the 1920s would, however, initiate a decades-long physical and ideological struggle between religious believers (Muslims as well as others) and advocates of Marxism-Leninism. The Soviet leadership was overtly hostile to Islamic institutions, and by the late 1920s had implemented policies designed to limit, and ultimately destroy, the faith in the Soviet Union.

Restrictions and suppression waned during World War II, when Josef Stalin, the Soviet leader, sought the support of his Muslim subjects in the effort to defeat Germany. As a result, four Muslim spiritual boards, each headed by a mufti, were established in the USSR, with Muslims in Kyrgyzstan falling under the jurisdiction of the mufti in Tashkent, Uzbekistan. Nevertheless, official efforts to eliminate religion in Soviet society continued until the policy of glasnost (openness) took hold in Kyrgyzstan during the late 1980s.

By severing connections to the rest of the Islamic world, limiting the availability of the Koran, and outlawing many aspects of the faith, the Soviet regime did, in fact, damage Islamic religiosity in Kyrgyzstan. Traditions such as Ramadan and daily prayer were abandoned by a majority of both Kyrgyz and Uzbeks, and few Muslims were allowed to make the hajj under Soviet rule—typically, a few dozen each year. Yet the general failure of nearly seventy years of Soviet policy directed against Islam is apparent in the Islamic revival that has swept Kyrgyzstan and other Central Asian countries since the late 1980s. Hundreds of new mosques, many of them funded from abroad, have appeared in Kyrgyzstan since that time. Most of these new structures have been constructed in the southern part of the country, but a substantial number were built in other parts of Kyrgyzstan.

Freedom of religion is enshrined in the Kyrgyz constitution, and compared with its neighbor Uzbekistan, the Kyrgyz government is relatively tolerant of unofficial religious movements, with a few exceptions. Officially Kyrgyzstan is a secular state, and religious political parties are banned. The teaching of religious subjects is not allowed in the public schools. According to Kyrgyz law, all religious organizations are required to register with the State Commission on Religious Affairs, the governmental body that oversees legal matters involving religion. A separate muftiate established in 1991 represents official Islam in the country and is supervised by the government. The mufti is an Islamic leader selected by

Muslims pray near the statue of former Communist leader and the founder of the Soviet state Vladimir Lenin, in the town of Osh. (Shamil Zhumatov/Reuters/Corbis)

the ulema, a group of Islamic scholars working in Kyrgyzstan. A large number of foreign missionaries are allowed to proselytize in Kyrgyzstan, but they, too, are required to register with the State Commission. Ironically, some Islamic groups as well as the Russian Orthodox Church in Kyrgyzstan do not view the activities of the missionaries favorably, especially as some of the evangelical movements have attracted a substantial following from among both the Slavic population and the Muslim population (Akbarzadeh 2001).

Some Islamic organizations are illegal in Kyrgyzstan, primarily because the Kyrgyz administration views them as extremist groups who seek to incite violence and destabilize the country. One such group, which certainly has been involved in violent activity, is the Islamic Movement of Uzbekistan (IMU). In 1999, the IMU initiated a campaign to topple the regime in Uzbekistan by invading the Fergana Valley region. The IMU insurgents were based in Tajikistan and crossed into Kyrgyzstan in August 1999 with the intent of reaching Uzbek territory. Along the way, they took several hostages, both local and foreign, and engaged the Kyrgyz army in several small-scale battles. In 2000, another series of attacks was launched from northern Tajikistan that penetrated both Batken oblast (province) in southern Kyrgyzstan and parts of Uzbekistan (Handrahan 2001). By this time, the IMU was receiving support from the Taliban regime in Afghanistan, and during the fall of 2001 soldiers from the IMU fought alongside Taliban forces against the U.S. military. Much of the IMU appears to have been eliminated by U.S. bombs, but Kyrgyz authorities on occasion continue to accuse the organization of attempts to recruit followers and incite uprising in southern Kyrgyzstan.

A second group branded as extremist in Kyrgyzstan, which may have a larger following than the IMU was ever able to build, is Hizb-ut-Tahrir (HT). HT is banned in all the countries of Central Asia as well as many nations in the Middle East but is allowed to function in a number of European countries, primarily the United Kingdom, where the organization is headquartered. Although viewed as radical and destabilizing by the Central Asian governments, including that of Kyrgyzstan, HT has not been conclusively connected to any acts of violence in the region. The primary goal of HT is to reestablish the Islamic caliphate, a position that has been vacant since the end of World War I. It is difficult to determine the number of supporters HT has in Kyrgyzstan because the group is extremely secretive and organized in a system that allows each follower to know the identity of only a few other members. There is an ethnic dimension to the organization's support as well; most of those joining appear to be Uzbeks from southern Kyrgyzstan, although there is some HT activity in the northern reaches of the country as well. Increasing poverty and unemployment rates among the predominantly Uzbek population in the south may lead some young people to join radical groups, but the threat of an Islamist regime taking power in the country seems remote at best because there is little support for such a government among the majority Kyrgyz.

EDUCATION

Before the twentieth century, few Kyrgyz had access to education. Their nomadic lifestyle made a system of regular, organized education virtually impossible. From the early 1920s, the Soviet administration invested in near universal and compulsory education for the Kyrgyz masses, and Kyrgyz society today, like its neighbors in most cases, has a high rate of literacy and basic education. The Soviet system was flawed in several aspects, however, and since independence Kyrgyz authorities have endeavored to reform and upgrade the educational system. Meeting the challenges of educational reform has proven difficult for a number of reasons, not the least of which have been a severe lack of funding and a shortage of teachers.

The Educational System

Several major changes have affected the educational system

Students and teacher in a classroom in Kyrgyzstan. (Nevada Wier/Corbis)

in Kyrgyzstan since independence. First, the now-discredited philosophy of Marxism-Leninism, which pervaded the teaching and materials under the old system, has been jettisoned, but because of a lack of funding and simple lag of time, new materials are still in short supply. Second, there is now much more emphasis on teaching in Kyrgyz, a factor that relates to the lack of materials because there were few textbooks or other materials produced in that language before the early 1990s. These educational materials must now be written and published, a process that requires time and money. In turn, the recent shift to Kyrgyz in many schools has led to a shortage of teachers in some instances because many Slavic teachers did not have the ability to teach in that language and simply emigrated to Russia.

Some remnants of the Soviet system persist, however. The most noticeable of these to a Western observer is the degree of respect and discipline in the typical classroom in Kyrgyzstan. Students stand when their teacher or an administrator enters the room and often will stand when responding to a question from the instructor. Discipline problems and truancy are much rarer than in the United States (although truancy rates have increased since independence), because teachers are a respected authority in Kyrgyz society, and in general, any person who has attained a relatively high level of education is accorded respect in the community. Students tend to study and learn more in groups than their counterparts in the United States, and it is typical for the same group of students to stay together as a class all the way through their primary educational years.

A child in Kyrgyzstan usually begins his or her formal education around age seven and by Kyrgyz law must complete eleven years of both primary and secondary levels. Kyrgyz government statistics report that there are more than 2,000 primary and secondary schools in the country, although many of these are small and located in rural areas. After completing the secondary grades, a student may choose to pursue further education at a university or institute or may seek training for a trade at a technical college. There are some forty institutions of higher learning in Kyrgyzstan, a surprisingly high number in a country of only 5 million people. There are graduate programs at a number of universities that enable students to pursue postgraduate degrees, and since independence some institutions have switched from the old Soviet degree structure to a Western system, conferring master's and doctoral degrees.

Changes in curricula have occurred at all levels of the Kyrgyz educational system in the last fifteen years. The social sciences and humanities have seen the most profound transformation because these subjects were previously covered in the framework of Marxist-Leninist ideology; since independence, such subjects, especially Kyrgyz history, have been examined in a more open way. At the postsecondary level, a host of new programs in business and public administration have been developed, as these disciplines were effectively absent in the university curriculum before 1991. Obviously, such programs are essential to the economic development of a country in which specialists in management, marketing, advertising, and other aspects of business are in short supply.

In recent years, some troubling trends have emerged in Kyrgyzstan's educational system. The quality of the educational infrastructure has steadily declined, another problem directly related to lack of funding. Many schools do not have basic amenities, and some are not even heated in wintertime, a serious problem given Kyrgyzstan's climate. Under such conditions, attempts to modernize classrooms with computers and other technology now routinely encountered in Western classrooms seem to be overreaching, but to compete in the global economy, Kyrgyzstan must pursue such goals as quickly as possible. Other trends appear to indicate a decline in the overall quality of education and an increase in the number of girls who leave school early. These may reverse as the economy improves, as has happened over the last several years. If such downturns do not fade, strategies to address them must become a priority for the Kyrgyz regime.

Literacy

In the last years of the Russian Empire, surveys indicated an abysmal rate of literacy in Central Asia, with less than 10 percent of the native population claiming an ability to read and write in Russian (although some individuals might have been literate in other languages, this alone would not raise the literacy rate significantly). For women, the literacy rate was well below 1 percent. In the 1920s, the Soviet government initiated a major program to eliminate illiteracy, with spectacular results. Within a decade and a half the literacy rate in Kyrgyzstan stood at around 70 percent, and by the 1980s the literacy rate in Kyrgyzstan, the second-poorest republic in the Soviet Union, was above 90 percent. Since independence and an economic decline in the 1990s, literacy rates have slipped somewhat, although they remain high when compared with nearby countries such as Afghanistan, Pakistan, and Tajik-istan.

Religious Education

Before the advent of Soviet power in Kyrgyzstan, there were few means to obtain an education for a young Kyrgyz beyond attending a *medresseh*, or Islamic seminary. Most of these institutions were located outside of the traditional Kyrgyz lands, and few young people had the opportunity to pursue even this limited avenue of educational attainment. Most of the medressehs were closed during the Soviet period, but since the late 1980s, many Islamic schools have opened in the country. The largest, the Islamic University of Kyrgyzstan, opened in Bishkek in 1991. The official Kyrgyz Islamic admin-istration, or muftiate, is officially in charge of the university, which receives funding from abroad as well. There are several hundred students studying at the university in an average year. Smaller Islamic institutes are found in several cities around the country.

CONCLUSION

The initial sheen of Central Asia's "island of democracy" has become tarnished, as the Akayev regime drifted toward authoritarianism through the 1990s. Corruption and nepo-tism plague Kyrgyz society, undermining the motivation of individuals determined to build a more civil society (Cokgezen 2004). Yet the promise of Kyrgyzstan is not com-pletely dashed—it is still accurate to hold that the country is the most democratic country in Central Asia, and certainly it is more democratic than the previous regime of the USSR. The education problems the country faces will not be resolved quickly or inexpensively, but the improvement in the econ-omy in the late 1990s may lead to better-quality schools in the long run. The most significant test of Kyrgyzstan's fledgling democracy will be the transfer of power from the provisional government, replacing the discredited Akayev regime, to a successor. If this process transpires according to democratic principles, Central Asia's drifting island of democracy may inspire changes in the remainder of the region's political landscape.

References

Akbarzadeh, Shahram. 2001. "Political Islam in Kyrgyzstan and Turkmenistan." *Central Asian Survey* 20(4), pp. 451–466.

Anderson, John. 1999. *Kyrgyzstan: Central Asia's Island of Democracy?* Amsterdam: Harwood Academic.

Bohr, Annette, and Simon Crisp. 1996. "Kyrgyzstan and the Kyrgyz." In *The Nationalities Question in the Post-Soviet States,* 2nd edition, edited by Graham Smith. New York: Longman Publishing.

Cokgezen, Murat. 2004. "Corruption in Kyrgyzstan: The Facts, Causes and Consequences." *Central Asian Survey* 23(1), pp. 79–94.

Handrahan, Lori. 2001. "Gender and Ethnicity in the 'Transitional Democracy' of Kyrgyzstan." *Central Asian Survey* 20(4), pp. 467–496.

Huskey, Gene. 1993. "Kyrgyzstan: The Politics of Demographic and Economic Frustration." In *Nations and Politics in the Soviet Successor States,* edited by Ian Bremmer and Ray Taras. New York: Cambridge University Press.

Kyrgyz Society and Contemporary Issues

Kyrgyz society is undergoing a double transformation. The most obvious set of changes are those that take the Kyrgyz people from a closed Communistic system that severely limited contact with the outside world to an open, globalized society connected to the rest of the world via satellite television and telephones, fax machines, foreign visitors, and the Internet. The second transition involves the resurrection of Kyrgyz culture, which for seventy years was subsumed beneath the façade of Soviet culture. The Kyrgyz are busily rediscovering and strengthening their traditions and thereby discovering who they are as a people and as a nation. In the eyes of most Kyrgyz, it is a process long overdue.

This dual modification in some ways appears contradictory. The new generation of Kyrgyz study the ancient ways of their ancestors, learn the traditional songs and legends of the Kyrgyz people, but at the same time adopt the modern blue jeans, T-shirts, baseball caps, and music videos of global culture. Young people in Kyrgyzstan, however, seem to see nothing paradoxical in recovering the suppressed rituals and customs of their grandfathers, while enjoying the latest offerings from Eminem, Britney Spears, or numerous popular musicians from Europe and Russia and following the latest fashion trends from New York, London, or Paris. They are comfortable melding both local and global influences into their lives, a fitting approach in a country that strives to recover its past while simultaneously struggling to integrate into global society as quickly as possible.

These multiple transformations are made more complex by the serious problems Kyrgyz society faces. Some of the country's minority groups, in particular the Slavs and Germans, feel excluded and threatened by the effort to recover Kyrgyz culture and have departed in large numbers since the country became independent. There are broad divisions emerging in Kyrgyz society between urban and rural, north and south, and rich and poor. Ironically, perhaps the most critical divergence is between two Muslim groups, the Uzbeks and the Kyrgyz, in the southern reaches of the country, a conflict that led to tragic bloodshed just before the country's independence. The focus of this chapter is to describe the basic features and dynamics of Kyrgyz society and to place in context the divisions that threaten it. The final section addresses Kyrgyzstan in the larger framework of the Central Asia region and the international stage.

ETHNICITY AND SOCIAL SYSTEM
Ethnic Groups

Like its neighbors Uzbekistan and Kazakhstan, Kyrgyzstan contains an ethnically diverse population. More than twenty distinct groups compose the majority of Kyrgyz society, with the Kyrgyz representing about two-thirds of the population. As recently as 1989, Kyrgyz made up only slightly more than 50 percent of the population, but their proportion has risen dramatically over the past decade, as large numbers of Slavs and Germans have left. Kyrgyz belongs to the Turkic language family and has two main dialects, spoken in the northern and southern sections of the country. Currently Kyrgyz is written using the Cyrillic script, but there are plans to switch to a modified Latin alphabet in the future. Russian is still used widely by Kyrgyz and other groups for interethnic communication.

Great controversy has surrounded the historical origins of the Kyrgyz people, and the question has acquired political overtones in modern Kyrgyzstan. In general, there is agreement among scholars that the ancestors of the Kyrgyz migrated into the territory of contemporary Kyrgyzstan from southern Siberia, beginning around the sixth century A.D. These early Kyrgyz were nomadic, and their movement was gradual and deliberate, requiring possibly 500 years before the western slope of the Tien Shan range was fully occupied (Abazov 2004, 8). The foundation of Kyrgyz identity is the epic poem *Manas,* which may have existed in oral variations for a millennium. The story tells of the life and struggles of Manas, a Kyrgyz hero, and his son and grandson, and Manas today is viewed as the founder of the Kyrgyz nation. The epic is long and is related by a *manaschi,* a bard who has memorized the entire tale and who typically presents his or her rendition accompanied by music. The traditional Kyrgyz nomadic society was subdivided into tribes and clans, and these connections remain an essential part of Kyrgyz identity. Many consider knowledge of one's ancestors an absolute requirement for being a true Kyrgyz, and one is traditionally expected to be able to recount all of one's ancestors back seven generations. There are three main tribes: the Ong Kanat (or "right wing"; there is no political connotation), the Sol Kanat ("left wing"), and the Ichkilik. Within these designations are further divisions into various clans and extended family groupings.

Kyrgyz men are distinguished by their hat, or *kalpak,* which is distinct from the *doppa* worn by Uzbeks. The Kyrgyz kalpak is made of felt and is usually white, often with black embroidery. Unlike the skullcap donned by Uzbeks, the Kyrgyz hat has a brim and is peaked, usually standing six to eight inches above the brim. In rural areas, especially during winter, both men and women will wear a *chapan,* a long, heavy cotton robe, and chapans are frequently given as gifts to friends and visitors. It is common for women to wear a scarf both in the countryside and in urban settings when in public. Central Asian women in general do not wear the *paranja* (veil), and in Kyrgyzstan this is particularly rare; only in some of the more conservative regions of the south does one occasionally encounter women wearing the veil. In Bishkek and some of the larger cities, especially in the north, many non-Islamic women follow Western standards of dress.

As was the case in other Central Asian republics, during the 1940s many minority groups were deported to Kyrgyzstan because Josef Stalin, the leader of the USSR, doubted the loyalties of these peoples. In this way, many Crimean Tatars, Koreans, Meskhetian Turks, and others were transported to Kyrgyzstan to join an already diverse community. Many of the Turks and Tatars have left since Kyrgyzstan became independent, but most of the Koreans have remained. A number of small Muslim minorities are present in Kyrgyzstan, including Uighurs, Tajiks, Dungans, and Kazakhs. The Uighurs share many characteristics with a much larger minority community, the Uzbeks, and are related to the large Uighur minority in western China. The Tajiks are Muslim but not Turkic and speak a language closely connected to Farsi, the language of Iran. They are concentrated along the southern boundary of Kyrgyzstan, and their numbers increased substantially in the early 1990s, when many entered Kyrgyzstan fleeing the civil war in Tajikistan. The Dungan people are ethnic Chinese who converted to Islam and migrated to Kyrgyzstan in the 1800s. Like the Uighurs, they are closely related to similar peoples in western China. Although none of these minority groups represents more than about 1 percent of the total population, their numbers belie their economic and technical importance to the country.

Kyrgyzstan's largest minority group is the Uzbeks, who surpassed the Russians in number in the 1990s. Uzbeks make up about 15 percent of the population and are concentrated overwhelmingly in the Fergana Valley in southern Kyrgyzstan. The majority in Kyrgyzstan's second-largest city, Osh, are Uzbek, and Jalalabad, the country's third-largest city, also contains a large Uzbek population. Tensions between the Kyrgyz and Uzbeks in this region have been serious, as indicated by ethnic rioting in 1990 near Osh that left at least 300 people dead, although some unofficial estimates place the number killed much higher (Lubin 1999). The violence exploded when local authorities allocated land to ethnic Kyrgyz that had previously belonged to a collective farm controlled by Uzbeks. The Uzbeks are more devout and conservative Muslims than most Kyrgyz and are distinguished from the Kyrgyz by both their language and style of dress. Although both peoples are Muslim and Turkic, intermarriage between Kyrgyz and Uzbeks is relatively rare.

As recently as 1989, Russians were Kyrgyzstan's largest minority group and accounted for more than 20 percent of Kyrgyzstan's population, but during the 1990s their numbers declined precipitously (Kaiser 1994). By 2000, Russians made up only about 11 percent of the population, a percentage that continues to decline. Other European groups in Kyrgyzstan, such as Ukrainians and Germans, have experienced even greater losses. The dramatic reduction in numbers for these groups is due mostly to massive out-migration, although they typically have lower rates of natural increase than Muslim peoples as well. Although there was a general trend of emigration by these groups even before the independence of Kyrgyzstan, the wave of emigration since 1991 has been spurred by feelings of discrimination among the Slavs and Germans, in both economic and cultural terms. As the Kyrgyz language is increasingly used in official documents and in the media and Kyrgyz culture is promoted as the national culture of Kyrgyzstan, the Russians and others have felt increasingly alienated and unwelcome. Their departure is detrimental to Kyrgyzstan's economic development, because many Slavs and Germans are professionals, businesspeople, and educators.

Social System

Social relationships among the Kyrgyz are strong and traditional, especially at the family, clan, and tribal levels. As nomadic peoples, the Kyrgyz family historically was composed of several generations, all of whom lived and moved as a single unit and typically shared a common dwelling, the *yurt.* A yurt is a large round tent constructed of a wooden frame, with felted carpets stretched over it. The yurt has become an important symbol of Kyrgyz culture in independent Kyrgyzstan—the Kyrgyz flag prominently features a *tundyuk,* or smoke vent located at the top of the yurt. Close family and clan ties remain a key part of Kyrgyz life, and it is not uncommon for three or more generations to share an apartment or at least to live in the same building. Collectivization of the Kyrgyz during the Soviet era did not destroy the tight family and clan connections—often an entire clan or extended family simply occupied the *kolkhoz,* or collective farm, shaping their traditional relationships to follow the Soviet model.

In urban areas, an important unit historically and today is the *mahalla,* or neighborhood. This social unit functions among the Islamic groups in Kyrgyzstan, but is especially strong among Uzbeks and among Kyrgyzs living in the southern part of the country. The elders, or *aksakals* ("white beards"), are the authority in the *mahalla,* and an individual's behavior reflects on the entire organization. Young people in trouble at school or with the police may seek help resolving their problems via the advice of the *aksakals,* and residents who are in difficult financial straits may receive assistance from the *mahalla.* In addition, certain ceremonies, such as weddings and funerals, are typically organized with the assistance of the *mahalla.* Considerable social control and pressure can be exerted on the individual through the *mahalla,* as antisocial behavior and other problems are not concealed within the family but are known to everyone in the neighborhood, and bring the condemnation of the entire community.

As in other societies, weddings and funerals carry great significance among the Kyrgyz. Weddings are usually large and

A Kyrgyz family during jailoo, *the summer pasturing period in the mountains. (Janet Wishnetsky/Corbis)*

expensive affairs, and a typical celebration might include several hundred guests and family members. The groom's family traditionally paid a bride price, or *kalym,* while both families exchanged gifts. During the Soviet period, large weddings and the payment of *kalym* were officially discouraged, but these traditions persisted and today are gaining popularity. A second occasion that is the cause of great joy and celebration is the birth of a child. Not only is the birth marked by a *toy,* or large feast, but other events are also celebrated with great fanfare and abundant food, such as the name-giving ceremony, the final removal of the umbilical cord, and a child's first haircut. Funerals, in contrast, are somber and sad observances. Upon a person's death, family and friends visit for three days before the burial occurs. Once the body is interred, the elderly men of the family visit the grave for seven days, offering prayers and reading aloud passages from the Koran. Forty days after the funeral, friends and family will again gather at the home of the deceased person in remembrance, and visitations by friends and relatives to the mourning family may continue for the next year.

WOMEN'S STATUS IN SOCIETY

Because of the less strict observance of Islamic traditions among the nomadic Kyrgyz people, Kyrgyz women historically played a more visible role in society. For example, at no time in their past did northern Kyrgyz women widely wear the *paranja;* this was a tradition usually observed only among sedentary Muslims in Central Asia, and in Kyrgyzstan mostly in the Fergana Valley. This is not to imply that Kyrgyz females enjoyed an equal status with men or that they enjoyed complete freedom in directing their lives, however. Young women could be kidnapped and forced into marriages, a practice that still surfaces in Kyrgyzstan today. Even if the girl did not desire the marriage, she might be forced to accept it, because once she had spent the night away, her virtue was in question, and her parents might well refuse to receive her back into their home. Bride kidnapping is reflected in a popular traditional game, *kyz kuumai,* in which a prospective suitor is required to catch his bride-to-be on horseback to marry her.

Under the Soviet system, women in Kyrgyzstan, regardless of their ethnicity, made significant advancement in education and government. For the first time in their history, many Kyrgyz women attended school, and many received a higher education at university or at trade schools. This continues in independent Kyrgyzstan and opportunities for advanced education are greatest for those living in the cities and for Slavic, Korean, and other non-Muslim women, although Kyrgyz women are well represented in the country's universities. Since independence, women have been active in politics, and several have been elected to the Jogorku Kenesh, the country's parliament. Kyrgyz and other Muslim women are conservative in relations with men outside their families and in public, however. Although shaking hands with a stranger is

Demonstrators, many of them women, rally in the southern city of Osh in March 2005. A month earlier, parliamentary elections that many felt were unfair had triggered numerous such protests in southern Kyrgyzstan. (AFP/Getty Images)

acceptable, public displays of affection, including hugging and kissing, are not considered appropriate, even with husbands or boyfriends, especially outside the major urban areas of the north.

About two-thirds of the women in Kyrgyzstan live in rural areas. In general, life is much more difficult and less comfortable in the countryside, and rural women are frequently employed in jobs that pay low wages and are physically demanding. Women often work as field hands, planting, cultivating, and harvesting the country's agricultural products, especially cotton, grain, and vegetables. Women also have their traditional responsibilities of homemaker and child rearing. Some international agencies estimate that the poverty rate in rural areas is greater than 50 percent, and unemployment remains high as well (Howell 1996, 56). Health care facilities are more difficult to access and of lower quality than in the cities, a problem that disproportionately affects women and children. Sadly, because of the difficult economic conditions, many women in Kyrgyzstan and elsewhere in Central Asia have been exploited by traffickers who lure women abroad (mostly to Europe and the Middle East) with promises of better jobs and then force them into prostitution. Typically these criminals seize their victims' passports and threaten them with physical violence so they will not return home.

The lifestyle of the non-Muslim minorities in Kyrgyzstan is different from that of Muslim women. For the remaining Slavs, Germans, Koreans, and others, social opportunities and standards are closer to those encountered in Western countries. The clothing styles favored by Slavic women, for example, are much less conservative than among most Kyrgyz, and especially among the more conservative Uzbeks in the south. Marriages are usually not arranged and girls in these groups marry at a later age, start families later, and have fewer children than their Muslim counterparts. Because they are mostly urbanized, non-Muslim women have greater opportunities for education and generally enjoy a higher standard of living and make an important contribution to the Kyrgyz economy as professionals and businesswomen.

RECREATION AND POPULAR CULTURE

The last twenty years have seen a revolution in popular culture in Kyrgyzstan and other former republics of the Soviet Union. As recently as the early 1980s, most aspects of Western popular culture, especially magazines, music, and film, were labeled decadent, and it was illegal to bring such items into the USSR. The Soviet government jammed radio and television broadcasts that might expose its citizens to information and aspects of culture that originated outside its borders. This is not to suggest that Western culture, and popular music in particular, were unknown to Soviet young people but that it was difficult for them to acquire recordings or other media from the West, with the exception of some musical forms, like jazz. Western clothing, especially Levi's blue jeans, brought top prices on the underground market in the Soviet Union.

This cultural blackout was lifted in the last five years of the USSR's existence, as the policy of glasnost (openness) displaced the repressive approach of earlier Soviet administrations. The subsequent complete collapse of the Soviet state and independence for its constituent republics led to a veritable tide of Western culture flowing into the region. By the early 1990s, the songs of popular Western musicians could be heard playing across Central Asia, and American and European films were available for viewing in theaters, small private video salons, and on television. Today in Bishkek and other cities in Kyrgyzstan, numerous kiosks on the streets offer the latest foreign movies on video and DVD, and although the players for these media are expensive by Kyrgyz standards, many people own them. Apartment buildings in the cities are often bedecked with satellite dishes, providing their owners direct access to broadcasts from around the world. Although foreign entertainment is popular, traditional Kyrgyz music and dance is as well. The following discussion describes some of characteristics of entertainment in contemporary Kyrgyzstan.

Traditional Music

The tradition of singing represents the very core of Kyrgyz identity given that the national epic, *Manas,* is an oral epic recounted by *manaschi.* These performers may sing the epic a cappella or accompanied on the *komuz,* a stringed instrument similar to a lute. Memorizing the *Manas* story requires great concentration and effort because it is quite long—some scholars estimate it to be the longest such tale ever created. Manaschi are revered in Kyrgyz society, partially because of the effort required to master the entire epic and partially

A female akyn *plays a* komuz, *the Kyrgyz national instrument. Akyns, or bards, are highly respected in Kyrgyz society. (David Samuel Robbins/Corbis)*

because they embody the historical roots of the Kyrgyz people (Stewart 2004). In recent years, special schools to train the younger generation in the art of relating the epic have been established in Kyrgyzstan, and a national competition is held annually to select the best manaschi. Other tales and folksongs are performed by the *akyn,* a singer who is also widely respected and admired in Kyrgyz society.

A variety of musical instruments in addition to the *komuz* accompany traditional singers and performers. The *temir komuz* is a kind of mouth harp that is played by both professional performers and amateur musicians. The *kyyak* is a stringed instrument played with a bow, and percussion is frequently supplied by various sizes of drums, the most common of which is referred to as a *dool* (Spector 1989). A popular instrument among the Uzbeks in Kyrgyzstan is the *daira,* a rhythm instrument that resembles a large tambourine and may be played alone or in accompaniment with other instruments or a singer.

Traditional dancing, marked by swaying movements and gestures with the arms and hands, is popular among both the Kyrgyz and Uzbeks. At weddings, a professional dancer, almost always a woman, may be hired to entertain the guests.

Modern Music and Music Video

Over the last fifteen years, the music of Western musicians has become popular with young people in Kyrgyzstan. In every bazaar of even modest size, several merchants sell tapes or compact discs of well-known American and European performers. Many times, these recordings have been illegally copied, and occasionally the quality is poor, but Kyrgyz music fans buy them anyway. The music kiosks are generally easy to locate, because their proprietors apparently believe the best way to advertise their music is to play it at ear-splitting volume, a practice to which nobody seems to object. Madonna, U2, Eminem, Usher, and other globally distributed artists appear to be as popular with youth in Kyrgyzstan as they are elsewhere in the world. In addition to the American and European singers and bands, musicians from Russia and other former Soviet Republics are also commonly offered. There are only a few musicians from Kyrgyzstan who record pop, rock, hip-hop, or other styles of modern music, although some of the traditional artists will sometimes record folk songs accompanied by synthesizers, electric guitars, or other nontraditional instruments.

Satellite television and the Internet are two vehicles that enable young people to stay up with the latest music videos available in the West. Television channels that feature mostly or exclusively music videos are not available to the average young person in Kyrgyzstan. Some channels, especially those from Russia, may occasionally provide programming that includes clips of videos from popular artists or full-length videos. Those videos that do receive airtime generally lack the explicit lyrics and sexual overtones that many videos shown on Western cable networks include, because Kyrgyz society remains conservative about such topics. Nevertheless, music videos represent a medium of entertainment that is increasingly popular with the younger generation in Kyrgyzstan, one that connects them to the global culture.

Television and Film

Several television channels are available in Kyrgyzstan, but these are concentrated mostly in Kyrgyzstan's main cities, especially Bishkek. Almost all broadcasting is via the airwaves, although a U.S. company is currently attempting to build the infrastructure in Bishkek to support cable broadcasts. Some stations are government-owned, but several independent stations operate as well, although they frequently are not available in certain parts of the country. Several channels from Russia are available, and some programming is offered from Turkey as well, but the majority of programs are presented in Kyrgyz. Reruns of foreign television serials and movies are popular forms of entertainment programming, especially soap operas. In rural areas, fewer channels are available, and the variety of programs is often limited.

Numerous foreign films are available in video kiosks in the country's main cities, and Kyrgyzstan has a domestic film industry as well. Action films from the United States and Russia appear to be especially popular, and many American movie stars are well-known in Kyrgyzstan. In the Soviet era, the state-sponsored film industry produced several feature films each year, and since independence, Kyrgyz filmmakers have successfully teamed with foreign partners to produce feature films and documentaries. *Beshkempir,* a Kyrgyz film produced in the late 1990s, won several international awards. Historical themes are also frequently the focus of Kyrgyz films, including the *Manas* epic.

Sports

Sports and athletic competition have long been popular among the Kyrgyz. In the days when most Kyrgyz were nomads, horseback riding was a prized skill, and a large number of traditional contests take place on horseback. There are long-distance races of nearly 25 miles, as well as contests of shorter distances, and riders race both in the saddle and bareback, depending on the rules of the specific contest. Men will engage in *oodarysh,* or wrestling on horseback, in which two riders attempt to throw the opponent from the saddle, and tests of skill, such as shooting a target while riding and picking up objects from the ground while at full gallop, are frequently part of outdoor festivals. The Kyrgyz also play *ulak tartysh,* a sport found in other parts of Central Asia in which two mounted teams struggle for a goat's carcass, which must be carried to the opposing team's goal. Women also take part in riding contests, most of which are races. Falconry, both on foot and from horseback, remains popular among the Kyrgyz in the countryside, and like the Uzbeks the Kyrgyz have resurrected *kurash,* a traditional form of wrestling that its practitioners claim has been studied in Central Asia for centuries.

Nontraditional games also have a large following in Kyrgyzstan. The most popular team sport is probably soccer, and Kyrgyzstan has numerous soccer clubs. Boxing is also popular, and several Kyrgyz boxers have done rather well in international competitions, including the Olympics. Kyrgyz athletes participate in tennis, swimming, basketball, and track and field competitions held annually. Kyrgyzstan's spectacular natural environment offers many opportunities for outdoor activities, especially skiing during the winter, and hiking, trekking, and hunting during the summer months. The peaks of the country represent a mostly undiscovered and unexplored terrain for mountain climbers, and Kyrgyzstan is becoming increasingly popular as an international destination for mountaineering.

For those who like activities on the water, it would be difficult to find a more beautiful setting than Issyk Kul. For many people, strolling in the many parks and open areas is an enjoyable pastime.

KYRGYZSTAN AND THE WORLD

Positioned at the juncture of China, Kazakhstan, Uzbekistan, and Tajikistan, Kyrgyzstan is poised to play the role of economic, cultural, and political intermediary between East and Central Asia. Considerable trade already moves across Kyrgyzstan in both directions, and it is possible that if the industrial economies of East Asia, particularly China, seek additional sources of energy in Central Asia, much of that oil and gas will transit the territory of Kyrgyzstan. Moreover, since independence, Kyrgyzstan has been viewed by many as the most progressive country in Central Asia in terms of constructing a civil society, and when compared with some of its neighbors such as Uzbekistan and Turkmenistan, the Kyrgyz regime appears to be well along the path to democratization and economic reform. Many citizens of Kyrgyzstan hope that Askar Akayev's sudden departure from the post of president in March 2005 will result in an acceleration of democratic reforms in the country and a reduction of corruption.

Since achieving independence, Kyrgyzstan's relations with two of its southern neighbors, Uzbekistan and Tajikistan, have been rocky and unstable. Friction with Uzbekistan has erupted over everything from disagreements concerning payments to Uzbekistan for natural gas deliveries to the mining of the border by Uzbekistan, allegedly to prevent Islamic militants from entering the country from Kyrgyz territory. In the 1990s, relations with Tajikistan were strained over the volume of refugees fleeing into southern Kyrgyzstan to avoid the violence of the Tajik civil war (Anderson 1999, 95). In general, however, Kyrgyzstan's relations with its neighbors since the collapse of the USSR have been positive, and these relations will become increasingly important because Kyrgyzstan controls a disproportionate amount of the key resource for Central Asia's future development: water. Indeed, Kyrgyzstan's abundant water virtually guarantees the country a vital strategic role in the coming years.

Kyrgyzstan has shown a great willingness to participate in both regional and international organizations to promote trade and security. Shortly after independence Kyrgyzstan joined most major international economic organizations. The country joined the Central Asian Union (later the Central Asian Forum) even before independence and is a member of the Eurasian Economic Community (EEC) and the Shanghai Cooperation Organization. The EEC is an organization composed of former Soviet republics committed to facilitating trade between its members, and the latter, made up of former Soviet states and China, is focused on reducing tensions between member states as well as addressing trade, terrorism, and other issues the region faces. Kyrgyzstan has also indicated a desire to join larger international bodies without the cooperation or support of its regional allies. Such was the case in 1998, when Kyrgyzstan became the first Central Asian country to join the World Trade Organization, a move that generated economic friction with Uzbekistan and Kazakhstan.

The United States has developed a generally warm and positive relationship with Kyrgyzstan since Soviet disintegration. U.S. administrations in the 1990s and afterward have viewed the country as an example for the entire region and have offered much support in the hope that other regimes in Central Asia would pursue reforms with the same intensity and vigor shown by the Akayev government. The terrorist attacks on the United States on September 11, 2001, abruptly magnified the importance of the U.S.-Kyrgyzstan partnership, as the Kyrgyz government quickly offered the use of its airspace in the U.S. campaign against the Taliban. Shortly thereafter, an agreement was struck to base U.S. forces near Manas (the facility was later named Ganci airbase), just outside of Bishkek, and to allow U.S. aircraft to use the airport there, even though the stationing of U.S. soldiers in Kyrgyzstan alarmed Russia, Kyrgyzstan's main trading partner and strategic ally. U.S. troops have remained at the Ganci base since 2001, a clear sign that both countries see their strategic relationship as lasting well into the future.

The Kyrgyz government has shrewdly maintained solid relations with Russia and China as well. Both countries are important trading partners and share many security concerns with the Kyrgyz administration, including the spread of Islamic militancy, drug trafficking, and nuclear proliferation. In response to Russian concerns over the U.S. base at Manas, the Kyrgyz government approved the establishment of a Russian military base at Kant, a small city east of Bishkek. Thus, the Kyrgyz regime has troops from both the United States and Russia stationed within its borders, adding to both its security and its ability to play the interests of one powerful ally against those of the other, thereby maximizing the benefits from both strategic partners. For the Chinese, Kyrgyzstan is an important strategic partner that also has the potential to supply a substantial portion of western China's future energy needs. A Kyrgyz official suggested in 2004 that Kyrgyzstan might export a billion kilowatts of electricity annually to western China with the help of Chinese investment, and the Chinese government has shown interest in developing Kyrgyzstan's modest oil resources. In its short history as an independent country, Kyrgyzstan has made great strides in building ties to powerful allies and trading partners.

References

Abazov, Rafis. 2004. *Historical Dictionary of Kyrgyzstan.* Lanham, MD: Scarecrow Press.

Anderson, John. 1999. *Kyrgyzstan: Central Asia's Island of Democracy?* Amsterdam: Harwood Academic.

Howell, Jude. 1996. "Coping with Transition: Insights from Kyrgyzstan." *Third World Quarterly* 17(1), pp. 53–68.

Kaiser, Robert. 1994. "Ethnic Demography and Interstate Relations in Central Asia." In *National Identity and Ethnicity in Russia and the New States of Eurasia,* edited by Roman Szporluk. Armonk, NY: M.E. Sharpe.

Lubin, Nancy. 1999. *Calming the Fergana Valley: Development and Dialogue in the Heart of Central Asia.* New York: Century Foundation Press.

Spector, Johanna. 1989. "Musical Tradition and Innovation." In *Central Asia: 120 Years of Russian Rule.* Durham, NC: Duke University Press.

Stewart, Rowan, and Susie Weldon. 2004. *Kyrgyz Republic,* 2d ed. New York: W.W. Norton.

PART TWO
REFERENCE SECTION

Key Events in Kyrgyz History

1000–200 B.C.

Scythian (Saka) nomads, a mysterious people of Iranian stock who left no written records but were masters at working gold, construct a loose-knit nomadic empire stretching from the Tien Shan to the Black Sea. The Scythians use the Fergana Valley as a base for invading toward the west for several centuries, at one point even attacking the Assyrian Empire in the Middle East. This pattern of periodic nomadic invasions from Central Asia to the west will hold for the next 2,000 years.

329 B.C.

Alexander the Great crosses the Oxus (Amu Darya) and campaigns against the trading settlements of Central Asia.

160 B.C.

A Turkic people, the Usun, cross the Tien Shan into the basin of Issyk Kul and gradually settle the Jeti-su (Land of Seven Rivers). The Usun establish a capital city, Chiguchen, on the shore of Issyk Kul and control the region until the advent of the Huns in the third century A.D.

A.D. 680–751

Muslim forces gradually bring the oasis cities in the major river valleys under control, converting the local population to Islam. In 751, a Muslim army defeats a Chinese force near the Talas River in northwestern Kyrgyzstan. This battle has profound repercussions for the region because it solidifies the Muslim hold on Central Asia and prevents the intrusion of Chinese influence, ensuring that it will be an Islamic, not a

Chinese, civilization that will shape Central Asia for the next millennium.

900

Kyrgyz tribes migrate from southern Siberia into the Chu, Talas, and Fergana valleys in a process that continues for several centuries.

940–1141

The Karakhanid empire is established, extending from Lake Balkhash to western China. One of the Karakhanid capitals is located at Balasagun in northern Kyrgyzstan.

1219

In retaliation for the execution of the members of a Mongol caravan, Genghis Khan invades eastern Central Asia and devastates the entire region. His successors continue to rule the region for a century and a half.

1370–1405

Reign of Amir Timur (Tamerlane) in Central Asia.

1762–1831

The Khanate of Kokand expands into the Chu and Talas river valleys in northern Kyrgyzstan, bringing Kyrgyz tribes under its authority. The khans of Kokand demand high tax payments from the Kyrgyz nomads, and various tribes of Kyrgyz frequently revolt against the khanate.

1865

Tashkent, a major city under the control of the Kokand khan, falls to Russian forces.

1876

The Khanate of Kokand is abolished, opening the way for Russian absorption of the Fergana Valley and northern Kyrgyzstan.

1898

Andijan Uprising. Muslims riot and attack Russian garrisons in several Fergana Valley towns, including Osh.

1916

In response to a government conscription order during World War I, thousands of Central Asians revolt. Intense fighting occurs in the Fergana Valley and in parts of northern Kyrgyzstan, with heavy casualties. In the region around Pishpek (Bishkek) alone, the population declines by more than 40 percent, mostly because of the violence. Many Kyrgyz nomads flee the fighting by crossing into China.

1917

In February, the tsarist regime falls. Later in the year, the Bolsheviks, a radical Marxist group, attempt to seize control of the government, resulting in civil war. Early the following year a Bolshevik committee takes control of Pishpek (Bishkek), but pockets of anti-Soviet resistance are widespread in Fergana Valley and eastern Kyrgyzstan.

1918–1920

Mikhail Frunze, a general of the Bolshevik army, campaigns in Central Asia, fighting both the White Army and a native insurgency, the Basmachi. After two years, the White forces are defeated, but the Basmachi continue activities for another fifteen years.

1928–1929

The Soviet program to collectivize agriculture is initiated in the Central Asian republics, with the confiscation of land from the "kulaks" (allegedly wealthy landowners). Many Kyrgyz flee across the border to China, and many others die attempting to migrate. Others slaughter their livestock rather than turn the animals over to the government.

1936
Formation of the Kyrgyz Soviet Socialist Republic (SSR). The elevation of the Kyrgyz to full republic status solidifies the concept of Kyrgyz national identity.

1938
Purges of Communist Party and mass execution of Central Committee near Chong Tash, outside of Frunze (Bishkek).

1940
Kyrgyz is shifted from the Latin to the Cyrillic alphabet.

1941–1945
In June 1941, Germany attacks the Soviet Union. During World War II, industrial enterprises and factories are shifted to Central Asia. In the early stages of the war, Stalin deports thousands of Germans from southern Russia to Central Asia, and many settle in northern Kyrgyzstan. In 1943, the Soviet regime agrees to the establishment of governing boards for the USSR's Muslims. Kyrgyzstan is placed under the control of the board based in Tashkent.

1961
Absamat Usubaliyev becomes first party secretary of the Kyrgyz Soviet Socialist Republic.

1989
The much-debated Law on Languages is passed by the Jogorku Kenesh (parliament), making Kyrgyz the official language of Kyrgyzstan. Many Slavic politicians and groups oppose the law because it requires a complete switch to Kyrgyz in all public institutions by 1999.

1990
In June, riots break out near the city of Osh between ethnic Kyrgyz and Uzbeks, resulting in hundred of casualties and

massive property damage. In October, Askar Akayev is elected to the newly created post of president.

1991

In August, a group of conspirators attempts to oust Mikhail Gorbachev, destabilizing the USSR. The coup fails, and the Kyrgyz SSR declares its independence on August 31. In December, the Soviet Union ceases to exist.

1995

Akayev wins reelection to the office of president. The celebration of the one thousandth anniversary of the *Manas* epic takes place.

2000

Akayev is reelected to the presidency in a controversial election.

2005

Elections held in February and early March are widely criticized as unfair. On March 24 demonstrators take over several government buildings, forcing President Akayev to flee the country. He later resigns as president, opening the way for a new presidential election later in the summer.

Significant People, Places, and Events

Abdurakhmanov, Yusup (1901–1938)   A leading Communist figure in Kyrgyzstan in the early Soviet period, Abdurakhmanov served as the first party secretary of the Communist Party of the Kyrgyz Autonomous Soviet Socialist Republic from the late 1920s until the early 1930s, when he was removed from power for alleged nationalist tendencies. In the late 1920s, Abdurakhmanov apparently played a part in the border delimitation between Uzbekistan and Kyrgyzstan, giving the Uzbek administration control over the enclave of Shakhimardan (see the reference section for Uzbekistan) in return for the inclusion of the city of Jalalabad inside Kyrgyz borders—Jalalabad was Abdurakhmanov's hometown. He was executed in the Stalinist purges of the late 1930s.

Aitmatov, Chingiz (1928–)   Aitmatov is the most famous author not only in Kyrgyzstan, but in all of Central Asia. He was active in politics from an early age and a member of the Communist Party of the Soviet Union. He worked for a time as a correspondent for the Russian newspaper *Pravda* and served in the higher apparatus of the Soviet Communist Party. By the 1970s and 1980s, Aitmatov's novels had gained a large following in the USSR, and his reputation as a masterful writer began to spread to the rest of the world. The work that most consider his tour de force is *The Day Lasts More Than a Hundred Years,* published in 1983. He has published several other novels and short stories, and many of his works have been made into movies in Kyrgyzstan.

Akayev, Askar (1944–) Askar Akayev was president of Kyrgyzstan from 1990 to 2005. Akayev had distinguished himself as a physicist during the Soviet era and held several posts in the Communist government from the 1980s until the collapse of Soviet power in 1991. In 1990, Akayev was elected to the new post of president of the Kyrgyz SSR, and the next year was elected by popular mandate to be the first president of independent Kyrgyzstan. He was reelected in 1995 and 2000, although after the mid-1990s his popularity waned, as he adopted a more authoritarian stance toward his critics and potential challengers. In 2003, he used a controversial referendum to acquire more political control. He was forced from office by demonstrations against his government in March 2005.

Aksy Events In March 2002, an outspoken opponent of the Akayev administration, Azimbek Beknazarov, was put on trial in Jalalabad Oblast in southern Kyrgyzstan. While the trial was in process, police and demonstrators supporting Beknazarov clashed, with at least eight protestors killed when police opened fire. This incident was blamed by many on the Akayev regime, and the government was shaken. Within a few weeks Akayev's entire cabinet resigned, and the president barely survived demands for his own resignation. The Aksy events highlighted the division and resentment between the north and south in Kyrgyz politics.

Baitik Khan Leader of the Solto, a Kyrgyz tribe that rebelled against the Khanate of Kokand in 1862 with the assistance of the Russian Empire. Kokand dealt with the Kyrgyz nomads under its jurisdiction particularly harshly, imposing heavy taxes on the Kyrgyz and frequently conducting military campaigns against them. In 1862, Baitik lured the military governor to a celebration and attacked his escort, killing him and his troops. Baitik then requested help from the Russians stationed at Verny (Almaty) in reducing the Kokand fortress near

Pishpek (Bishkek). The Russians, who wished to dismantle Kokand's influence in the region, joined the Kyrgyz tribesmen in ousting Kokand's garrison.

Balasaguni, Yusuf (1016–?)   Balasaguni was one of the most influential Islamic philosophers of the early Middle Ages. He was born in the city of Balasagun (Balasaguni means "the man from Balasagun") a major trading city of the Karakhanid empire in what is today northern Kyrgyzstan. He was educated in the great center of Islamic learning in Central Asia, Bukhara, and read and wrote at least three languages: Arabic, Persian, and his native Karakhanid Turkic. He evidently rose to high prominence at the Karakhanid court, where he wrote his masterpiece, the *Qutadghu Bilig,* or "The Knowledge That Brings Contentment," a descriptive and philosophical commentary on politics and everyday life. Significantly, Balasaguni chose to write in his native Turkic, rather than the more scholarly languages of Arabic or Persian.

Bishkek   The capital city of Kyrgyzstan, Bishkek is the country's most populous urban area, with just over 1 million residents. In the nineteenth century, it was known as Pishpek, and from 1926 to 1991, it was called Frunze in honor of Mikhail Frunze, a famous Bolshevik military officer who grew up in the city. The city still features a statue of Vladimir Lenin, a decade after most other places in the region removed him, quite literally, from the public square; near the train station is an enormous statue of Frunze. A sizable Slavic community still lives in Bishkek, and the city now sports several universities, many of them built in the last decade.

Cholpan Ata   A resort town located on the north shore of Lake Issyk Kul, during Soviet times Cholpan Ata was famous for its spas and rest houses. The site has been occupied for thousands of years, as the rock carvings located in the mountains above the town attest; some of the drawings are well over three thousand years old. Today the town survives almost exclusively on tourism and has some of the best beaches on the shores of Issyk Kul. Cholpan Ata is also near the terminus of a trekking trail that connects the north shore of Issyk Kul with the Malaya Almatinka gorge, near Almaty, Kazakhstan.

Chong Tash   The site of one of the most infamous episodes of Stalinist brutality in Kyrgyzstan. In 1937, most members of the Central Committee of the Kyrgyz Communist Party were arrested and transported to this remote village, where they were summarily executed. In total, almost 150 people were shot, and their bodies were then dumped into a local well. For decades, the fate of these individuals was unknown, until the late 1980s when witnesses came forward and revealed the whereabouts of the victims. The father of the Kyrgyz writer Chingiz Aitmatov was one of the victims. Today the site of the massacre is marked by a stone memorial.

Frunze, Mikhail (1885–1925)   Frunze was a famous Bolshevik general who fought first the White forces in Central Asia and then struggled to suppress the Basmachi rebellion as well. Frunze was an ethnic Moldavian who had been raised in Pishpek (Bishkek) and later studied in St. Petersburg, where he engaged in radical activities and was arrested several times. During the Russian Civil War, he was selected to lead the Bolshevik forces in Central Asia and was highly successful against a combined army of Whites and local soldiers. He died in 1925, allegedly during surgery, but some historians believe he was killed on Stalin's orders. After his death, the city of Bishkek was named in his honor until 1991.

Ganci Airbase   In the aftermath of the terrorist attacks on September 11, 2001, in the United States, the U.S. administration sought closer cooperation with several Central Asian states. The Americans were especially interested in having access to military facilities in Central Asia, in preparation for a campaign against the Taliban in Afghanistan. In October 2001 the Kyrgyz government agreed to lease land and facilities near Manas International Airport, near Bishkek, to the U.S. military and NATO. The base was intensively used during the war against the Taliban in 2001–2002. The base is named after a New York City firefighter who died in the collapse of the World Trade Center.

Isfara Conflict   Isfara is a small city situated in Tajikistan, near the border with Kyrgyzstan. In 1989, Tajiks and Kyrgyz clashed near the city over the usage and rights to local water supplies. Agriculture on both sides of the border is dependent on irrigation, and heavy demand in the summer of 1989 led to tensions between the communities. Local police attempted to separate the factions, which became increasingly hostile, but tempers spilled over (some reports suggest that many in the crowd on both sides were drunk). Rioting broke out, resulting in several deaths and many injuries. The incidents serve as a reminder of the increasing importance of water in the region.

Issyk Kul   A gorgeous mountain lake in north-central Kyrgyzstan. The name means in Kyrgyz "hot lake," and in fact the lake does not freeze even during the long, cold winters that characterize the region. The lake is slightly saline, and some have suggested that springs supplying warm water along the lake's bottom also prevent the lake from freezing. Issyk Kul is a major tourist destination for Central Asians, who flock to the sandy beaches around its shores during the summer months. Ample archaeological evidence shows that humans have lived on the shores of the lake for thousands of years. The Soviet navy used the lake for testing torpedoes, but today Issyk Kul is simply used for relaxation and recreation.

Jalalabad   A city situated at the eastern terminus of the

Fergana Valley. It is the capital of Jalalabad oblast, and the third largest city in the country, holding about 80,000 inhabitants. Jalalabad became a processing center for the region's cotton and other agricultural products in the late Soviet era, when the city grew substantially. About a third of the city's residents are Uzbek, with most of the remainder consisting of Kyrgyz, along with smaller numbers of Slavs, Koreans, Tatars, and other groups. Recent years have seen a downturn in the local economy and a significant increase in unemployment in the city, as many Soviet-era enterprises shut down and the labor force increased.

Kant A small city established by German immigrants in the nineteenth century. After the Russian Empire took control of northern Kyrgyzstan in the late 1800s, German farmers were offered "free" land in the Jeti-su (Semireche) region, or "Land of the Seven Rivers." A sizable German community settled between Pishpek (Bishkek) and Issyk Kul, and a number of villages in this part of the country have German names. Since the 1970s, the Germans have been leaving Kyrgyzstan (and Central Asia as a whole), and the German community is much smaller today than it was just after World War II. In 2002, the Kyrgyz government allowed Russia to build an airbase near Kant, partially in response to the U.S. presence at Ganci Airbase near Bishkek.

Karakol There are at least two towns in Kyrgyzstan named Karakol (the name means "Black Fist" in Kyrgyz); the Karakol referred to here was formerly called Przhevalsk and is located at the eastern end of Lake Issyk Kul. The town was named for the famous Russian explorer and naturalist Nikolai Przhevalsky in the late 1800s after he died there from typhus and was buried near the shore of Lake Issyk Kul. In 1991, it reverted to the former name of Karakol. It is an administrative center and popular tourist destination, both for mountain climbing in the adjacent Tien Shan and for those enjoying the attractions of Lake Issyk Kul.

Kulov, Felix (1948–)   Kulov was a leading opposition figure in Kyrgyzstan during the late 1990s. Kulov played an important role in the first years of independence, because he served the Kyrgyz administration in a number of capacities. He was elected the country's first vice president in 1992, was elected the *akim* (governor) of Chu oblast (province) in 1993, and in 1997 left that position to become the head of the country's security agency. In 1999, he was fired and charged with corruption, but the charges were dropped. Kulov then founded a new political party, Ar Namys, and supported an opposition candidate against President Akayev in the 2000 presidential election. After the election, Kulov was arrested and convicted on charges of corruption. He was freed by his supporters during the rioting that led to the downfall of the Akayev government in March 2005.

Kurmanjan Daatkha (1811–1907)   Kurmanjan Daatkha was a remarkable Kyrgyz leader in the nineteenth century— the more so because she was a woman. The widow of a Kyrgyz chieftain who was killed fighting the khan of Kokand, she rallied the disparate Kyrgyz tribes but recognized that the Kyrgyz lacked the sophisticated weaponry and tactics of the khan's forces. In need of powerful allies, Kurmanjan turned to the Russians, who had an interest in weakening the khanate, which stood in the way of additional Russian expansion in the region. In 1864, Kurmanjan officially allied her people with the Russian Empire and became the only Central Asian woman in the nineteenth century to hold the rank of colonel in the Russian army.

Manas   The great legendary hero of the Kyrgyz people and the epic named after him. It is unclear whether an actual historical figure named Manas ever lived or that he engaged in the adventures that the epic describes. Some scholars believe that Manas is a composite of several ancient leaders of the Kyrgyz. The story that bears his name is the world's longest epic poem and is actually a trilogy, describing the life and times of Manas, his son Semetey, and his grandson, Seitek. The age and origin of the epic is difficult to determine because it was passed through generations orally before portions were written down for the first time in the nineteenth century.

Manas Mausoleum Called the Manas Gumbez in Kyrgyz, this is the alleged burial chamber of the epic hero Manas, seen as the founding father of the Kyrgyz nation. The building is made of red clay bricks and is surprisingly small. On the front of the structure is an Arabic inscription, and although the building is difficult to date, Soviet archaeologists believed that the building was constructed no earlier than the fourteenth century A.D. Since independence the Kyrgyz government has invested heavily in the site, building a large museum nearby that features artifacts and displays on Manas and his exploits.

Masaliyev, Absamat (1933–) Masaliyev served as the first party secretary of the Kyrgyz Communist Party from 1985 to 1991. He was defeated by Askar Akayev in the first election for president in 1990, the year before Kyrgyzstan became independent. Masaliyev remained active in politics in the 1990s and was elected to the Jogorku Kenesh, the Kyrgyz parliament.

Naryn The largest city in south-central Kyrgyzstan and the capital of the oblast (province) of the same name. The city sits at the edge of the Tien Shan range at an elevation slightly above 6,000 feet. Naryn received a considerable amount of investment under the Soviet regime, but since independence the local economy has declined, as factories and businesses have closed and unemployment has risen. The city is the jumping-off point for many trekking and climbing expeditions in the Tien Shan.

Ormon Niyazbek-uulu (1791–1854)   A Kyrgyz noble who led a resistance movement against the Khanate of Kokand in the 1840s. Ormon managed for a while to unify many of the tribes in northern Kyrgyzstan, in an effort to create a quasi-state for the Kyrgyz. He fought not only the Kokand government, but also the Kazakhs and some of his own people, when they attempted to leave the confederation he had formed. He was killed while fighting in 1854.

Osh   The second-largest city in Kyrgyzstan and one of the oldest cities in Central Asia, Osh (the name means "food") is the primary hub of the Kyrgyz section of the Fergana Valley in southern Kyrgyzstan. For centuries, Osh was a major trading center on the Silk Road and became an important religious center as well because of the presence of a shrine just outside the city, Solomon's Throne, which attracts pilgrims from all over Central Asia. The central bazaar in Osh is one of the largest and most colorful in the entire region. The city holds a large Uzbek population, and in 1990, Osh and the surrounding area was the site of violent rioting between Uzbeks and Kyrgyz.

Osh Riots   The bloodiest single episode of ethnic violence to rock Central Asia in the late Soviet era occurred in the southern city of Osh in 1990. A dispute over land allocated to a local *kolkhoz* (collective farm) erupted into widespread rioting between ethnic Uzbeks and Kyrgyz, which quickly spread to surrounding communities. The violence continued for nearly a week before authorities were able to reestablish order, and the number of people killed reached at least 200, with unofficial estimates running as high as a thousand dead. Thousands of people were hurt, and hundreds of homes and buildings damaged or destroyed. The brutality of the fighting shocked many people in the USSR, and the echoes of this tragedy continue to haunt the city.

Otunbayeva, Rosa (1950–) Otunbayeva is a former member of the Akayev administration, and today an influential politician in Kyrgyzstan. She held several posts in the Soviet government during the last years of Soviet power, and after Kyrgyzstan's independence was ambassador to the United States for several years and then ambassador to the United Kingdom during the late 1990s. She later broke with the Akayev regime and became an outspoken critic of its policies.

Przhevalsky, Nikolai (1839–1888) Przhevalsky was one of the greatest explorers and geographers of the nineteenth century, a century replete with such men. Przhevalsky was an officer in the Russian military but spent the greater part of his adult life exploring the wilds of Inner Asia. Several times he visited Tibet and Mongolia and on one excursion discovered the small wild horse that is named for him. He was a player in the so-called Great Game between the British and Russian empires and served his country well, gathering information on the territory and peoples that lay beyond Russia's southern boundary. On a hunting expedition in eastern Kyrgyzstan, he drank contaminated water, was sent to the Russian hospital at Karakol on Lake Issyk Kul, and died there at age forty-nine.

Saimaly Tash A remote archaeological site in western Kyrgyzstan, Saimaly Tash is notable for the spectacular, well-preserved petroglyphs that cover the area. Some of the drawings found at Saimaly Tash have been dated to 3000 B.C., and many appear to be from the Scythian culture, which may have used the location for religious rituals. Later petroglyphs indicate that various peoples who moved into the region attached significance to Saimaly Tash, and the carvings represent the best-preserved and most numerous collection of ancient art in Central Asia.

Talas   An administrative center and industrial city on the Talas River in northwestern Kyrgyzstan, Talas is located about 80 miles southeast of Taraz in southern Kazakhstan. The local economy has declined significantly since independence, as many industrial enterprises have closed. The Manas Mausoleum is located a short distance from the city, however, and the Kyrgyz government has invested heavily in developing tourism in the region.

Tokmak   An industrial city located in north-central Kyrgyzstan, almost on the border with Kazakhstan, Tokmak was established as a fortress by the khan of Kokand in the early 1800s, near the ancient city of Balasagun, a major city of the Karakhanid Empire. In the 1860s, Cossack forces in the Russian army captured the city, and it gained a large population of Russian and German immigrants over the next two decades. It was the center of intense fighting during the 1916 uprising in Central Asia.

Tokonbayev, Aaly (1904–1988)   One of the more influential Kyrgyz writers and poets of the Soviet period, Tokonbayev stands second only to Chingiz Aitmatov as a shaper of modern Kyrgyz literature. He was the longtime editor of *Kyzyl Kyrgyzstan* (Red Kyrgyzstan), the largest circulation Kyrgyz-language newspaper during the Soviet era. Tokonbayev wrote numerous poems and translated the works of several foreign writers into Kyrgyz.

Toktogul (1864–1933)   The most famous *akyn* (bard) of Kyrgyz epic songs. His full name was Toktogul Satylganov, but he is always referred to simply by his given name. Toktogul was an acknowledged master of the *komuz,* a stringed instrument that the akyn uses for accompaniment. He was a supporter of the Bolshevik Revolution and the Soviet regime and has a city, a large manmade lake, and the Kyrgyz government prize for excellence in performing arts all named in his honor.

Turgunaliyev, Topchubek (1941–)   Turgunaliyev is a major opposition figure in Kyrgyzstan who played a central role in the formation of the Democratic Movement of Kyrgyzstan in 1990, an umbrella organization composed of groups opposed to Communist rule. Turgunaliyev was highly critical of the administration of Absamat Masaliyev in the waning years of the Soviet Union, and his influence was crucial in successfully electing Askar Akayev to the position of president in 1990. In the 1990s, however, Turgunaliyev became a vocal critic of the Akayev government and was brought up on charges of corruption in 1997. After serving several years, he was released and continues to be active in Kyrgyz politics.

Usubaliyev, Turdakun (1919–)   Usubaliyev was the first party secretary of the Kyrgyz Communist Party for nearly a quarter of a century, from 1961 to 1985, and thus was the most powerful politician in the Kyrgyz Soviet Socialist Republic (SSR). He was successful at attracting large industrial investments from Moscow in the 1960s and 1970s for the Kyrgyz SSR and viewed the Soviet system as a means of developing and modernizing the Kyrgyz economy. He was removed from his position when Mikhail Gorbachev became the general secretary of the Soviet Communist Party in 1985.

Uzgen   An ancient Silk Road city about 20 miles east of Osh, Uzgen is located in the Fergana Valley of southern Kyrgyzstan. The city holds several structures from the Karakhanid dynasty and is a regional administrative center. In 1990, it was the scene of vicious ethnic fighting between Uzbeks and Kyrgyz over land rights and usage.

Language, Food, and Etiquette in Kyrgyzstan

LANGUAGE

The issue of language has been a contentious one in Kyrgyzstan since the late Soviet period. According to the country's constitution, Kyrgyz is the "state" language, while Russian is an "official" language. Unlike their cousins the Kazakhs, the Kyrgyz retained the widespread use of their native tongue during Soviet times, although most learned Russian as well. The majority of ethnic Kyrgyz are conversant in both languages, but few Slavs and other Russian-speaking minorities in the country mastered Kyrgyz when the country was part of the USSR, and few have done so since independence. To run for the office of president, a candidate must show competence in the Kyrgyz language. In the late 1990s, the Kyrgyz government passed legislation that will require students to show proficiency in Kyrgyz by 2010. The emphasis on adopting Kyrgyz as the primary language of communication has led many Slavs and others to emigrate over the last decade.

Kyrgyz belongs to the Kipchak branch of the Turkic languages and is closely related to Kazakh and Karakalpak in Central Asia. There are three broad dialectical divisions of Kyrgyz, based on geographic regions: the northern dialect, southeastern dialect, and southwestern dialect. In the nineteenth and twentieth centuries Kyrgyz was influenced by Russian and adopted many words from that language, especially technical and scientific terminology. Kyrgyz was written in the Arabic script until 1926, when a shift to the Latin alphabet was instituted, and in 1940 another change occurred when the Cyrillic alphabet was adopted for the written language. Kyrgyz has recently come under the globalizing influence of English, and many slang phrases and expressions are borrowed from the music, movies, and videos that young people listen to and watch. In addition, English is now the most popular foreign language for young people in Kyrgyzstan to study.

Kyrgyz, like other Turkic tongues, adds ending and particles to the major parts of speech to change or negate their meaning. This makes Kyrgyz an agglutinative language and means that a great deal of information may be contained in a single word or phrase. For example, the English sentence "I will not go" may be rendered in Kyrgyz and related languages by a single word, which contains all the component parts of the English sentence. Although this implies that basic words in Kyrgyz tend to be longer than in English, it also means that the cadence and rhythm of Kyrgyz tend to be faster than the typical conversation in English between native speakers.

Following are several useful and common phrases in Kyrgyz:

Salom alaikum	Hello, good day, greetings (literally, "Peace to you").
Jakshi sizbu?	How are you?
Jakshi	Well, good.
Jakshi kalingidzar	Good-bye
Hope	Okay, alright, yes
Rakmat	Thanks
Kaida?	Where is . . .?
Ooba	Yes
Jok	No
Kancha?	How many, how much?
Men tushumbay jatamin	I do not understand.
Siz angliischa suiloi suzbu?	Do you speak English?

FOOD AND BEVERAGES

Hospitality is a common traditional virtue of nomadic societies, and the Kyrgyz are no exception. Meals are a social event, not simply a procedure of obtaining nourishment. Sharing food with a guest is considered a cause for celebration, and in most cases, the best the host has will be served. Meals are traditionally served while sitting on the floor or ground (this will be the case if one is in a yurt, the traditional "tent" of the Kyrgyz), and the food is placed on a cloth, or *dastarkhan.* The guest will likely be given a place of honor, perhaps next to the host or the eldest member of the family. Food will be passed around or simply placed on one's plate (usually in large portions), and guests should try anything that is offered, regardless of its appearance.

Certain protocols must be observed when eating in Kyrgyz society. Islamic prohibitions against using the left hand at the table or dastorkon are observed by many Kyrgyz, even though other practices forbidden to Muslims, such as the consumption of alcohol, are widely ignored. When sitting, it is important not to place one's feet near the food, not should the sole of the foot point at another person at the meal. Generally, it is best to sit cross-legged, or to rest on one's shins and lower legs, with the feet angled behind. Bread is treated with special reverence—never place a piece of bread upside down, even next to a plate or bowl, and bread should never be thrown out with other trash, even when stale. Most people will give old bread to birds or animals.

Common Kyrgyz Dishes

Kyrgyz cuisine is often similar to that of their cousins the Kazakhs, especially the basic meat dishes. Meat is present in large quantities at every Kyrgyz meal—in general, vegetarianism is rare in Central Asia, and native Central Asians are rather puzzled and bemused by the concept. Mutton is by far the most common meat, although beef is eaten frequently as well. Much to the shock of many American visitors, horse meat is considered a delicacy among the Kyrgyz, just as it is among Kazakhs. At a feast, the head of a sheep or horse may be served, and the guest may be required to do the carving, usually with the help of the host.

Mutton Dishes. A Kyrgyz meal is likely to begin with *shorpa,* a soup containing pieces of mutton along with chopped potatoes and vegetables. *Beshbarmak,* a mutton stew with noodles, is somewhat similar to the version of this dish found among the Kazakhs, only the meat may be shredded or chopped and is served in a savory broth. *Kesme* is another type of soup that is popular, made from potatoes, thin noodles, and chunks of meat. A common dish is *lagman,* a mixture of chopped mutton, vegetables, and spices served over long, thick noodles. *Kulchetai* is another variation of soup made with noodles and mutton. Shashlik, frequently eaten as a quick lunch or snack on the street, consists of skewers of meat and fat from the tail of the sheep, although it may be made from beef or ground meat as well. *Assip* is a kind of sausage made from mincemeat and rice. In the southern region of Kyrgyzstan, *manti* and *samsa* are especially popular. Manty are steamed dumplings filled with chopped onions and meat, and samsa are baked pastries usually filled with meat and fat from a sheep's tail, although samsa can be made with other fillings as well.

Horse-Meat Dishes. Horse meat is eaten more rarely than other meats and is considered a special treat. The Kyrgyz are fond of *kazy karta,* a type of sausage made from horse intestines, and *choochook,* a sausage made from horse fat taken from the animal's neck.

Breads and Related Foods. Bread is part of every meal, and typically is served as *non* (Russian: *lepyoshka*), a round flatbread that is baked in a *tandir,* a traditional clay oven. At the table, the host will typically tear the bread into pieces and distribute them around the table. There are many types of specialty breads, served as treats at celebrations or snacks. *Tan mosho* is a fried bread, somewhat like a pretzel, that is dusted with sugar and served as a dessert or snack. *Sanza* are fried buns that are often eaten for breakfast or as a snack with tea. *Boorsok* is another traditional bread, as is *kattama,* a layered bread. A special treat often served with any bread is *halvaitar,* a sweet spread made from flour, lamb fat, and sugar. Noodles and rice are common ingredients in soups and other dishes, and kasha, porridge made from rice, oats, buckwheat, or other grains, is a common breakfast food.

Milk Products. For centuries the traditional Kyrgyz lifestyle was built around animal husbandry, and milk products from a variety of animals have been an important part of the diet of the Kyrgyz for probably thousands of years. *Kaimak* is sour cream and is served with soups, bread, and others dishes. *Airan* is a thin yogurt drink typically made from mare's milk, and a variety of cheeses are part of the diet as well. A common snack, especially for children, is dried curd, which is rolled into small balls. Milk, either from cows or goats, may be bought from street vendors or in the bazaar. Adults typically do not drink milk.

Common Kyrgyz Beverages

Tea. Tea is more than a beverage in Central Asia; serving and drinking tea are social rituals. Green tea is available, but black tea is the most popular variety. It may be taken sweetened, but Kyrgyz typically do not drink tea with milk or cream, except in the case of *atkanchai,* a special tea that is made with milk, butter, and sour cream. Tea is always drunk hot and typically is made from loose tea leaves, not bags. Tradition holds that water from the teapot be poured into a *piloshka,* or small bowl for tea, and then added back to the pot three times before the tea is ready to be drunk.

Alcoholic Beverages. Among Muslims in Central Asia, the prohibition against alcohol is infrequently observed. This is due in part to the adoption of Slavic drinking customs, but in fact among the nomadic Kyrgyz and Kazakhs, alcoholic beverages were commonly drunk well before they became subjects of the Russian Empire. A favorite among Kyrgyz people is *kumiss,* made from mare's milk. A stronger spirit called *chagirmak* is distilled from kumiss. Of course, a wide variety of alcoholic drinks are available for purchase in stores and supermarkets, including vodka (the universal favorite), cognac, wine, and beer.

Soft Drinks. The typical soft drinks that one finds all over the world are available in Kyrgyzstan and are drunk mainly on special occasions—most Kyrgyz do not drink soda with their everyday meals. Soft drinks are rarely served chilled, but rather at room temperature, although one may find a street vendor in the summer months offering cold beverages. There are several traditional drinks the Kyrgyz enjoy in addition to commercial soft drinks. *Jarma* is made by boiling wheat and is often served chilled. *Bal* is a hot beverage made from boiling honey and spices in water—an excellent fortifier on cold mornings.

ETIQUETTE

Standards of conduct and behavior in Kyrgyzstan differ among ethnic groups and also typically vary according to geographic situation. By and large, rural dwellers tend to hold to more traditional, conservative standards than do their counterparts in the cities. The observations and descriptions that follow are therefore not intended to apply to everyone in Kyrgyzstan but do represent expectations that are commonly encountered in much of Kyrgyz society. These should be approached as general standards of behavior and are meant to inform foreign visitors, many who come from a different cultural background. As is the case anywhere, a guest or visitor who is aware of the expectations and values of his or her hosts is less likely to offend inadvertently.

Taking Off Shoes. Shoes are removed immediately upon entering many dwellings—this applies to private homes, apartments, and especially yurts—as well as mosques. The streets and byways of Central Asia are notoriously dusty, and shoes (and the feet in general) are assumed to be dirty. In the case of entering someone's home, a pair of house shoes will usually be supplied to the visitor. This is done to keep the home clean and is a custom observed widely in the Middle East and South Asia.

Use of Hands and Feet. In Muslim cultures, there is frequently a prohibition against using the left hand for certain purposes. Generally speaking, the left hand is traditionally used for bodily functions and handling items that are dirty or unclean—therefore, when taking a meal, one should not touch food or pass a dish or food to someone with the left hand. Among Slavs and other non-Muslims in Kyrgyzstan, this custom is not commonly observed, but one should observe his or her hosts to be certain. The feet should never approach the table or a tablecloth placed on the floor in traditional style, nor should the bottom of one's foot face someone directly, particularly an elderly person or one's host or hostess.

Social Hierarchy and Respect. Respect for the elderly is a central component of Kyrgyz values and mores. One's elders, especially grandparents, are viewed as a source of wisdom and counsel, and in rural areas it is not uncommon for a young man to consult with the *aksakals* (literally, "white beards"), or village elders, before he makes an important decision. To be discourteous or impolite to an elderly person is considered extremely bad behavior and will likely draw the condemnation of the entire community. At meals the eldest person of the household is accorded the place of honor, unless there is an honored guest, when the guest will typically be seated next to the elder as a sign of respect and courtesy.

Public Display of Affection between Opposite Sexes. In rural locales, holding hands, kissing, and hugging in public between men and women is generally frowned on. This is especially true for young, unmarried people, but even married couples will rarely have much physical contact in public. The situation in larger communities is somewhat different, especially in Bishkek, where there are stronger influences of Western behavior. Among non-Muslims, touching between male and female in public is viewed much more casually.

Sitting. Meals may often be eaten on the ground in Kyrgyzstan, and one should sit with the feet well away from the tablecloth. As noted earlier, the best tactic is to sit cross-legged or to fold the feet under one's legs and sit on top of them. This will avoid pointing the bottom of one's foot directly at another person, which is considered rude.

Nose Blowing. Blowing one's nose during a meal is considered uncultured, and one should leave the table if it is necessary to use a handkerchief. This basic rule of thumb should be followed in most public venues—restaurants, classrooms, theaters, and so on. Tissues are rarely available, and Central Asians almost always carry a handkerchief.

Bargaining. Haggling over price is not considered bad manners in the bazaars and small shops in Central Asia, and in fact is an expected part of the shopping process. One who fails to negotiate a lower price, often much lower than that initially offered, will be considered foolish and ignorant of local custom. In larger department stores, prices are fixed, and one usually does not negotiate, but even this is not universally true and may depend on the seller.

Business Cards. Since the fall of the Soviet Union, many professional people in Kyrgyzstan have adopted the habit of exchanging business cards, and this practice appears to be growing. If doing business with someone, it is standard procedure to offer one's card.

Clothes. Acceptable dress varies greatly in Kyrgyzstan, according to one's age, ethnic group, gender, and geographic location. Despite the warm temperatures during the summer in many locations, shorts are rarely worn by women, and virtually never by men—the only exception would be swimming apparel. Kyrgyz females generally dress modestly in long skirts or dresses and do not wear trousers or jeans. Russian females, on the other hand, will dress much like their counterparts in Western Europe and North America, although again, shorts are usually not a garment worn regularly in public. Matronly women of all ethnic groups will frequently don a scarf or *babushka* (Russian for "grandmother") when they venture outside, and men are fond of the *ak kalpak* (white hat); one will see many Kyrgyz men sporting this headgear in the rural regions of the country. If entering a mosque, women must cover their heads with a scarf or handkerchief, and shoes should be removed. If invited to dinner at someone's home, it is best to dress at least semiformally, because Central Asians dress up more than Americans for such events.

Kyrgyzstan-Related Organizations

BUSINESS AND ECONOMIC

The following is a brief listing of various groups and organizations focused on commerce and business development in Kyrgyzstan. Many more may be found on the Internet, as the business environment in Kyrgyzstan is expanding, and new opportunities and businesses are appearing regularly. When calling locations in Kyrgyzstan from outside the country, one must dial the country code (996) and then the number.

Consulate General of the Kyrgyz Republic
866 UN Plaza, Suite 514
New York, NY 10017
Telephone/Fax: (212) 319-2838
E-mail: visa@kyrgyzconsulate.org
Web site: http://kyrgyzconsulate.org
    The Consulate General's Web site has general information on procedures for starting a business in Kyrgyzstan and other information on doing business in the country.

Institute of Business, Management and Tourism
22A Manas Street
Bishkek, Kyrgyzstan
Telephone: (312) 21-34-42
Fax: (312) 21-34-26
E-mail: azamat@ecology.freenet.bishkek.su
    The institute is part of the state educational system and is dedicated to the training and education of citizens "in the fields of management, bank activity, hotel-tourism business." It also works to retrain and improve the skills of businesspeo-

ple and specialists and conducts research and collects data on small businesses in Kyrgyzstan.

Kyrgyz Stock Exchange
172 Moskovskaya Street
Bishkek, Kyrgyzstan 720010
Telephone: (312) 610-589
E-mail: kes@kse.kg
Web site: http://www.kse.kg

Kyrgyzstan Community and Business Forum
Room 213a
237 Panfilova Street
Bishkek, Kyrgyzstan 720040
Telephone: (312) 226-632
E-mail: nazgul@kyrgyzstan-cbf.org
Web site: http://www.kyrgyzstan-cbf.org

The Community and Business Forum "aims to build relationships by creating networks between local communities and business. At the centre of this network are local NGOs [nongovernmental organizations], who are in a position to identify and address the priority social and economic issues in their villages." The CBF monitors and advises businesses and serves as a source of information. It supports a small grants program to promote these goals.

Kyrgyzstan Development Gateway
Web site: http://eng.gateway.kg

The Kyrgyzstan Development Gateway Web site is a treasure trove of information on business and economic development in Kyrgyzstan. There are dozens of links to reports and sources of data on a wide range of topics. An excellent resource for researching economic and business-related topics.

Logos A&M
40 Rector Street
New York, NY 10006
Telephone: (212) 233-7061
Fax: (212) 233-7167
Web site: http://www.logosgroup.com

Logos is a company that assists U.S. businesspeople in establishing businesses in foreign countries.

CULTURE, EDUCATION, AND EXCHANGE

Association of Independent Scientists-Lawyers of the Kyrgyz Republic
42 Chui Prospect, Room 220
Bishkek, Kyrgyzstan 720065
Telephone: (312) 29-18-43, 22-23-05
Fax: (312) 28-27-76

An organization devoted to "the formation of a democratic legal state and the development of the legal conscience of society." The association assists in the training of lawyers via drafting laws, providing legal advice, and assisting in the incorporation of new technologies. There are five schools designed to assist in the training of members of the legal profession, and the association is connected to the Human Rights Center and the Center of Independent Expertise.

Association for Support of Woman Artists and Art Critics of Kyrgyzstan
20 Moldibaeva Street, Apartment 65
Bishkek, Kyrgyzstan 720055
Telephone: (312) 21-45-85
E-mail: orosgan@janay.bishkek.su

This group supports professional women artists, encourages young people to develop artistic talents, and works to maintain the tradition Kyrgyz art forms. They periodically support exhibitions for women artists.

Center for Social Research of the National Academy of Sciences of Kyrgyzstan
Chuiskii Prospect 265-A
Bishkek, Kyrgyzstan 720071
Telephone: (312) 24-37-35
Fax: (312) 21-85-22
E-mail: academy@eawarn.bishkek.su

The goals of the Center for Social Research are to gather data through surveys on various social and political issues, to analyze that information in the context of the politics and interethnic relationships in Kyrgyzstan, and to create databases and support conferences and publications relating to these issues. The center also offers courses in Russian, Kyrgyz and other foreign languages.

Congress of Women of Kyrgyzstan
120 Bokonbaeva Street
Bishkek, Kyrgyzstan 720040
Telephone: (312) 66-42-13
Fax: (312) 66-42-13
E-mail: zamira@congress.cango.net.kg
Web site: http://wcongresskr.freenet.kg

The CWK works to expand the activities of women in human development and business. It supports the United Learning Center, an institution that offers courses on basic business operations, beginning computer skills, and a variety of language courses.

GOVERNMENT

Embassy of Kyrgyzstan
1732 Wisconsin Avenue, NW
Washington, DC 20007
Telephone: (202) 338-5141
Fax: (202) 338-5139

Consulate General of the Kyrgyz Republic
866 UN Plaza, Suite 514
New York, NY 10017
Telephone/Fax: (212) 319-2838
E-mail: visa@kyrgyzconsulate.org
Web site: http://www.kyrgyzconsulate.org

TOURISM

There are plenty of reasons to plan a visit to Kyrgyzstan. Although distant, the country is a bargain for Western travelers, and the scenery is magnificent. For those interested in skiing, climbing, trekking, and other outdoor sports, the opportunities in Kyrgyzstan cannot be surpassed. The traditional hospitality of the Kyrgyz, their ancient and fascinating culture, and the country's history all make a journey there worthwhile.

Central Asian Tourism Corporation
Kyrgyzstan.com
1410 York Avenue, Suite 5A
New York, NY 10021
Fax: (212) 327-4881
E-mail: info@kyrgyzstan.com
Web site: http://www.kyrgyzstan.com
    An informative site for all kinds of tourist activities in Kyrgyzstan.

Edelweiss Travel Company
68/9 Usenbaev Street
Bishkek, Kyrgyzstan 720021
Telephone: (312) 28-07-88
Fax: (312) 68-00-38
E-mail: edelweiss@elcat.kg
Web site: http://www.edelweiss.elcat.kg

Shepherds' Life Association
Tel: (353) 52-25-34
E-mail: maksapnana@elcat.kg
Web site: http://www.tourism.elcat.kg

For those looking for an out-of-the-ordinary cultural experience, Shepherds' Life Association offers "homestays" during the *janloo,* or summer migration. One can stay in a yurt with a Kyrgyz family and take part in Kyrgyz traditional life.

Annotated Bibliography of Recommended Works on Kyrgyzstan

The following section describes sources on Kyrgyzstan that provide additional information on some of the topics addressed in this chapter. The list follows the order of the general topics presented in the narrative section and is selective. There are many sources on the country beyond those listed, and a search of the Internet and library holdings is recommended for specific topics.

GEOGRAPHY AND HISTORY OF KYRGYZSTAN

Abazov, Rafis. 2004. *Historical Dictionary of Kyrgyzstan.* Lanham, MD: Scarecrow Press.

An outstanding contribution to the scholarship on Kyrgyzstan. Abazov provides a historical sketch that deftly summarizes both Kyrgyz history and the contemporary political and economic landscape. The entries seem directed at current political figures, and a few historical figures and places are omitted, but this is a must-have reference book for the serious student of Kyrgyzstan.

Anderson, John. 1999. *Kyrgyzstan: Central Asia's Island of Democracy?* Amsterdam: Harwood Academic.

Anderson, a seasoned observer of Central Asian politics, offers a summary of Kyrgyzstan's development focused on the 1990s. In addition, the first chapter reviews the country's history prior to independence. This book is a good introduction to the events and difficulties that Kyrgyzstan has endured since the collapse of the Soviet state, despite the somewhat dated character of some of the information.

Kaiser, Robert. 1994. "Ethnic Demography and Interstate Relations in Central Asia." In *National Identity and Ethnicity in Russia and the New States of Eurasia,* edited by Roman Szporluk. Armonk, NY: M.E. Sharpe.
An examination of demographic dynamics in Central Asia, with a focus on migration and the status of nonmajority groups in the various new states. The volume contains an extensive table of ethno-territorial disputes in Central Asia, highlighting the recurrent issue of border demarcation and territorial control in the region.

Lydolph, Paul. 1990. *Geography of the USSR.* 5th ed. Elkhart, WI: Misty Valley.
Published the year before the USSR imploded, this text is still useful in many ways. Obviously the political geography included is badly out-of-date, but the description of the physical features of Central Asia remains accurate and enlightening, as does a surprising amount of the economic geography presented on Central Asia.

Stewart, Rowan, and Susie Weldon. 2004. *Kyrgyz Republic,* 2d ed. New York: W.W. Norton.
This is the ideal travel guide for Kyrgyzstan, but it is much more than a simple travel guide because it contains a wealth of information about the culture and history of the Kyrgyz people. The format is especially attractive, featuring glossy photographs, well-produced and detailed maps, and informative vignettes on various aspects and attributes of the country.

Wixman, Ronald. 1984. *The Peoples of the USSR: An Ethnographic Handbook.* Armonk, NY: M.E. Sharpe.
An excellent reference work for anyone interested in the myriad peoples of the former USSR. Although the political

framework of the Soviet Union collapsed, the people living in the region have by and large remained the same. All the ethnic groups resident in Kyrgyzstan and Central Asia are described, giving details on linguistic and religious characteristics.

THE ECONOMY OF KYRGYZSTAN

Abazov, Rafis. 1999. "Policy of Economic Transition in Kyrgyzstan." *Central Asian Survey* 18(2), pp. 197–223.

A highly detailed review of the economic situation of Kyrgyzstan through the decade of the 1990s. Abazov offers a balanced assessment of the policies pursued by the Akayev administration in the effort to transition from a Soviet-style command economy to free-market capitalism. He notes that although Kyrgyzstan has made progress in this regard, dangers of "crony capitalism" still lurk, and the "shock therapy" approach of the early 1990s created social problems that remain unresolved.

Dabrowski, Marek, and Vladislav Jermakowicz. 1995. "Economic Reforms in Kyrgyzstan." *Communist Economics and Economic Transformation* 7(3), pp. 269–297.

A dated but still useful review of Kyrgyzstan's economic development patterns and strategies in the years just after achieving independence.

Howell, Jude. 1996. "Coping with Transition: Insights from Kyrgyzstan." *Third World Quarterly* 17(1), pp. 53–68.

Howell's research focused on the coping strategies of households in countries suffering high levels of poverty. He applies a theoretical model previously utilized in Africa for examining coping strategies in famine areas to Kyrgyzstan in the early 1990s, when the Kyrgyz economy was declining. Using data gathered from interviews, Howell demonstrates how Kyrgyz families survived the economic downturn after independence.

International Monetary Fund. 2004. "Kyrgyz Republic: Poverty Reduction Strategy Paper Progress Report," IMF Country Report No. 04/200. Washington, D.C.: IMF. Available at: *http://www.imf.org.* Accessed January 30, 2005.

This is a fairly technical treatment of the issue of poverty in Kyrgyzstan, but like most of the IMF publications, it contains a great deal of statistical data and a general introduction that describes the characteristics and causes of poverty in the country. Much of the information is unavailable from other sources.

Koichuev, Turar. 1996. "Kyrgyzstan: Economic Crisis and Transition Strategy." In *Central Asia in Transition: Dilemmas of Political and Economic Development,* edited by Boris Rumer. Armonk, NY: M.E. Sharpe.

This is a comprehensive discussion of the Kyrgyz economic situation in the mid-1990s, only a few years after the introduction of the *som* and when the economy was struggling on nearly all fronts. Koichuev is certainly no optimist and suggests that fifteen to twenty years will be required before the economy shows measurable signs of successfully making the transition from a command to a free-market system.

KYRGYZ INSTITUTIONS

Cokgezen, Murat. "Corruption in Kyrgyzstan: The Facts, Causes and Consequences." *Central Asian Survey* 23(1), pp. 79–94.

A unique examination of a pervasive problem in Kyrgyzstan and across Central Asia. The author begins with a discussion of the cause and consequences of corruption and notes how it weakens economic performance. A compelling case is made that the level of corruption is so high in Kyrgyz society so as to seriously inhibit economic growth and transition. The article features several tables and charts on corruption.

Filonyk, Alexander. 1994. "Kyrgyzstan." In *Central Asia and the Caucasus after the Soviet Union: Domestic and International Dynamics,* edited by Mohiaddin Mesbahi. Gainesville: University Press of Florida.

A clear exposition of Kyrgyzstan's socioeconomic condition in the mid-1990s. Filonyk is optimistic about Kyrgyzstan's role as an "island of democracy" in the region, as were many commentators in the years just after the country achieved independence. The topics of Islam in Kyrgyzstan and Kyrgyz foreign policy are briefly addressed toward the end of this article.

Handrahan, Lori. "Gender and Ethnicity in the 'Transitional Democracy' of Kyrgyzstan." *Central Asian Survey* 20(4), pp. 467–496.

An interesting piece that attempts to link gender and ethnicity and makes the argument that gender issues have been largely overlooked as a key component of the political process in Kyrgyzstan.

Huskey, Gene. 1993. "Kyrgyzstan: The Politics of Demographic and Economic Frustration." In *Nations and Politics in the Soviet Successor States,* edited by Ian Bremmer and Ray Taras. New York: Cambridge University Press.

Huskey presents a sophisticated, insightful analysis of the various factors involved in emergent Kyrgyz nationalism. He argues that no concept of "nationalism" was present among the Kyrgyz until the arrival of the Russians and that it was at least in part the conflict and friction between the Kyrgyz and the colonial power that gave birth to a national consciousness among the disparate Kyrgyz clans and tribes.

Kasybekov, Erkinbek. 1999. "Government and Nonprofit Sector Relations in the Kyrgyz Republic." In *Civil Society in*

Central Asia, edited by M. Holt Ruffin and Daniel Waugh. Seattle: University of Washington Press.

A highly informative discussion of the difficulties involved in the formation of nongovernmental organizations (NGOs) in Kyrgyzstan, the relations between existing NGOs and the Kyrgyz government, and the issue of the role of NGOs in poverty alleviation in the country. The discussion is from the point of view of an insider, because Kasybekov has been active in NGO formation and activity in Kyrgyzstan.

Namatbaeva, Tolkun. 1995. "Democratic Kyrgyzstan: What Lies Ahead?" In *Central Asia: Conflict, Resolution, and Change.* Chevy Chase, MD: CPSS Press.

A general review of the various social and political difficulties facing the Kyrgyz state in the early years of transition to a quasi-democracy. The author proposes an interesting theory as to why President Akayev occasionally appeared to pull back from democratic processes and reforms: his counterparts in neighboring countries, especially Islom Karimov in Uzbekistan, fear the establishment of democracy on their border and therefore exert pressure on Akayev to adopt a more authoritarian domestic policy.

KYRGYZ SOCIETY AND CONTEMPORARY ISSUES

Heyat, Farideh. 2004. "Re-Islamization in Kyrgyzstan: Gender, New Poverty and the Moral Dimension." *Central Asian Survey* 23(3–4), pp. 275–287.

Heyat provides a glimpse into the process of "re-Islamization" in Kyrgyzstan, meaning the recovery of Islamic traditions lost under the Soviets, but also the incorporation of more conservative Islamic values, which were not previously a component of Kyrgyz Islam. This process, combined with the declining economic situation in the country, has greatly affected social behavior.

Hvolef, Erlend. 2001. "The Social Use of Personal Names among the Kyrgyz." *Central Asian Survey* 20(1), pp. 85–95.

This is a fascinating anthropological study of the importance and status of names in traditional society. Hvolef frames the changing role and structure of names in a political context, examining how names and their characteristics changed from the traditional nomadic Kyrgyz society, to modifications that occurred after the Bolshevik Revolution, to the role individual naming plays in the overarching notion of identity in independent Kyrgyzstan.

International Crisis Group. 2002. *Kyrgyzstan at Ten: Trouble in the "Island of Democracy."* Osh: International Crisis Group.

The International Crisis Group conducts research and provides analysis on the economic, social, and political situation on the countries of Central Asia, among others. This report offers a compelling argument that the chances for democracy and a politically pluralistic society emerging in Kyrgyzstan have declined during the 1990s, as the Akayev government has taken a progressively harder line with opponents and critical media outlets.

Kolstoe, Paul. 1995. *Russians in the Former Soviet Republics.* Bloomington: Indiana University Press.

Kolstoe includes a chapter on the Russian community in Kyrgyzstan and Kazakhstan, apparently on the basis that the two peoples are culturally and historically related, and that therefore the situation of Russians in each location is somewhat similar as well. The section on Russians in Kyrgyzstan is well written and clearly identifies the major challenges facing the Russian minority in the country.

Lubin, Nancy. 1999. *Calming the Fergana Valley: Development and Dialogue in the Heart of Central Asia.* New York: Century Foundation Press.

A policy study that captures the Fergana Valley as a regional unit, rather than abiding by the international borders that now divide this agricultural heartland. Lubin and her collaborators make a compelling case for intervention in the socioeconomic conditions found across the region. There is considerable information and analysis presented on the Osh riots of 1990.

Madi, Marat. 2004. "Drug Trade in Kyrgyzstan: Structure, Implications and Countermeasures." *Central Asia Survey* 23(3–4), pp. 249–273.

Madi traces the origins of the drug trade in Kyrgyzstan and its consequences for the country. He outlines the major players in the drug business and Kyrgyzstan's role as a major transfer point for drugs moving out of Central Asia, identifying specific routes that smugglers use to move the contraband through Kyrgyzstan's neighbors and across the rugged terrain. One of his most interesting points is that many of those accused of Islamic militancy in the region are actually motivated by drug profits.

Spector, Johanna. 1989. "Musical Tradition and Innovation." In *Central Asia: 120 Years of Russian Rule.* Durham, NC: Duke University Press.

A comprehensive look at the musicology of Central Asia. Spector covers musical style, instrumentation, music theory, and many other aspects of musical expression among the Kyrgyz and other Central Asian peoples. There are few scholarly studies on Central Asian available in English, and Spector's work, published more than fifteen years ago, remains almost the only contribution of its kind.

Index

About the Author

Reuel Hanks received his Ph.D. from the University of Kansas after completing his dissertation on nationalism and Islam in Uzbekistan during the Gorbachev years. He is currently associate professor of geography at Oklahoma State University and serves as the editor of the *Journal of Central Asian Studies*. He was a Fulbright Scholar in Tashkent in 1995 and in 1997 led a Fulbright-Hayes Faculty Development Seminar to Uzbekistan. He has published more than a dozen articles on Islam and ethnic geography in Uzbekistan and Central Asia and is the author of *Uzbekistan,* an annotated bibliography in the World Bibliographical Series, published by ABC-CLIO.